Textbook of
Environmental Biotechnology

Contents

Environmental biotechnology is a vast and rapidly growing field, which continues to revolutionise the understanding of basic life sustaining processes in the environment, by identifying and exploiting the biomolecules and their, utilities to provide clean technologies, in order to counter environmental problems. This technology plays very crucial role in environmental management. There are several applications in agriculture, including the use of specific bacteria to enhance nutrient supply to soil and also in pollution control, as the use of micro-organisms for waste water treatment. The technology is focused to improve production process with minimum waste generation, waste recycling, development of bioresources, manipulation of micro-organisms according to waste, remediation of contaminated habitats, degradation of chemicals, pesticides, heavy metal removal, remediation of surface and ground water. Environmental degradation is due to rapid industrialisation, expanding population, exploitation of natural resources, and this lead to global warming, ozone depletion, acid rain and health hazards.

This Textbook of Environmental Biotechnology contains 13 chapters.

Chapter 1 focuses on the scope of environmental biotechnology and discuses environmental science, environmental engineering and its limitations. Chapter 2 is devoted to environment and ecology and provides information on components of environmental and ecosystems. Chapter 3 looks at the need of environmental pollution. Various types of pollutions, their causes, effects and control are discussed. Chapter 4 considers the role of microbial metabolism. The chapter discusses various types of valuable micro-organisms their mechanism and metabolic pathways. Chapter 5 concentrates on analytical techniques for environmental monitoring. The chapter also discusses wastewater, air quality sound and radioactive monitoring along with minimum national standards for waste disposal.

Chapter 6 discusses management and treatment of waste. Various types of waste, their collection and treatments are discussed in detail. Chapter 7 considers the role of biological waste treatment. Various types of aerobic and anaerobic treatment processes are discussed along with the factors affecting these processes. Chapter 8 is devoted to bioreactors for waste treatment. Various types of biological treatment bioreactors on the basis of microbial growth pattern are discussed. Chapter 9 focuses on effluent treatment. Various aerobic

Textbook of Environmental Biotechnology

and anaerobic treatment processes along with step involved in treatment process are discussed. Chapter 10 serves as foundation to understand bioremediation. The chapter discusses various types of biodegradation, *in situ* and *ex situ* bioremediation along with treatment of soil and industrial wastes. Chapter 11 concentrates on bioenergy from waste. Various types of energy resources and biofuels along with their advantages, disadvantages and future prospects are discussed.

Chapter 12 provides information on value added products from organic waste such as biofertilisers, single cell protein, biofuels, mushroom and enzymes, etc. Chapter 13 is devoted to global environmental issues at national and international level as climate change, global warming, ozone layer, acid rain, sustainable development, protect biodiversity, various environment protection acts and legislations, international policies, summits and declarations to protect environment etc.

I am thankful to Mr Pravin Kr. Sachan, Assistant Professor, Department of Biochemical Engineering and Food Technology at Harcourt Butler Technical University, Kanpur, who helped me in editing the book. Appreciations are also extended to Mr Harinder Singh, Senior DTP operator, who drew and labelled the flow diagrams and worked long hours to bring the book on time. I am also thankful to the editorial team of Woodhead Publishing India Pvt. for their wholehearted cooperation in bringing out the book in time.

It may not be wrong to hold that this Textbook of Environmental Biotechnology is essential reading for students pursuing B.Tech/M.Tech, (Biotechnology, Environmental Engineering, Food Biotechnology, Biochemical Engineering). Besides students, this book will prove useful to industrialists and consultants in the respective fields.

It has been prepared with meticulous care, aiming at making the book error free. Constructive suggestions are always welcome from users of this book.

Pramod Kumar

Vipin Kumar

Foreword

Biotechnology has always been a fascinating subject as it unveils the manifestations of Nature. Environmental Biotechnology is more fascinating, because it envisages how the marvels of nature can be utilised by human beings. The twenty first century belongs to the biotechnologists. The development of science and technology has caused immense ecological damage due to overexploitation of the natural resources. Biotechnology can solve most of the problems caused by overexploitation of resources and mismanagement of waste, generated from product manufacturing industries. The application of Environmental Engineering principles, which are based on chemical processes turn into biological processes using microorganisms. It has given rise to the field of Environmental Biotechnology, is used to treat industrial effluents in a cost effective manner, which forms the subject matter of this book.

I am happy to note that Mr. Pramod Kumar having long experience of teaching Biotechnology Engineering is a faculty and Head, Department of Biotechnology at Hindustan College of Science and Technology, Mathura. With his academic brilliance in Biotechnology Engineering, he has authored this book, mainly to cater to the needs of students pursuing their B.Tech and M.Tech in Biotechnology.

This book is written in a manner that is simple to understand. Most of the complicated aspects of Environmental Biotechnology have been explained in a lucid style. The book addresses the Environmental Biotechnology principles with special reference to biological processes.

I am extremely happy to note that this text book is probably the best one of its kind, particularly at a time when industrial pollution is causing serious problems. The waste management and its treatment is challenging task to technical community working in this domain.

I recommend this book to the Biotechnology Engineering and Biochemical Engineering students, faculty members and young biotechnology engineers for better understanding. I wish the author all the best and the text book all success forever.

Prof. (Dr.) Rajeev Kumar Upadhyay
Director
Hindustan College of Science & Technology

Scope of Environmental Biotechnology

1.1   Introduction

It has been observed that population of world is exponentially increasing day by day and it is reaching over seven billion. To provide sufficient food, water, air and shelter to this population of the world is a big challenge. Nature has given us sufficient resources but we have to use these resources in right way. We are in era of globalisation and running very fast on road of development. During this economic growth race, we are exploiting natural resources and time will come when all these resources will finish. We should move towards sustainable development that means 'development without harming nature'.

Industrialisation plays an important role to enhance the economic growth rate of the country but the adverse effect of industrialisation results water pollution, soil pollution, air pollution, noise pollution, generation of solid waste, liquid waste, and gaseous waste.

Some industries are generating hazardous waste during product formation, sometimes waste is disposed without proper treatment that causes huge lose of flora, fauna and environment. It has been observed that ground water is too polluted due to peculation of heavy metals and hazardous wastes. The quality of air is being very poor due to emission of harmful gases. Soil fertility is another problem that we are facing is due to excess use of chemical fertilisers and chemical insecticides. The emission of harmful gases and generation of harmful wastes causing the environmental pollution.

1.2   Environmental science

The word environment is derived from French word 'Environner' which means our surroundings. All the living and non-living things are included in the environment. According to Environment Protection Act (EPA) 1986, environment is sum of water, air and land, interrelationship among themselves and also with the human beings, other living organisms and property.

Pollution may be defined as undesirable change in physical, chemical and biological characteristics of water, soil and air that can harm all living beings.

Environmental biotechnology is using technical approaches of biological sciences to deal with the environmental problems. A combination of biotechnological approaches is used to resolve the problems facing every one in the form of soil pollution, water pollution, air pollution, radioactive pollution, etc.

Environmental biotechnology involves specific application of biotechnological tools and techniques to resolve the problems of environmental pollution. Environmental biotechnology deals with environmental monitoring, environmental quality improvement, proper use of resources, and treatment of the waste by various approaches and techniques, replacement of non-renewable sources by renewable sources, development of microbial strains capable for degradation of hazardous pollutants, restoring biodiversity, monitoring the ecological changes and risk management. Environmental biotechnology components are shown in Fig. 1.1.

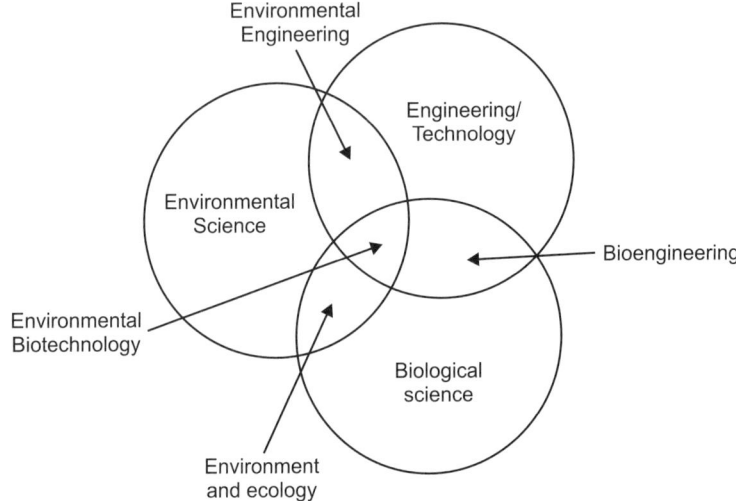

Figure 1.1: Environmental biotechnology components.

Sustainable development is the need of the day, to do this we should understand environment in deeper sense. Environmental science can play a key role to understand about environment. This deals with basic science as physics, chemistry, mathematics and biology. We can say that it is multidisciplinary dealing with every aspects of life. Environmental science provides a holistic view of the environment and human relationship with environment.

1.3   Environmental engineering and its limitations

Environmental engineering is fast growing field of engineering. This discipline provides concepts to use resources in right way, use methods which leads development towards sustainable development. Environmental engineering concepts help us to reduce effect of pollutants. It provides knowledge for management and treatment of waste using chemical reaction processes. The knowledge of environmental engineering techniques helps us to measure and monitor the changes which are taking place day to day and causes environmental pollution.

Environmental engineering aspects are helpful for measurement of pollution and also for treatment, but treatment process using chemical compounds to degrade and dispose generated waste. These chemical compounds are also creating problems when used in high concentration.

These chemical compounds are also a product; a huge cost is involved to manufacture these compounds. That's why environmental engineering based concepts have their own limitation. The treatment process is very costly and that is the reason, why this approach is not sufficient to attract the industrialist to use this for long time in future. Industry people are looking towards alternate method that could be more efficient, less costly and create no harmful effects on environment.

1.4 Environmental biotechnology, present and future prospects

Waste and pollutants are generated by various activities of man, e.g., domestic, agricultural, manufacture, transport, etc. This waste if not properly managed then it may contaminate air, water, and soil. The natural production processes use solar energy and produce materials containing the elements such as C, N, H, O, P and S. All the products are biodegradable. In contrast, synthetic production processes designed by man are inefficient in energy use, utilise as raw materials those elements present on earth, and many of the products of these processes are non-biodegrade. In addition, these processes generate by-products, waste or effluents, which are released in the environment cause damage to ecosystem.

To minimise the damaging effects of man made activities on the environment, man is developing technologies to clean up the pollution generated by other technologies. Man is also developing production technologies, which are 'cleaner' and generate less pollution. Both these technological approaches minimise damage to the environment. Environmental biotechnology uses biotechnological approaches for management of environmental problems. In nutshell, environmental biotechnology is the integration of natural and engineering sciences to achieve the application of organisms, cells, their parts and molecular analogues for products and services.

To solve the limitation of environmental engineering approaches and get advantage over it, biological components can be used in place of chemical agents. Biotechnology is emerging field of this era, where biological agents like micro-organisms are playing key role for degradation of organic waste and biotransformation of other hazardous chemical compounds by different types of microbial processes. Biotechnology can play a major role to understand global environmental challenge and also helpful to treat waste up to permissible limit in low cost.

Micro-organisms are present everywhere in nature, by sound knowledge of growth and metabolism patterns of these micro-organisms; one can use these in better way. Here environmental biotechnology will lead the problem solving approaches with the blend of technology, environmental science, engineering and biological agents as micro-organism.

Now a day's xenobiotic compounds are producing more harmful effects on the environment and making environment polluted. Xenobiotic compounds are not natural compounds these are man-made compounds like polythene, plastic, etc. These compounds are very dangerous for environment, human health, animals and vegetation.

In chemical processes a high pH waste is generated. It is very difficult to treat such type of waste using microbial treatment process because micro-organisms are not generally survive at very high pH (above 10 pH) but some micro-organisms can grow slowly at this pH. Such types of problems can be resolve by the use of biotechnology. Recombinant DNA technology can play major role to modify micro-organisms.

Such improved micro-organisms are called genetically modified or Recombinant micro-organisms. Recombinant micro-organisms are developed to meet out such type of problems. For example 'Super Bug' an oil eating bug first time developed using genetic engineering to genetically modify *Pseudomonas putida* by Dr. Anand Mohan Chakerborty. He named this genetically engineered micro-organism super bug. Super bug was developed for microbial degradation of oil spilled on coastal areas.

Organic waste is also generated in large amount. India is agriculture based country so large amount of agrowaste is generated during the harvesting and processing of the crops. Other sources of organic waste are domestic waste, excreta of animals, slaughter house waste, dairy waste, food industries waste, sugar industries waste, tannery waste, paper and pulp industry waste, brewery waste and effluent, distillery effluent, etc. Approximately two kilogram per capita waste is generated per day.

Such huge amount of waste produces bad odour and other harmful gases during microbial degradation in natural condition. So organic waste is also one of major causes of environmental pollution. Environmental biotechnology plays a vital role for utilisation of organic waste and conversion of organic waste in to the value added products with the help of different microbial processes. Biofuels, organic fertilisers, bofertilisers, bioinsecticides, etc., can be produced by different microbial conversion process of organic waste.

Major examples of biofuels are biogas (CH_4), bioethanol, biohydrogen, biodiesel, etc., which are produced by micro-organisms utilising organic matter or organic waste.

Environment and Ecology

2.1 Introduction

Environment is the combination of biotic and abiotic factors, which surrounds us and other organisms. Abiotic factors affect human being in least which includes water, air, soil, light, temperature, etc. The other factor is biotic factor which influence the environment much more compare to abiotic factors. Biotic factors include all forms of life like animals, plants, micro-organisms, etc. Human is an integrated part of the environment and have very close relationship with each other. The social life of human is also affected by its environment where human lives. It has been seen that water, soil, climate and language of human differ after distance to distance. That may leads to generate various types of social and cultural activities around the world.

In India only several regional languages and culture is present right from Kashmir to Kanyakumari. The people at hills have different life styles compare to people in the plain area. Similarly people around the world differ in their food, cloth, traditions, festivals, etc. All these are influenced by the factors around them.

The term ecology was coined by A. G. Tensley. Ecology is focused on the study of interaction between an organism of some kind and its environment. In ecology, the role of an organism or species play in its ecosystem is called ecological 'Niche'. An organism niches includes everything that affected by the organism not depending upon its lifetime. We study ecology to understand how nature interacts with living systems and how living systems respond to nature. Thus, ecology is a study to achieve new goal to help scientist to develop technical methods to protect the natural environment.

Environmental biotechnology can play an important role to balance interaction level of biotic and abiotic systems by developing these advanced methods for protecting environment and ecological system.

Dr. A. M. Chakrabarty developed a genetically modified strain of *Pseudomonas putida* which having oil eating capacity. Oil spills adversely affect the aquatic life due to lack of gaseous exchange that results the death of aquatic flora and funna.

Ecology has been defined as a study of interaction among living beings (animal, plants) and their environment. Ecology may be studied with particular reference to animals or to plants. Thus, it can be divided in to animal ecology and plant ecology. Animal ecology, however, cannot be completely understood except against a proper knowledge of plant ecology. The animal and plants are given equal emphasis; the term bioecology is often used. The term 'Synecology' is the study of communities with environment, and 'autecology' the study of species with environment.

2.2   Components of environment

There are three major components of environment. These are as following:

1. Physical component.
2. Biological component.
3. Social component.

2.2.1   Physical component

In physical component of environment we can includes air, water, soil, light, temperature, climate, etc. The physical components are also known as abiotic components of the environment.

These environmental components are responsible for determination of living conditions for the human population. Physical component of the environment is again divided into three parts as following:

1. Atmosphere (gas)
2. Hydrosphere (liquid)
3. Lithosphere (solid)

Structure of atmosphere: The atmosphere is broadly divided into four major zones. These zones are named as Troposphere, Stratosphere, Mesosphere and Thermosphere. The zones are pictorially represented in Fig. 2.1.

These three parts represent the three important states of matter constituting the environment. This physical component of environment only consists of abiotic components like air, water and soil. All these abiotic components influence much more to all living organisms including human. Water and temperature are the most important abiotic components affecting living beings as water is necessary for survival of livings. Water plays an important role to keep optimum temperature of the body and its metabolic activities. All living things work in a particular range of temperature. When temperature will not be in that range, growth of living beings will be affected. Air is one of the main physical component, which is required for respiration. All living beings including plants and animals require oxygen for their survival. In metabolic

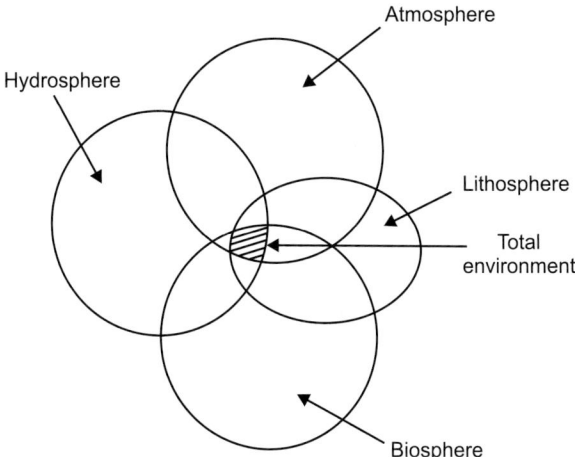

Figure 2.1: Components of environment.

process, oxygen is taken into the body and comes out in from of CO_2. On the other hand the plants consume CO_2 for food preparation during photosynthesis and gives out oxygen to the surrounding.

Soil is another important component for all living beings to create their habitat. It is the soil in which plant grows and man constructs houses to live in. Soil helps to retain ground water which is available for drinking and other farming activities.

2.2.2 Biological component

The biological component of environment is also called as biotic component. This biological component consists of all living things like plants, animals and small micro-organisms like bacteria, algae and fungi. Biological component interacts with the abiotic component of the environment. Interaction of these two components forms various ecosystems like forest ecosystem, pond ecosystem, marine ecosystem, desert ecosystem, etc. Biosphere is self sufficient and large ecosystem. All ecosystems consist of three different types of living organisms; these are producers, consumers and decomposers.

Producer consist of mainly green plants and other photosynthetic bacteria which produces various organic substances such as carbohydrates, proteins, etc., with the help of water, soil and light energy. Consumers depend on green plants for their nutrition as these green plants produces organic food materials. Decomposers decompose dead plants and animals and results in to various important minerals for the running of the natural cycles.

2.2.3   Social component

The third component of environment is social component. This component is mainly consists of various groups of population of different living beings like birds, animals, etc. Human is the most self sufficient and intelligent living organism. Like other living creatures on earth, man builds house, prepares food and releases waste materials to the environment. It has been said about human by Greek philosopher, Aristotle that human is a social animal. He makes various laws, policies for the proper functioning of the society.

These three components of the environment give rise to four important zones like Atmosphere, Hydrosphere, Lithosphere and Biosphere. There is continuous interaction among these four zones. These interactions involve the transport of various elements, compounds and different form of energy. These zones are explained as follows.

Atmosphere

Atmosphere consists of mixture of gases and suspended particles, form complex system called atmosphere. At the time of the planet origin atmosphere was not present. The atmosphere has been derived from the Earth itself in past by chemical and biochemical reactions. The gases like oxygen, argon, nitrogen, carbon dioxide and water vapour, etc., together make up the total volume of atmosphere. Together with suspended particulate matter, viz., dust and soot constitute the gaseous turbidity particularly in troposphere.

The vertical structure of atmosphere is very much related to radiant energy absorption and this can be described in terms of variable of temperature (Fig. 2.2). Below 60 km there are two main zones of absorption at the Earth's surface and in the ozone layer. The absorbed energy is redistributed by radiation, conduction and convection.

There are two temperature maxima: one maxima is at the Earth's surface and second is above 50 km from earth surface. There is mainly convectional mixing above each of these maxima. Temperature in these mixing layers decreases as height increases from heat source. The lower part of these two zones is known as troposphere and the upper is the mesosphere. These zones are separated by a slitly mixed layer in which the atmosphere tends towards a layered structure known as the stratosphere.

Tropopause is present between the ionosphere and the stratosphere which marks the approximate upper limit of mixing in the lower atmosphere. The average height of this is usually given as 11 km, but this varies depending on different latitude present over the earth. In tropical latitude its average height is 16 km and in polar latitude it is only 10 km.

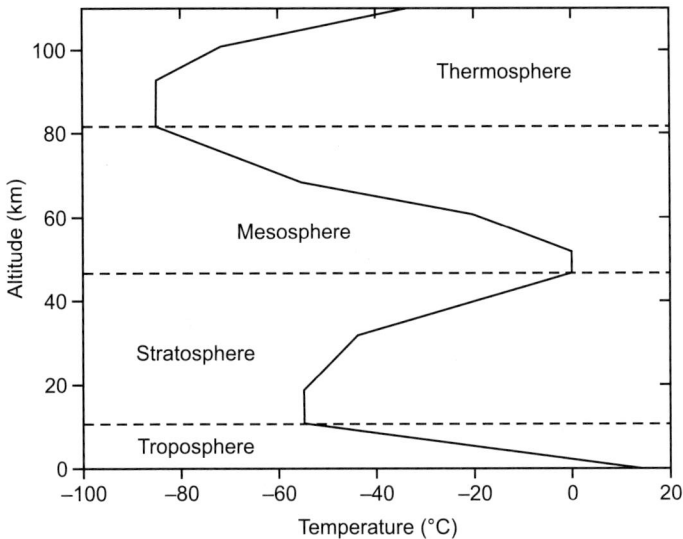

Figure 2.2: Temperature profile of atmospheric layer.

There is another zone of heating, above the mesosphere which is more than 90 km from the Earth's surface. In this zone shortwave ultraviolet radiation is absorbed by many oxygen molecules present at this height. This is known as thermosphere. Ionisation occurs in thermosphere zone which produces charged ions and free electrons. Exosphere present at a height of approximately 700 km where the atmosphere has an extremely low density. However, this simple model of vertical structure can be simplified to provide a model of the atmosphere as two concentric shells the boundaries of which are defined by the stratopause at approximately 50 km above the Earth's surface and a hypothetical outer limit of the atmosphere, at approximately 80,000 km. There is 99% of the total mass of the atmosphere in the stratosphere and troposphere below the stratopause. Beyond the stratopause a thick layer of nearly 80,000 km contains only 1% of total atmospheric mass and experiences ionisation by high-energy, short wavelength solar radiation.

Hydrosphere

Hydrosphere consists of water present on surface and its surrounding interface. It is important molecule for survival of life. Water possesses a number of physical and chemical properties, which help the molecule to act as best suited medium for life activities. Hydrological cycle acts as closed system where movement of water from earth surface to atmosphere takes place. On the earth surface, water is the most abundant and most important substance on the Earth's surface. Whole water of earth surface is divided in ocean, glaciers and ice caps. The oceans cover approximately 71% water of the planet, and rest water covered by glaciers and ice caps and additional areas. Water is also found in lakes and streams, in soils and underground reservoirs, in the atmosphere, and in the bodies of all living organism. Water is used at home, in industry, in agriculture, and for recreation. These applications differ widely in the quantity and quality of the water that they require. We are consuming all available sources of water inland waters, ground water, and even oceanic water. The demand for global water resources increasing day-by-day that could fulfill the need of the day. Today the availability of pure fresh water has been decreasing severely. Thus there is need to understand the global problem and develop good habit to consume pure fresh water and their fruitful storage and conservation. A simplified outline of hydrological cycle is given in Fig. 2.3

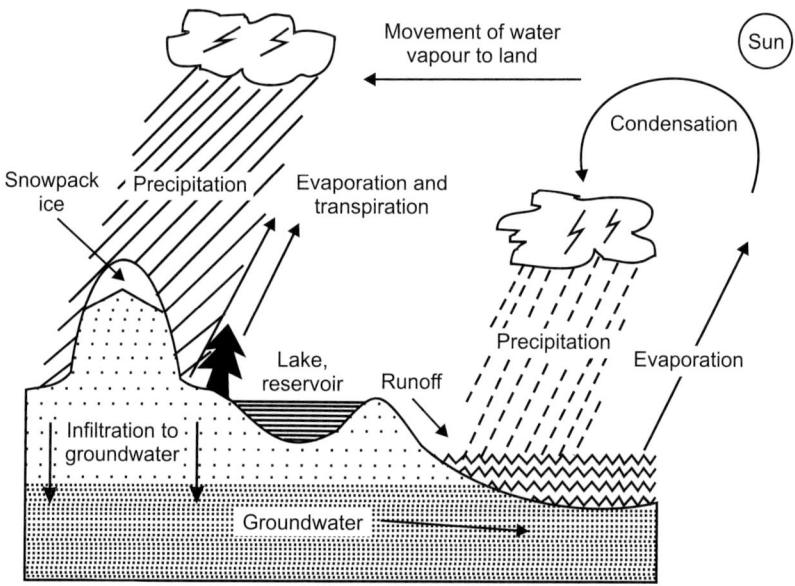

Figure 2.3: Hydrological cycle.

Lithosphere

Lithosphere is the outer boundary layer of solid earth which forms a complex interface with the atmosphere and hydrosphere. This is the environment in which life has originated. The inner boundary is adjacent to rock, which is at high temperature near its melting point. Lithosphere is nothing but a crustal system made up of various layers. These layers are known as core, mantle and outer crust. Various elements constitute such crustal layer in mixture of different proportions. In general, the earth curst is composed of three major classes of rocks, like igneous rocks, sedimentary rocks and metamorphosed rocks.

There are two types of crusts – Continental crust which consist of granitic rocks containing silicon, aluminium and the others. Oceanic crust which is basaltic in composition consists of more basic minerals. Interaction between the crustal system of the lithosphere, atmosphere and biosphere takes place where continental crust is exposed above sea-level. At the land/air interface crustal material becomes exposed to inputs of solar radiant energy, precipitation and atmospheric gases. These inputs are often modified through the effects of the living systems of the biosphere. Under the influence of these inputs, crustal rocks are broken down by weathering process and are transferred to fine porous crustal layers called soil.

Biosphere

The zones on the Earth in which life is present is called biosphere. It develops on earth since 4.5 billion year through the process of evolution. At the top of the lithosphere, throughout the hydrosphere and into the lower atmosphere, life of diverse type exists. These bio-resources and their surrounding constitute the 'Biosphere' where mankind acts as the most developed creation. Very complex steps are involved in the origin of life on earth and require several centuries. Considerable uncertainty surrounds the details of atmospheric composition, the processes involved and even the sequence of some events leading to formation of living cells. The conventional view observed that the earliest organism on the planet were heterotrophic prokaryotic bacteria. Autotrophic prokaryotes and eukaryotes appeared as stepwise evolutionary changes. Life on Earth requires water, a source of energy (sun light) and various nutrients found in the soil, water and air. Appropriate combinations of these essentials cannot be found high in the upper atmosphere or deep underground. These exists only in a narrow layer near the surface of the Earth.

2.3   Ecology and ecosystem

Every living being either small or big depends on the environment for its existence. Living being also competes with others for essentials in life. Living beings form groups and different groups compete with each other for survival in life. The study of interrelationships between organisms and group of organisms is called the science of ecology. The word ecology has its roots from two Greek words 'ikos' meaning a house or dwelling or place of living or habitat and ecology is hence the study of interrelationship among plants and animals and their interactions with the physical environment.

Ecology can be classified as Autoecology and Synecology.

1. Autoecology or species ecology: This is the study of an individual species, i.e., behaviour, adaptation and interaction of a particular species in its environment.

2. Synecology or ecology of communities: This is the study of communities and their interaction with the environment.

2.3.1   Concept of ecosystem

An ecosystem is defined as a collection of plants, animals or living organisms living together and interacting with the physical environment in which they live. An ecosystem is a closed boundary system and the flow of mass in and out of the system is very less as compared to the internal movement of mass. Ecosystems may be large or small. Examples of large ecosystems are rain forests, deserts, salt marshes, coral reefs, lakes and ponds, open ocean, grasslands, etc.

2.3.2   Component of ecosystem

Ecosystem components consist of both living or biotic and abiotic components, which are called environmental factors or ecological factors. A factor is component of environment which directly or indirectly affects the life of an organism.

Abiotic components

The physical factors of the environmental component which have a major influence on the life of organisms.

The abiotic components are of two types. These are:

1. Climatic factors.

2. Edaphic factors.

Climatic factors: Climatic factors consist of light, temperature, rainfall and ice, wind, humidity, etc. The climate of an area is the result of several factors such as latitude, elevation, distance from the sea, and monsoon activities and ocean currents.

Temperature: Temperature is most important component, it affects the metabolic rates of reactions in plants and animal both. Reaction rate will approximately double with every 10°C increase in temperature. Plant species require a range of temperature to survive. Below a minimum temperature they are inactive, and above a maximum temperature physiological reactions stop. Normally in many plant species growth is possible above 6°C. In areas with extremes of temperature, such as the tundra and tropical deserts the plants have mechanisms to adapt such adverse conditions.

Light energy: Energy obtained from sun light affects the magnitude of photo-synthesis reactions in plants. Different plant species have their characteristic light requirements in respect of light intensity, duration and wavelength. Some plants, known as helophytes, require high intensity light, whereas sciophytes can grow in shady or low light conditions.

Water: Water is an important factor for plant to proceed biochemical metabolic or physiological processes, including photosynthesis. Plants growing on lands obtain their water requirements from the soil through their roots by the osmosis process. Plants known as hydrophytes grow in fresh water and they cannot survive in drought. Xerophytes survive for long periods in drought, and halophytes are able to survive in saline water. Mesophytes require moderate conditions (neither waterlogged nor drought) and are found mainly in temperate areas.

Edaphic factors or soil factors: These edaphic factors are pH, mineral and organic matter in soil and texture of soil.

Soil: It is the major source of nutrients and moisture in almost all the land ecosystems. Soil is formed due to rock weathering .The rocks brake down into a collection of different inorganic or mineral particles. The type and rate of the weathering of the rocks as well as the nature of the vegetation growing on it is dependents on climate. Nutrients are recycled in the soil by the plants and animals in their life cycles of growth, death and decomposition. Thus humus material essential to soil fertility is produced.

Soil mineral matter: This soil matter is derived from the weathering of rock material. These minerals consist of two types, viz., stable primary materials like quartz and various secondary materials like clays and oxides of Al and Fe.

Soil texture: Texture of soil is the different size range of mineral particles varying from fine clay to coarse gravel. The different percentages of each size range produce soils with different characteristics.

Soil organic matter: This soil organic matter is called humus that is formed by the decomposition of plant residue (agro waste) and animal matter. The rate of digestion or decomposition depends upon the nature of the material and the climate. The humus produced and incorporated into the soil, is known as clay-humus complexes, which are important soil nutrients.

Biotic components

The living component of an ecosystem is called biotic component, it consist of plants, animals, and micro-organisms (bacteria and fungi). They carry out different functions and based on their role they are classified into three main groups. These are:

1. Producers
2. Consumers
3. Decomposers

Producers: Producers are mainly green plants those having chlorophyll and able to perform photosynthesis. These plants produce carbohydrates by photosynthesis process. Plants convert solar energy into chemical energy using water and carbon dioxide in this photosynthesis process. These plants are called autotrophs since they produce their own food. Part of the food produced by the autotrophs are utilised for their own consumption for survival and growth while the remaining is stored in the plant parts for future consumption. This becomes the food for other biotic components in the environment.

Consumers: Consumers are living things and they do not have chlorophyll, and hence they are unable to produce their own food. They depends on the producers for their food requirements. Consumers are called Heterotrophs. Consumers are classified into four categories.

1. Primary consumers (first order consumers) or herbivores: They are also called first order consumers. They eat the producers or plants. Examples are cattle like cow and goat, deer, rabbit, etc.
2. Secondary consumers (second order consumers) or primary carnivores: They are also called second order consumers. They eat herbivores examples are snakes, cats foxes, etc.
3. Tertiary consumers (third order consumers): They are also called third order consumers. They feed on secondary consumers. They are large Carnivores. Example is wolf.
4. Quaternary consumers (fourth order consumers): They are also called fourth order consumers. They feed on secondary consumers. They are very large carnivores and feed on tertiary consumers and are not consumed by other animals. Examples are lions and tigers.

Decomposers: Decomposers are termed as Saprotrophs. These are mainly micro-organisms like bacteria and fungi. They feed on dead organic materials of producers and consumers. They decompose the complex organic matter into simple compounds during their metabolic process. These simple compounds are nutrients, which are absorbed by the producers.

2.3.3 Concept of energy flow in ecosystem

The sun is the ultimate source to fulfil all our energy needs. It is working as a continuously exploding hydrogen bomb where hydrogen is converted to helium with the release of energy. This produced energy is mostly in the region of 0.2 to 4 mm in the electromagnetic spectrum (ultraviolet to infra red). Around 50% of the radiant energy is in the visible range. The energy reaches the earth at a constant rate is called the solar flux or solar constant, which is the amount of radiant energy crossing per unit area in unit time. Chlorophyll containing plants convert this solar energy into carbohydrates and sugars using carbon dioxide and water.

This process is known as photosynthesis. The generalised form of the photosynthetic reaction is as follows:

$$6CO_2 \; + \; 12H_2O \;\; \rightarrow \;\; C_6H_{12}O_6 \; + \; 6O_2 \; + \; 6H_2O$$
$$\text{Carbon dioxide} \quad \text{Water} \qquad\qquad \text{Glucose} \quad \text{Oxygen} \quad\;\; \text{Water}$$

The plant produces carbohydrates by photosynthesis undergo further modifications such as production of proteins and nucleic acids by combining with nitrogen, phosphorous and sulphur. Cellulose is formed after poly-merisation of starch. The energy obtained from sun thus enters the living beings through photosynthetic reactions and is passed from one organism to another in the form of food. The flow of energy is unidirectional and is governed by the thermodynamic law that states that energy is neither created nor destroyed and can transform into different forms. When energy travels from producers to different levels of consumers in an ecosystem there is loss of energy at each level due to the energy dissipated in the form of heat during the metabolic processes of the organisms. Energy travel in ecosystem is shown in Fig. 2.4.

Thus as we move step by step away from the primary producers the amount of available energy decreases rapidly. Hence only 6 to 7 feeding levels are possible. These feeding levels are referred to as Tropic levels.

Ecosystems are arranged by trophic (feeding) levels between various producers, the autotrophs, and consumers, the heterotrophs:

First trophic level (producer): Contains the autotrophs which build energy containing molecules. They also absorb nitrogen, phosphorous, sulphur and other molecules necessary for life. They provide both an energy-fixation base as well as the nutrient-concentration base for ecosystems. Two types of autotrophs: photoautotrophs - plants and some protista. Chemoautotrophs - bacteria

Second trophic level (primary consumer): It contains the primary consumers which eat the primary producers including herbivores, decomposers and detritivores, e.g., insects, grasshoppers, deer and wildebeest.

Third trophic level (secondary consumer): It contains the secondary consumers, primary carnivores which eat the herbivores, e.g., Bonobo, mice, spiders and many birds.

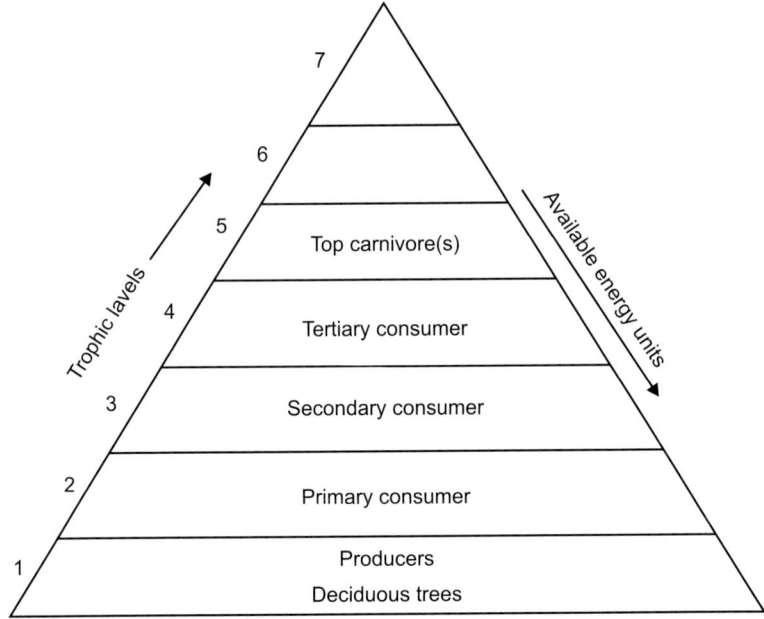

Figure 2.4: Energy travel in ecosystem.

Fourth trophic level (tertiary consumer): It contains the tertiary consumers, secondary carnivores who eat the primary carnivores, e.g., Crocodile, weasel, owl, sharks and wolves.

2.3.4   Food chain, food web, ecological pyramids

Autotrophs

The food chain is an ideal model of flow of energy in the ecosystem. In food chain the plants or producers are eaten by only the primary consumers, primary consumers are eaten by only the secondary consumers and so on. The producers those can produce their own food are called autotrophs.

Any food chain has three main tropic levels, viz., producers, consumers and decomposers. The energy efficiency of each tropic level is very low. Hence shorter the food chain greater will be the availability of food. The typical food chain in a field ecosystem might be grass, rabbit or mouse, snake, hawk.

Food webs are more complex and are interlinked at different trophic levels. Organisms have more than one alternative for food and hence survivability is better. Hawks don't limit their food to snakes, snakes eat things other than mice, and mice eat grass as well as grasshoppers, and so on. A more realistic depiction of eating habits in an eco system is called a food web. An examples of food chain is shown in Fig. 2.5.

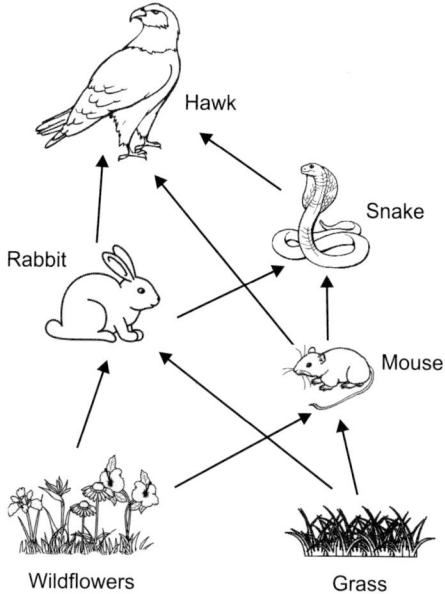

Figure 2.5: Food chain.

Food web

Charles Elton introduced the food web concept in year 1927, which he referred to as food cycle. Charles Elton described the concept of food web as: The carnivore animals prey upon the herbivores. These herbivores get the energy from sunlight. The later carnivores may also be preyed upon by other carnivores. Until a reach where an animal has no enemies it forms a terminus on this food cycle. There are chains of animals that are linked together by food, and all are dependent on plants in the long run. This is referred to as a food chain and all the food chains in a community is known as the food web. A food web of forest ecosystem is given in Fig. 2.6.

A food web is a graphical depiction of feeding connections among species of an ecological community. Food web consists of food chains of a particular ecosystem. The food web is a illustration of various methods of feeding that links the ecosystem. The food web also defines the energy flow through species of a community as a result of their feeding relationships. All the food chains are interconnected and overlapping within an ecosystem and they make up a food web.

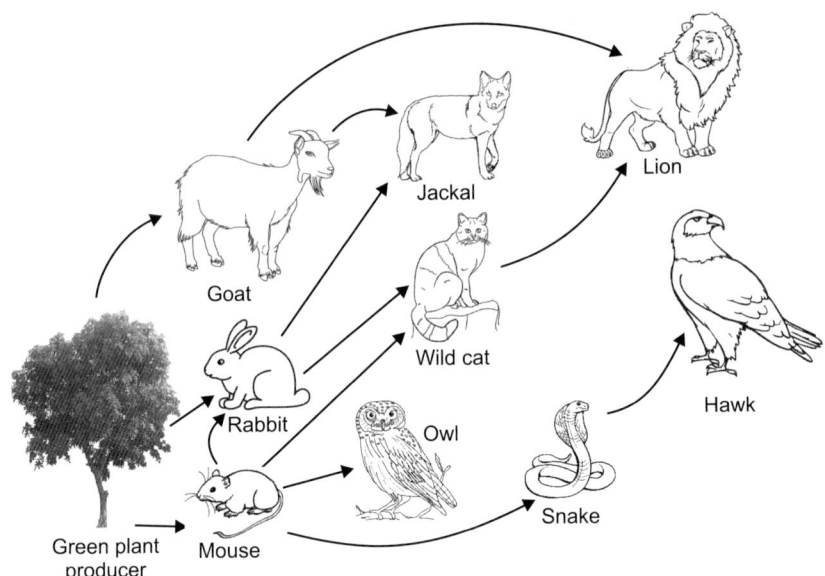

Figure 2.6: Food web of a forest ecosystem.

In natural environment or an ecosystem, the relationships between the food chains are interconnected. These relationships are very complex, as one organism may be a part of multiple food chains. Hence, a web like structure is formed in place of a linear food chain. The web like structure if formed with the interlinked food chain and such matrix that is interconnected is known as a food web. Food webs are an indispensible part of an ecosystem; these food webs allow an organism to obtain food from more than one type of organism of the lower trophic level. Every living being is responsible and is a part of multiple food chains in the given ecosystem.

Ecological pyramids

Ecological pyramid represent the trophic levels of different organisms based on their ecological position as producer to final consumer. The food producer present at the base of the pyramid and on the top. Other consumer trophic levels are in between. The pyramid consists of a number of horizontal bars presenting specific trophic levels. The length of each bar represents the total number of individuals or biomass or energy at each trophic level in an ecosystem. An ecological pyramid is a graphical representation designed to show the biomass or bio productivity at each trophic level in a given ecosystem. These are trophic pyramid, energy pyramid, or sometimes food pyramid. Biomass is the amount of living or organic matter present in an organism.

Biomass pyramids represent the quantity of biomass how much it is present in the organisms at each trophic level. The productivity pyramids represent the production or turnover in biomass. Ecological pyramids originates with producers on the bottom such as green plants and proceed through the various trophic levels such as herbivores that eat plants, then carnivores that eat herbivores, then carnivores that eat those carnivores, and so on. The highest level is the top of the chain. An ecological pyramid of biomass shows the relationship between biomass and trophic level by quantifying the biomass present at each trophic level of an ecological community at a particular time. It is a graphical representation of biomass present in per unit area in different trophic levels. Flow of energy through the food chain will be in a predictable way, entering at the base of the food chain, by photosynthesis in primary producers, and then moving up the food chain to higher trophic levels.

The transfer of energy from one trophic level to the next is inefficient. It may also be useful and productive to examine how the number and biomass of organisms vary across trophic levels. Both the number and biomass of organisms at each trophic level should be influenced by the amount of energy entering that trophic level. When there is a direct correlation between energy, numbers, and biomass then biomass pyramids and numbers pyramids will result. However, the relationship between energy, biomass, and number can be complicated by the growth form and size of organisms and ecological relationships occurring among trophic levels.

2.3.5   Types of pyramids

The ecological pyramids are of three categories:

1. Pyramid of numbers.
2. Pyramid of biomass.
3. Pyramid of energy or productivity.

Pyramid of numbers

Pyramid of numbers represents the population of trophic level as how much total number of individuals of different species present at each trophic level. Pyramid of numbers may be upright and may be completely inverted that will depend upon count of individual present and so. The pyramid of number does not completely define the trophic structure for an ecosystem as it is very difficult to count all the organisms present overthere. Pyramid of numbers in grass land and pond ecosystem are shown in Fig. 2.7.

Pyramid of numbers – upright: In this pyramid, the number of individuals is decreased from lower level to higher trophic level.

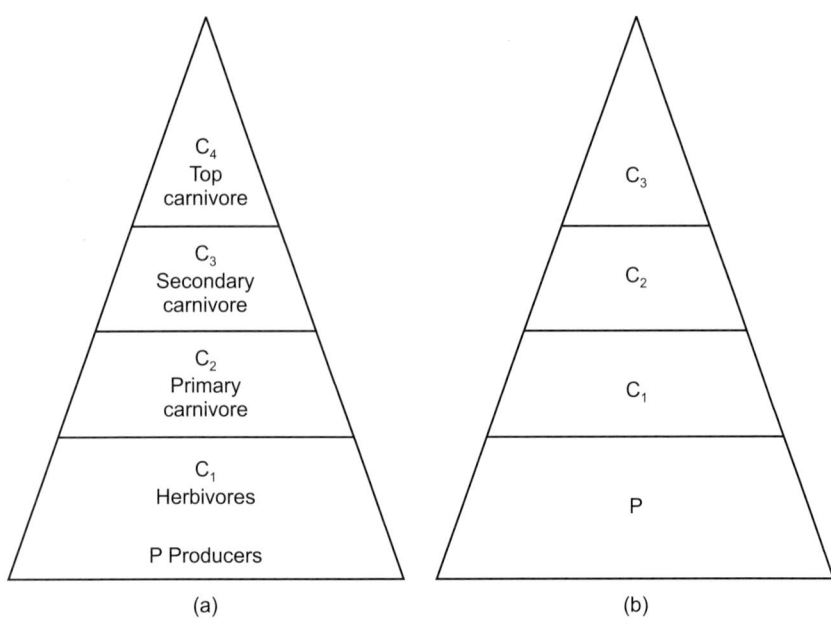

Figure 2.7: Pyramid of numbers in (a) grass land, and (b) pond ecosystem.

Grassland ecosystem and pond ecosystem is good example of pyramid of numbers. At base (lowest trophic level) grass is present in abundent amount. The next higher trophic level is primary consumer – herbivore (example – grasshopper). The number count of grasshopper is less than that of grass. The next energy level is primary carnivore (example – rat). The number of rats are less than grasshopper, because, they feed on grasshopper. The next higher trophic level is secondary carnivore (example – snakes). They feed on rats. The next higher trophic level is the top carnivore. (example – Hawk). As we reach each higher trophic level, the numbers of individual decreases from lower to higher trophic level.

Pyramid of numbers – inverted: In this type of pyramid, the number of individuals is increased from lower level to higher trophic level. Example, tree ecosystem (Fig. 2.8).

Pyramid of biomass

Pyramid of biomass (Fig. 2.9) represents the total dry weight of organisms. It is usually determined by collecting all organisms occupying each trophic level separately and measuring their dry weight. This will help to solve the size difference problem because all kinds of organisms at a trophic level are weighed. The measuring unit of biomass is g/m^2. The biomass of a species is

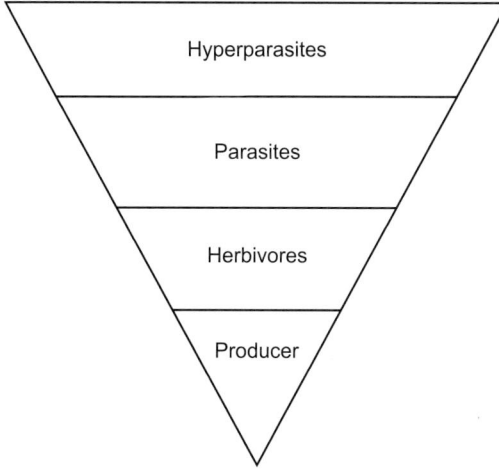

Figure 2.8: Inverted pyramid of number - tree ecosystem.

expressed in terms of fresh or dry weight. Measurement of biomass in terms of dry weight is more accurate. Certain mass of living material of each trophic level at a particular time called as standing crop. The standing crop is measured as the mass of living organisms (biomass) or the number in a unit area.

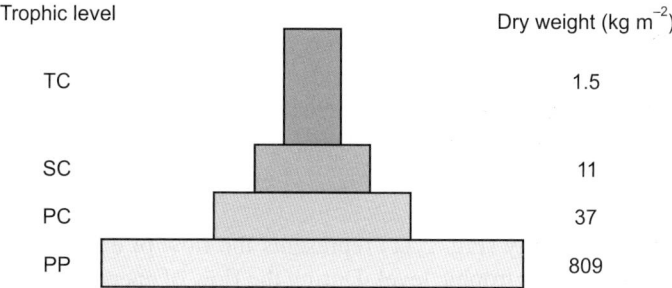

Figure 2.9: Pyramid of biomass represents sharp decrease in biomass from lower to higher trophic level.

Pyramid of biomass – upright: The pyramid of biomass on land contains a large base of primary producers with a smaller trophic level present on top. The biomass of producer known as autotrophs is at the maximum. The biomass of next trophic level from base, i.e., primary consumers is less than the producers. The biomass of next higher trophic level, i.e., secondary consumers is less than the primary consumers. The top, high trophic level contains very less amount of biomass. Upright pyramid of biomass in terrestrial ecosystem is shown in Fig. 2.10.

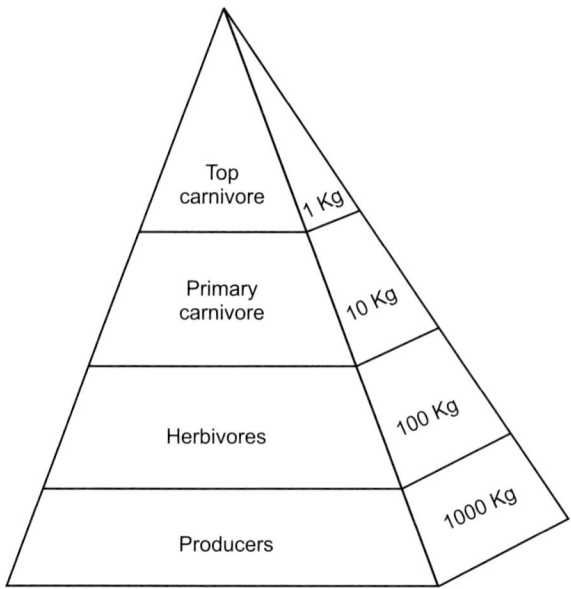

Figure 2.10: Upright pyramid of biomass in terrestrial ecosystem.

On other hand, in many aquatic ecosystems, the pyramid of biomass may present in an inverted form. Pyramid of numbers for aquatic ecosystem is upright.This is because the producers are small phytoplankton that grow and reproduce very rapidly. Here, the pyramid of biomass has a small base compare to the consumer biomass at any instant actually exceeding the producer biomass and the pyramid represent in inverted shape.

Pyramid of energy

The pyramid of energy (Fig. 2.11) represents the flow of energy from lower trophic level to higher trophic level. During the flow of energy from organism to other, there is considerable loss of energy. This loss of energy is in the form of heat. The primary producers like the autotrophs contain more amount of energy available.

The least energy is available in the tertiary consumers. Thus, shorter food chain has more amount of energy available even at the highest trophic level. An energy pyramid is most suitable to compare the functional roles of the trophic levels in an ecosystem. An energy pyramid represents the amount of energy at each trophic level and loss of energy during transfer to another trophic level. Hence the pyramid is always upward, with a large energy base at the bottom.

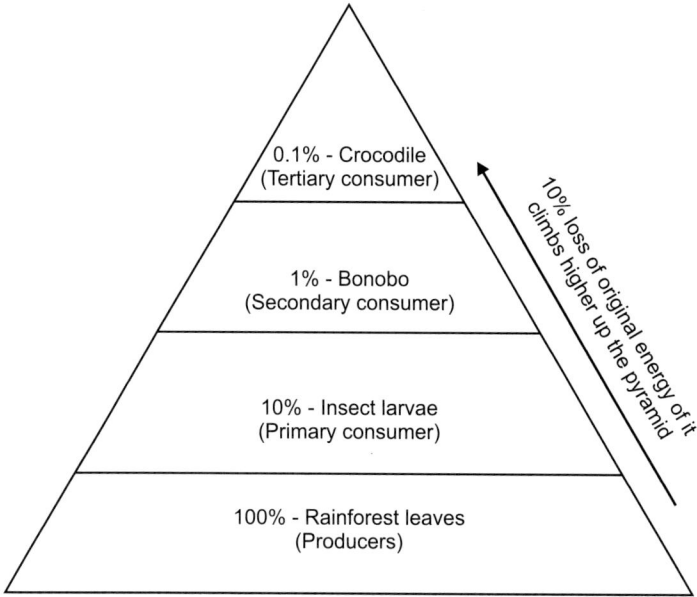

Figure 2.11: Pyramid of energy.

Suppose an ecosystem receives 1000 calories of light energy in a given day. Most of the energy is not absorbed by plants; some amount of energy is reflected back to space. Green plants utilise only a small portion of that absorbed energy, out of which the plant uses up some for respiration and of the 1000 calories, only 100 calories (10%) are stored as energy rich materials. Now suppose an animal eats the plant containing 100 calorie of food energy, that animal uses some of it for its own metabolism and stores only 10 calorie as food energy. A lion that eats that animal gets an even smaller amount of energy. Thus usable energy decreases from sunlight to producer to herbivore to carnivore. Therefore, the energy pyramid will always be upright.

Environmental Pollution

3.1   Introduction

When industry produces a product for consumption in society, waste is also generated. There is huge number of industrial units working in different sectors working all over the world. All these units generate a big quantity of waste along with products. If this waste will not be treated properly, it will cause pollution problems. Industrial pollution deteriorates the environment in a range of ways and it has negative impact on human lives and health.

Pollutants can kill animals and plants, imbalance ecosystems, degrade air quality, damage buildings and adversely affect quality of life. Any form of pollution that can trace its immediate source to industrial practices is known as industrial pollution. Most of the pollution on the planet can be traced back to industries of some kind. In fact, the issue of industrial pollution has taken on grave importance for agencies trying to fight against environmental degradation. Countries facing sudden and rapid growth of such industries are finding it to be a serious problem which has to be brought under control immediately.

Environmental pollutants are present in three forms namely, gases, liquid and solids. The pollutants emitted through industrial chimney and exhausts, mainly oxides of nitrogen, HC, CO_2, H_2S, SO_2, Cl_2, etc., cause air pollution. There are no direct biological methods by which these pollutants can be trapped.

3.2   Requirement and introduction of environmental biotechnology

Biotechnology can be defined as the application of scientific and engineering principles to the processing of material by biological agent. Micro-organisms follow different metabolic pathways to degrade material in to new form.

Environmental biotechnology applies the principles of microbiology to various environmental issues.

These environmental issues are as follows.

1. Treatment of industrial effluent and municipal wastewater.
2. Improvement in the quality of drinking water.
3. Protection of rivers, lakes and coastal waters.

4. Prevention of spreading pathogens through water and air.
5. Production of desirable product by use of waste like, methanol, methane, SCP, etc.
6. Global changes.
7. Environmental monitoring.
8. Restoring of environmental quality.
9. Resource/residue/waste recovery/utilisation/treatment through application of rDNA technology.
10. Substitution of non-renewable resources by renewable ones.
11. Strain improvement for degradation of highly – Toxic pollutants with the production of chemicals.
12. Biological diversity.
13. Risk management.

If more sincere efforts are made by those who are concerned, then only biotechnology assume the status of trusts and sought after technology in the environment protection field.

Potential biological treatments are:

1. *In situ* degradation of specific waste, using specialised cultures.
2. Inoculation of conventional waste treatment system which with adapted, specialised cultures.
3. Decontamination and detoxification of spoilages.
4. Heavy metal removal, recovery.
5. Bio-scrubbing of odour and waste noxious gases.
6. Generation of biomass (single cell protein, mushrooms) from waste.
7. Bio-gasification and ethanol production from waste.

3.3   Definition of environmental pollution

An undesirable change in the physical, chemical or biological characteristics of our air, water and land that may or will harmfully, affect human life. Or an addition or excessive addition of certain materials to the physical environment (water, air, land) making it less fit or unfit for life.

Pollutant: Pollutants are the material or agent which cause adverse effect on the natural quality of any component of environment or agent which causes environmental pollution, e.g., kitchen garbage, smoke, pesticides, noise, industrial effluent.

3.3.1   Types of pollutants

1. On the basis of form: (i) primary pollutants: these are the pollutants which are emitted into the atmosphere directly from the source, e.g., SO_2, CO_2, CO, (ii) secondary pollutants: these are formed in atmosphere as a result of some chemical reactions or photochemical reaction between two reactors or two primary pollutants. Example H_2SO_4, Mist, O_3, PAN (Peroxy acetyle nitrate).

2. On the basis of their existence: (i) quantitative pollutants: substances which occur in environment or nature but excess or beyond a threshold value become pollutants, e.g., CO_2, NO_2, and (ii) qualitative pollutants: do not occur in environment but passing in human activity create pollution, e.g., fungicides, herbicides.

3. On the basis of their natural disposal: (i) biodegradable: which degrade slowly by the active of microbe or naturally, e.g., kitchen waste, and (ii) non-degradable, e.g., aluminium cans, mercuric salt, long chain phenolic compound, plastic, etc.

4. On the basis of origin: (i) natural: volcanic eruptions add tons of toxic gases. Oils, mercury, lead, sulphur, etc. in rivers waters, and (ii) anthro-pogenic: it is manmade pollution, e.g., industrial waste, agricultural waste, automobiles, smoke from chimney.

3.3.2   Type of water pollution

Waste discharge from various sources pollutes water, which leads to land pollution too, in four ways. Accordingly there are four types of water pollution.

1. Physical pollution
2. Chemical pollution
3. Physiological pollution
4. Biological pollution

Physical pollution

Physical pollution of water is caused by the solid constituents of industrial effluents and sewage water. The nature of these solids varies depending on the type of industry. Most of the solids can be separated from the liquid by some physical process like settling and filtration.

Chemical pollution

Solid and colloidal chemicals that can be separated easily by any physical method, even by ultrafiltration, cause chemical pollution. These may be either organic or inorganic in nature. Due to discharge of effluents containing inorganic soluble chemicals such as acids, salts, and alkalies, the pH of a natural water source may change which is not desirable.

The same thing is true in the case of land pollution also. Heavy metals such as Cr, Ba and As are also responsible for toxicity of water.

When highly oxidisable chemicals, such as condensed types of tanning and reducing types of bleaching agents, are discharged, included oxygen deficiency occurs in aquatic life, causing respiration problems. It is therefore essential that all such oxidisable chemicals present in wastewater be peroxidised such H_2SO_4.

This will prevent the depletion of occluded oxygen by effluent chemicals in receiving water. To affect this amount of oxygen needed to stabilise the chemical oxygen demand (COD) of wastewater must be determined.

Physiological pollution

After removal of suspended particles and stabilisation of chemicals, the effluent may become harmless in general. However such a harmless effluent may still not be acceptable to the public due to the following reasons.

1. The effluent may impact colour, produce odour, or even change the taste of receiving water and the fish living it.
2. Colloidal solids which do not settle easily cause the receiving water to become turbid. This reduce the penetration depth of the sunlight and lower the rate of the natural process of purification by photochemical reaction.

Biological pollution

Biological pollution is caused by the organic matter present in wastewater or solid waste. The various types of micro-organism present in air water and soil decompose these polymeric complex compound into simpler ones and finally convert them into CO_2 and H_2O by consuming large quantity of dissolved oxygen (DO), thereby rendering the water or surrounding oxygen deficient.

3.3.3   Water pollution

Physical, chemical biological, substances of such quantity that its natural quality is altered as to impair useful.

The quality of water is very important to mankind. It is directly connected to human health (can-cause disease like diarrhea, dysentery, cholera, jaundice, etc.). Water which has lost its pure nature is called polluted water.

Properties of polluted water

1. Mild ore stronger colouration (yellowish brownish, etc.).
2. Bad taste.
3. Offensive small
4. Too much water plant in the water body.
5. Oil and grease floating on water surface.

The major sources of water pollution:

1. Artificial sources: Artificial sources are domestic waste, mainly sewage, industrial waste and agriculture waste.
2. Natural sources: Related with adverse with weather conditions such as, intense rain, floods. This may consists of runoff from land carrying silt, vegetable matter, manure, etc. Erosion of river banks and valley slopes.

Types of water wastes or pollutants and their properties:

1. Pathogenic organisms
2. Oxygen – demanding substances
3. Plant nutrients
4. Toxic organics
5. Inorganic chemicals
6. Sediment
7. Radioactive substances
8. Heat and oil

Effects

1. In sewage some chemicals (phenolic compounds, Cr, Hg, Pb, etc.), are present which advisely effects aquatic life plant and animals that leads to die of these living things.
2. Wastewater contaminated with feces leak out and gets mixed with ground water then drinking water may borne many diseases.
3. Extra nitrate in water leads to many problems.
4. Certain type of anemia in babies which cause suffocation and death.
5. Miscarriage (natural abortion) in women.
6. Cancer of digestive tracts.
7. Not good for plant roots are damaged and their stems and branches become thin.
8. Bacteria viruses or fluorides, nitrates, sulphate, etc., present in drinking water cause disease of serious nature.

9. Organic matter present in water, consumes the DO for biological decomposition, thus rendering it unfit for aquatic life.
10. When toxic chemicals from industrial effluents join the water sources, water becomes unfit for domestic use as well as for agriculture.

Harmful effects of ground water

1. Effect on man: (i) major cause for the spread of epidemics and chronic disease in man. It causes typhoid, jaundice, dysentery, diarrhea, tuberculosis and hepatitis, (ii) water contaminated by fibres i.e. asbestos cause fatal disease like asbestos and lung cancer, and (iii) ground water in excessive rainfall areas contains iron in toxic amount 20 ppm for drinking purpose permissible limit of iron is only 0.3 ppm, (iv) woolen industry contribute large amount of toxic metals such as Hg, Ni, Cu, Cr, Fe and cyanides to ground water causing skin and stomach disease in man effect of rain water.
2. Effect on soil: (i) irrigating agricultural field severely damages crops as decrease grain production, (ii) affect on soil fertility by killing bacteria and soil micro-organism, and (ii) affect plant metabolism severely and disturbs the whole ecosystem.

Effect of mercury poisoning: By industrial effluent

Harmful effect of sewage and domestic water:

1. Sewage is an excellent medium for growth of pathogenic bacteria, viruses and protozoa. *Vibriocholera* found in sewage causes cholera, *salmonella typhosa* causes typhoid, even after treatment.
2. Domestic sewage, which is primarily, composed of spent water containing wine, soopy wastes, food materials.
3. Several pathogenic micro-organism introduced in water course cause deleterious effects and chronic diseases in human and animal.
4. Sewage containing oxidisable and fermentable matter causes depletion of DO in water bodies affecting aquatic life and production of objectionable odours in water.
5. Solid and suspended matter creates river or water beds and blanket which cause reduction of aquatic life.

Harmful effect of industrial waste

1. Industrial effluent cause deleterious effects on living organisms and may bring about death or sublethal pathology of kidneys, liver, lungs, brain and reproduction system.

2. Effluent like methyl mercaptan and pentachlorophenol lower the photo-synthetic rate of aquatic communities by hindering sunlight penetration into water column.

3. Free chlorine discharged by factory cause heavy fish mortality in river.

4. Hg creates fetal disease like minimata in Japan.

5. As, Pb, CN, etc., cause cellular degeneration in brain which result in figidita, coma, stupov and numbness,

6. Acid and alkali make water corrosive.

7. Excess minerals cause water hardness which are then unsuitable for domestic and industrial purpose.

8. Tannery contains pathogen bacteria *Anthrax bacilli* and chromium also cause skin and eye irritation problem and also decrease soil ferities.

9. Heated effluent create unpleasant for water bodies.

Agricultural waste

Plant nutrients, pesticides, insecticides herbicides, fertilisers, farm waste, manure, sediments, plant animal debris contain organic material which causes water pollution.

Effects on humans

Excessive use of fertiliser lead the accumulation of nitrate in water which cause serious disease in children like methemoglobin anemia (blue bodies) and also nitrite interfere with O_2 carrying capacity of blood causing suffocation and damage respiratory as vascular system.

Methemoglobin	10% in blood cause disease
	20% headache and giddiness
	60% unconsciousness, stiffness
	80% death occurs.

Effects on plants

1. Fertiliser crop yield but at the expense of protein loss.

2. Super phosphates may lead to Fe, Cu, Zn deficiency in plant.

Measurements

For drinking and portable water, the following permissible limits have been prescribed by various agencies like WHO, BIS are shown in Table 3.1.

The parameter which need to be followed for drinking water are.

Table 3.1: Drinking water standards.

Parameters	Desirable maximum limits (mg/L) (except colour, turbidity and pH)
Colour (Hazens scale)	5–10
Turbidity (NTU)	10
Taste and odour	Acceptable
pH	6.5–8.5
TDS	1000–1500
Hardness	200–250
Chlorides	250
Sulphates	150
Flourides	0.8–1.5
Nitrates	45
Fe	0.1
Zn	5.0
Hg and phenol	0.001 (each)
Cr, CN, As, Cu, Mn, Se, Pb, Cd	0.01 to 0.1 (each)
Coliform count (MPN)	Zero
Alkyl benzene sulphonate (detergent)	Less than 1

Water quality for different purposes

Bureau of Indian Standards (BIS) has prescribed standards of quality of water required in different industries.

1. For irrigation purpose water should have less than 30 mg/L of BOD, 30 mg/l of (SS) suspended solid and less than MPN value of faecal coliforms.

2. For textile industry (mg/l):

Fe	0.5
TDS	50
SS	500
Hardness	100
pH	6–8

3. For tanning (mg/l):

Turbidity	20
Hardness	100
Alkalinity	100
pH	8

3.3.4   Soil pollution or land pollution

Soil is polluted by wastes produced in industries, automobiles and agricultural and domestic practices.

Sources and effects

1. Agricultural operations involve the use of fertilisers and pesticides. A number of nitrogenous and phosphorous fertilisers are available in market. Excess of Na, Mg, Ca, K, S, Zn, Fe inhibit plant growth and reduce crop yield.
2. Organic wastes enter the soil pores and decompose. Pathogenic bacteria spread injection. Hook worm and helminthes also cause diseases.
3. Compounds containing arsenic, Hg, Cr, Ni, Pb, Cd, Zn, Fe are toxic to life. Fluorides also affect the plant development.
4. Water logging and salinity increase the dissolved salt content in ground water and also the soil. Some plants are very sensitive to soil pH and salinity so land becomes unfit for irrigation due to water logging conditions.

Remedial measures

1. Understand soil water, plant relationship and protect the mineral cycles of fixation, nitrification is an indication of soil fertility.
2. Treat sewage before land disposal.
3. Preserve and protect top fertile soil. Control soil erosion by proper tree plantation measurement.
4. Prevent entry of leachates in to soil layer.
5. Carefully use fertilisers and pesticides or use alternate natural methods. Use of excess fertiliser result in loss of micronutrients and frequent use in pesticides eliminates soil friendly bacteria.
6. Plough or mix the soil to improve aeration, porosity and permeability.
7. Rotate the crop pattern to allow the soil replenish the nutrients or leave the land uncultivated for some time.
8. Cultivate grass and grow papaya trees only, on polluted waste land.

Parameters for soil analysis

Following parameters to understand the nature of soil and extent of pollution.

1. Soil classification, porosity, permeabity and particles size.
2. Moisture content, dissolved salts, acidity, alkalinity, pH, hardness.

3. Organic and inorganic substances.
4. Biological activity.
5. Soil nutrients like, N, P, K.
6. Fruits, vegetable and crops should also be tested for the residual chemicals as their quality depends on soil pollution.

3.3.5 Air pollution

The gases released into the air by activities of man are present in higher concentration. They cause harm to plant, animals and human beings.

On the basis of state of matter these are of three types.

Particulates

They include both solid and liquid particles. Small solid particles and liquid droplets are collectively known as particulates. They are present in atmosphere in fairly large amounts and pose a serious air pollution problem. Particulate pollutants are classified according to their particle size and nature in to fumes, dust, ash, carbon smoke, lead asbestos, mist, spray, oil, grease, etc.

Suspended particulate matter (SPM): Suspended particulate matter may be defined as all solid and liquid particles in the air that are small enough not to settle out on the earth's surface under the influence of gravity.

Respirable particulate matter (RPM) or PM$_{10}$: Particles of size less than 10 μ can enter in to the lungs. Particulates of this size and below can not be prevented by the filtering mechanism available in our respiratory tract and hence their entry in to the lungs. Special attention is given to RPM due to its potential harm to human respiratory system. It requires highly advanced method to control these particulates.

Dust: it is formed due to breaking of larger particles into smaller one or a result of some mechanical operation example, grinding, sawing, blasting, etc. The size of dust particle varies between 10–10000 μ. Dust particles have tendency to settle down on the ground under influence of gravity.

Smoke: it result from incomplete combustion of organic matter such as wood, coal, tobacco. It consists mainly of carbon and other combustible materials. It has a tendency to travel for off distances with air. The size of smoke particle varies from 0.5–1 μ in diameter.

Fumes: Results from condenstation of vapours of some solid material as a result if melting processes such as calcinations and distillation. The size of fumes varies between 0.03–0.3 μ.

Fly ash: This is inorganic residue left after burning of any type of coal. It consists of finely divided, non-combustible particles contained in the gases arising from combustion of coal. Fly ash shares characteristics of dust, smoke and fumes. Particle size range is $1.0-1000\ \mu$.

Liquid particulates

1. Spray: It results form automisation of liquid for example in use of insecticides and herbicides. The particle size in usually less than $10\ \mu$.
2. Mist: It results from condensation of vapours of some liquid. Mists are usually less than $10\ \mu$ in diameter. If mist concentration is high enough to obscure visibility, then it is called a fog.

Aerosols

Aerosols or particulates when liquid or solid particles are suspended in gaseous medium, e.g., dust, smoke mist, fog.

Gases

These are further classified as fumes inorganic and organic, e.g., SO_2, NO_x, CO, CO_2, CH_4, H_2S, HF, O_3, etc. On the basis of origin pollutants:

1. Primary pollutants: These are the pollutants which are emitted into atmosphere directly from the source, e.g., SO_2, CO, CO_2.
2. Secondary pollutants: These are formed in atmosphere as results of some chemical reaction or photochemical reaction between two reactants or two primary pollutants, e.g., H_2SO_4, mist, O_3, PAN, etc.

Pollutant

The agent which causes environmental pollution is called a pollutant, e.g., kitchen garbage, smoke, pesticides, noise, emissions from industries and automobiles, effluent from industries, etc.

Pollution is an undesirable change in the air, water or land of our environment that harmfully affects human, animal and plant life in different ways. Based on the nature of the pollutant pollution can be of several types.

1. Lead pollution
2. CO_2
3. Smoke
4. Noise
5. Pesticide
6. Radioactive

7. Mercury

8. Plastic

Based on creation:

1. Natural pollution: These are some pollutants in nature itself. These are oil and natural gas, mercury, lead, sulphur, etc., in river waters, lava from volcanoes, etc.

2. Man made pollution: Wastes from factories, exhausts from automobiles, pesticides from farms smoke from chimney, etc.

On the basis of degradability:

1. Biodegradable pollutants: Pollutants that can be easily decomposed by natural processes are called biodegradable pollutants, e.g., various types of kitchen waste.

2. Non-biodegradable pollutants: All material that do not degrade or degrade only very slowly in nature are called non-biodegradable pollutants, e.g., aluminium cans, mercuric salt, long chain phenolic compounds, plastics, etc.

Based on the area affected pollution are different types:

1. Local

2. National

3. Continental

4. Planetary.

Sources of air pollution

Sources which contribute pollutants to the air are:

Stationary combustion sources: Burning of fuels in industries, residential establishments, hotels and bakeries, thermal plant and brick field: (i) oxides of carbon: CO, CO_2, (ii) oxides of sulphur: oxides of sulphur in fossil fuels produces SO_2, SO_3^-, (iii) oxides of nitrogen: oxides of nitrogen present in the coal and petroleum produce NO and NO_2 on combustion in form of reddish brown haze called brown air, and (iv) Hydrocarbons: Hydrocarbons produced naturally during decomposition of organic matter and by certain types of plant (pine trees).

Mobile combustion sources: These include locomotives, automobiles, aircraft, etc. The major pollutants from these sources are: (i) gaseous pollutants: CO, HC, NO_2, (ii) particulate lead: Petroleum use in automobiles contain $Pb,(CH_3)_4$, Pb $(C_2H_5)_4$, and (iii) aerosols: chemicals, which are passed into the air in the form of vapour or fine mist. Jet aeroplanes emit aerosols containing CFC (which cause depletion of ozone layer).

Industrial processing and other sources: (i) gaseous pollutants CO_2, SO_2, NO_2, (ii) CFM are widely used as propellants for aerosols, as refrigerants, (iii) particulate from industry include metal dust, fly ash, cotton dust, radio active substances. And harmful metals As, Be, Cd, Ge, (iv) burning of plastic and its processing produce Polychlorinated Biphenyls (PCBs) (cause damage liver and impair vision), (v) from agriculture burning and pesticides spray, (vi) pollen spares and microbes cause allergies and diseases, (vii) tobacco smoke contains number of HC.

Secondary air pollutants: Formed from primary pollutants by photochemical reaction: (i) photochemical smog and (ii) acid rain.

3.3.6   Effects of air pollution

Global effect of air pollution

Acid rain: It include rain water, precipitation and dew which is acidic in nature. The gases present in atmosphere such as CO_2, NO_x (oxides of nitrogen) and CO_2 reacts with water to produce acids such as H_2SO_4, HNO_3 and carbonic acid.

$$SO_2 + \tfrac{1}{2}O_2 + H_2O \xrightarrow{\text{(HC, NO}_x)} H_2SO_4$$

These acids cause damage to aquatic life, building material, cause soil erosion, change in pH of soil, increased concentration of toxic elements for plant such as cadmium and Zn which reduce the plant nutrients such as potassium. It also increases water pollution as a shift in pH towards lower sides results into slow biodegradation of organics present in water bodies receiving polluted water.

Acid rain can be controlled by controlling release of gases like SO_2 and NO_x into the atmosphere.

In case of Taj Mahal:

$$CaCO_3 + H_2SO_4 \longrightarrow CaSO_4 + 2H_2O \xrightarrow{\text{Rain water}} \text{Earth}$$
$$\text{Limestone} \qquad\qquad\qquad \text{Zypsum}$$

Major cause is Mathura refinery. Building is left with yellow spots other sources are coal burning, locomotives. By using of LPG and locomotives have been electrified.

Rain tends to be naturally acidic with a pH of 5.6 to 5.7 due to the reaction of atmospheric CO_2 with water to produce carbonic acid. This small amount of acidity is sufficient to dissolve minerals the earth's crust and make them available to plant and animal life, but it is not acidic enough to inflict any major damage. Other atmospheric substances from volcanic eruptions, forest fires and other similar natural phenomena also contribute to the acidity in rain. Thus, even with the enormous amounts of acids created by nature annually, normal rainfall is able to assimilate them to the point where they cause little, if any, known damage. But, it is the contributions of SO_x, NO_x, etc., from anthropogenic activities that disturb this acid balance and convert natural and mildly acidic rain into precipitation with far-reaching environmental consequences.

Acid rain represents one of the major consequences of air pollution, because of large SO_x and NO_x emissions from big industrial areas. The longer the SO_x and NO_x remain in the atmosphere, the greater are the chances of their oxidation to H_2SO_4 and HNO_3 due to photochemical and catalytic chemical reactions. Acid rains may cause extensive damage to materials and terrestrial ecosystems, such as water, fish, vegetation, stone, steel, paint, soil and mankind.

Reduction of SO_x emissions can be accomplished by: (i) removing the sulphur content before the fuel is burnt with the help of techniques such as coal cleaning, coal gasification and desulphurisation of liquid fuels, (ii) removing the sulphur content during combustion, as in fluidised-bed combustion and removal of sulphur emissions after combustion, as in stack or flue gas desulphurisation systems or scrubbers.

The future of SO_x control from traditional fuel sources lies in the perfection of these techniques. Reduction of NO_x emissions from stationary combustion sources can be achieved by modification of furnace and burner design, and/or modification of operating conditions. The combustion modification techniques available now include using two-stage combustion, precisely controlling air, injecting water during combustion, recirculating flue gases, and/or by altering design of firing chambers. Reductions in NO_x emissions from mobile combustion sources may be achieved by lowering the combustion temperatures in the engine and catalytic removal of NO_x from exhaust gases using devices such as a three-way system that simultaneously reduces carbon monoxide, hydro-carbons and NO_x.

Green house effect: The CO_2 layer present in atmosphere allows some radiations to reach earth during day. However, it does not allow radiations from the earth back into the atmosphere after the sunset. This happening is resulting in an increase in the temperature of earth. Carbon dioxide is released by volcanoes, oceans, decaying plants as well as human activities, such as deforestation and combustion of fossil fuels. Automobile exhausts account for 30% of CO_2 emissions in developed countries. Methane is released from coal mines, decomposition of organic matter in swamps, rice paddy cultivation, guts of termites in forest debris and stomachs of ruminants.

Chlorofluorocarbons (CFCs) are used as coolants in refrigerators, propellants in aerosol sprays, plastic foam materials like 'thermocoles' or 'styrofoam' and in automobile air-conditioners.

In fact, the 'greenhouse gases' (particularly CO_2 and water vapour) are responsible for keeping our planet warm and thus sustaining life on the earth. If the greenhouse gases were very less or totally absent then the average temperature on the earth would have been at subzero levels. But, however, if the concentration of greenhouse gases increases, they may trap too much of heat, which may threaten the very existence of life on earth. For instance, the CO_2 present in the atmosphere of the planet *Venus*, is about 60,000 times more than that on earth. Hence, the average temperature of *Venus* is about 425°C, making the existence of life impossible there.

Melting of ice in antorctic and arctic poles. This will cause a rise in water level of sea and pose rise of sinking of coastal cities. This behaviour of CO_2 is similar to glass chamber in nursery. Reforestation and reduction in CO_2 conc. In the air some preventive measures to control green house effect.

Besides CO_2 about 30 more gases have been found to cause green house effect example methane, NO_x and chlorine from Chlorofluorocarbon (CFC) compounds slightly increase in surface temperature, say 1°C can adversely affect the world food production cause of fertile to poor soils.

An advantage of rise in earth temperature appears in more cloud formation and hence more rains which can be helpful in reforestation and vegetation.

The projections from computer modelling regarding the climatic changes that could be triggered off due to 'global warming' reveal alarming scenarios. Even a 1.5°C rise in surface temperature can adversely affect food production in the world. Thus, the wheat growing zones in the northern latitude may be shifted from the USSR and Canada to the polar regions, i.e., from fertile soils to poor soils near the North Pole. The biological productivity of the ocean would also decrease due to warming of the earth's surface layer, which in turn, may reduce the transport of nutrients from deeper layers to the surface by vertical circulation. Computer modelling also indicates the following effects due to 'global warming': melting of the polar ice caps; dry areas becoming drier; humid areas like the Amazon suffering more intense tropical storms; drastic drop in food production, particularly in lands within 35 degrees north and south of the Equator; increased breeding of pests and diseases due to more humid conditions; shorter, wetter and warmer winters and longer, hotter and drier summers, particularly in mid-continental areas.

Global warming may also trigger increased thermal expansion of oceans and melting of glaciers, which may result in an increase in the sea-level by 20 cm to 1.5 metres by the latter part of the 21st century. Thus, cities like Mumbai,

Miami, London, Venice, Bangkok and Leningrad may become extremely vulnerable. Defences against the rising sea-levels and expanding oceans are very difficult and expensive, which many nations cannot afford. Further, a global temperature rise, is likely to cause more floods, hurricanes and tornadoes.

Ozone hole: It is observed that the ozone layer present in stratosphere is undergoing damage due to chlorine being released from CRC compounds used in air propellants (spray) and refrigeration and also cause of aerosols and NO_2 considering the safe existence of O_3 layer in stratosphere pollution control board has put a ban on production and use of CPF by 2010.

The net result is regeneration of Cl radical which sustains the chain reaction means one Cl atom can destroy one lack O_3 molecule.

The ozone layer present in the stratosphere acts as a protective shield for life on Earth. It strongly absorbs ultraviolet radiations from the sun in the region 220–330 nm and thereby protects life on earth from severe radiation damage, such as DNA mutation and skin cancer. Thus only a small fraction of UV radiation reaches the lower atmosphere and the Earth's surface.

Ozone is formed in the stratosphere by photochemical reaction:

$$O_2 \text{ (Oxygen molecule)} + hv \text{ (242 nm)} \rightarrow 2O \text{ (Oxygen atom)}$$

$$O + O_2 + M \text{ (third body, such as } N_2 \text{ or } O_2) \rightarrow O_3 + M$$

The third body absorbs the excess energy liberated by the above reaction and thereby the ozone molecule is stabilised. Thus, ozone is constantly formed in the stratosphere. However, it is also destroyed by chlorine, released due to volcanic activity and also by reaction with: (i) nitric oxide, (ii) atomic oxygen and (iii) reactive hydroxyl radical, which are also present in the atmosphere.

In the atmosphere, nitrogen oxide (NO) comes from chemical and photo-chemical reactions, supersonic jets, nuclear explosions, etc., Cl_2 comes from CFC's and volcanoes and OH comes from biomass burning and from natural water systems.

Ozone, in the stratosphere, is also destroyed by manmade chlorofluoro-carbons (CFCs), which are used as coolants in refrigerators, air-conditioners, propellants in aerosol sprays and in plastic foams, such as 'thermocole' or 'styrofoam'. The CFC molecules, escaping into the atmosphere, decompose to release chlorine in the ozone layer (by photo-dissociation) and each atom of chlorine, thus liberated is capable of attacking several ozone molecules.

$$Cl + O_3 \rightarrow ClO + O_2$$

This reaction is followed by:

$$ClO + O \rightarrow Cl + O_2$$

which regenerates Cl atoms, so that a long chain process is involved, which conserves Cl atoms. Control of SO_x emissions from the anthropogenic activities is contemplated along the following lines: Removing SO_x from flue gases before letting them out into the atmosphere: Chemical scrubbers such as: (i) lime stone and (ii) citric acid are suggested to absorb SO_2 from the flue gases.

Because depletion in ozone danger of increasing UV radiation over earths biosphere can create lot of skin disease skin cancer, in plants reducing photo-synthetic rate and yield decrease, chest pain, coughing and irritation.

Photochemical smog

Photochemical smog is initiated by the photochemical dissociation of NO_2 and the consequent secondary reactions involving unsaturated hydrocarbons, other organic compounds and free radicals, leading to the formation of organic peroxides and ozone. This phenomenon takes place during sunny days with low winds and low level inversion. Photochemical smog and the consequent formation of aerosols reduce visibility, cause irritation to eyes and damage plants and rubber goods. The oxidation of SO_2 can also take place by interaction with the free radical $HO\cdot$ present in photochemical smog.

Chemical oxidation of SO_2 may also take place in water droplets, present in aerosols. This reaction is accelerated in the presence of NH_3 and catalysts, e.g., oxides of Mn, Fe, Cu, Ni. Solid particles, such as soot, bring about catalytic oxidation of SO_2 by providing a heterogeneous phase for contact. Soot is formed during combustion of solid and liquid fuels in domestic and industrial operations and automobile emissions. Sulphur dioxide is a pollutant responsible for smog formation, acid rains and corrosion of metals and alloys.

Oxidation of organic compounds

Organic compounds such as hydrocarbons, aldehydes and ketones absorb solar radiation and undergo various photochemical and chemical reactions involving free radicals. Some of these reactions are catalysed by particulate matter such as soot and metal oxides. Some of the resultant intermediates and final products contribute to photochemical smog formation.

Inversion

As we move upward from the earth surface, the temperature of air decreases at a rate of 1.8°C/1000 ft. This is known as normal lapse rate. Reverse of this known as inversion, a condition in which as cold layer of air near the earth surface is surrounded with relatively warmer layers of air. Favourable condition for inversion is stable atmosphere and no vertical movement or mixing of air. During inversion conditions the concentration of pollutants near the earth surface is maximum and the visibility is poor.

There are two types of inversion:

1. Radiation inversion: This usually is observed during winter season. When after sunset earth surface cools down, thus also cooling the layer of air adjunct to it. This type of invension has short duration and in the morning when sun rays heat the earth surface inversion conditions. Sun rays heat the earth surface inversion conditions disappear. If the temperature of earth surface falls below dew point it encourages fog formation.

2. Subsidence inversion: This type of inversion has long during and oceans when high pressure area is surrounded by low pressure area. Under these conditions air sinks to button resulting in to increase in its temperature as a result of compression.

Plume behaviours: Plume is path followed by emissions from stacks (chimney).

Looping: Looping (Fig. 3.1) occurs in strong lapse conditions when instability occurs in atmosphere. In this condition plume behaviour will be wavy and the concentration of pollutants on ground level near the stack will be high. The atmosphere is unstable which allows and encourages the vertical flow of plume to a greater extent. During this atmospheric condition, the large convective eddies are formed. These eddies take the plume in vertical direction and down vertically as it disperses vertically.

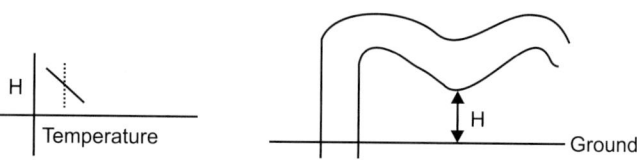

Figure 3.1: Looping.

Coning: The plume behaviour appears like an inverted cone in both horizontal and vertical direction. This pattern of coning (Fig. 3.2) is formed under weak lapse condition. This normally occurs under cloudy and windy conditions.

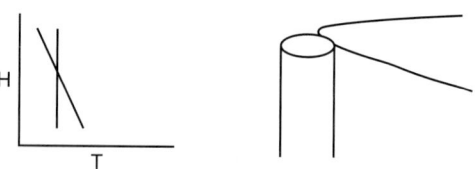

Figure 3.2: Coning.

Fanning: Fanning (Fig. 3.3) occurs when strong inversion condition present in atmosphere. The pollutants reach to the ground level at comparatively greater distance than coning more horizontally and very little vertically. This occurs at night in very stable boundary layer with strong surface inversion and weak variable winds. The inversion dose not allows the vertical movement of the plume and that's why there is no dispersion or little dispersion occurs vertical direction.

Figure 3.3: Fanning.

Fumigation: Fumigation (Fig. 3.4) occurs when inversion conditions exist above lapse condition. It is most undesirable conditions because of the concentration of pollutants near the ground level is maximum. This condition is usually occurs for short duration but results in the highest ground level concentrations.

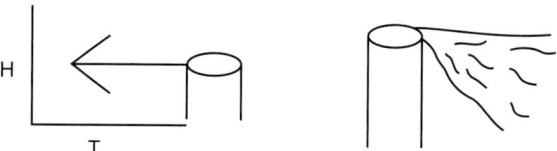

Figure 3.4: Fumigation.

Lofting: Lofting (Fig. 3.5) is most desirable type of plume behaviour. In this plume behaviour the concentration of pollutant near the ground is minimum. It occurs when lapse condition exist above inversion conditions. Depending on the height of the stake and the rate of deepening of the inversion layer the lofting condition may be very transitory or it may persist for long time (several hours).

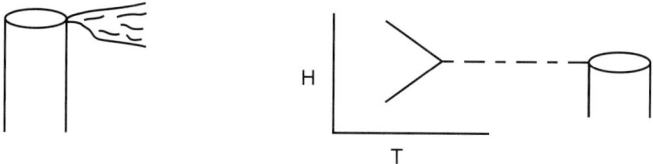

Figure 3.5: Lofting.

Trapping: In this behaviour the plume is trapped between two inversion layers. Plumes released in unstable atmosphere disperse their material throughout the air in uniform way. Trapping (Fig. 3.6) can lead to very high ground level concentrations when the inversion layer is low and there are weak winds.

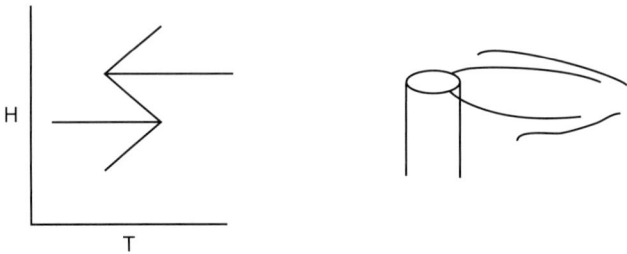

Figure 3.6: Trapping.

Effects on human health

1. The pollutants present in air mixture are creating hazardous effects. Dust, smog causes several respiratory troubles such as bronchitis, asthma, lung cancer, emphysema. In these diseases, small bags in lungs become filled with too much air causing breathing difficulties and heart problem.

2. Fly ash and metal dusts cause headache, loss of appetite, dizziness, insommia, anaemia, weakness and miscarriage.

3. SO_2 causes drying of mouth, sore throat and eye irritation.

4. Air borne organic matter such as spores, pollen, bacteria, fungi, fur, feather cause several decease like hay fever.

5. SO_3, NO, CO combines with haemoglobin of the blood and hence reduces the oxygen carrying capacity of blood.

   (a) Pb produced from automobile. Human body is not capable to metabolise Pb and if it enter in to human body, it remains there in almost every system of human body include respiratory system and blood forming system. Due to this animal produces low milk, less of appetite and there is incomplete growth.

   (b) Dust or other particulates restrict sunlight and affect photosynthesis adversely.

   (c) SO_2 present in more amounts in exhaust causes chlorosis, plasmolysis, membrane damage, metabolic inhibition.

   (d) Fluorides destroy tissues in leaves.

   (e) Hydrocarbon cause premature leaf fall, fruit drop, shedding of floral buds.

(f) Ozone damage chlorenchyma which cause distruction of several plants.

(g) Pb presence leads to weakening and death of tissues, branzing, silvering, browning leaves.

Methods of measurements of air pollution

Suspended matter the pollutant emitted into the air may as follows:

1. Solid material: Solid material such as grit, coarse enough to settle down fairly in the ground.

2. Finer material: Finer material tends to remain suspended in the air but can be collected by filtration technique. Large concentration of such material can affect visibility and blacking building and clothing size 1–100 μ.

There are gaseous impurities also which can be separated from air by chemical means like SO_2 which cause corrosion and health hazards.

Principle and applicability for suspended particle

Suspended particles present in air along with other gaseous composition may be separated by use of filtration unit driven by motor. In this process air drawn by means of high flow rate blower at a flow rate (1.13 to 1.7 cm^3/min) into a covered housing equipped with a filter. Filter is made up of glass fibres. This allows suspended particle having diameter less than 100 μ to pass to the filter surface. Particle with in size range of 100–0.1 μ collected on glass fibre filters. The mass conc. ($\mu g/m^3$) of suspended particle in ambient air is computed by measuring the mass of calculated particle and volume of air sampled.

Apparatus

Above mentioned apparatus for this purpose have three units: (i) face place and gasket, (ii) the filter adapter assembly, and (iii) motor unit. This apparatus shall be capable of passing environmental air through 406 cm^3 portion of a clear 20 cm × 25 cm glass fibre filter at a rate of at least 1.6.5 m^3/min.

Analysis

$$\text{Air flow rate } Q \text{ in } \frac{m^3}{min} \frac{V_a}{T}.$$

where, V_a = Air volume (m^3)

T = Time of flow (minute)

Sample volume: Volume conversion convert the initial and final parameter readings to true air rate.

$$\text{Air volume sampled V in } m^3 = \frac{(Q_1 + Q_2)T}{2}$$

Q_1 = Initial air flow rate in m^3/min

Q_2 = Final air flow rate in m^3/min

$$\text{Mass concentration of suspended particles} = \frac{W_f - W_1}{(min.\mu g/m^3)} \, 10^6$$

W_f = Final mass of filter in gm

W_I = Initial mass of filter in gm

V   = Air volume sampled in m^3

Control of air pollution

To control air pollutants present in air, following are the common strategies:

1. Control at source or point source: This can be done by installation of control equipment at the origin point of pollutant.
2. By change in new raw material that will release lesser quantity of pollutants or may not release one or more than one pollutants. That is being released by former raw material.
3. Change in process: The new process should be searched for less pollutant release.
4. Change in equipment design or replacement of old equipment by new ones.
5. Proper cleaning and maintenance of equipment.
6. Dilution of pollutants by use of tall stacks.

Methods of control of particulate by use of control equipments

Gravitational settling chamber: The time taken by the particle to travel from inlet to outlet is considerable greater than time required by the particle to fall vertically in to the dust hopper (Fig. 3.7).

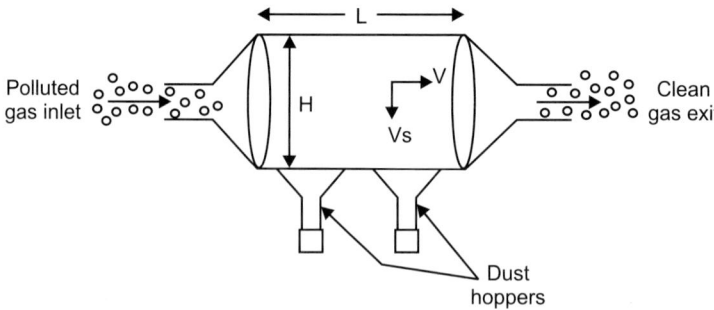

Figure 3.7: Gravitational settling chamber.

Considering limiting condition that the particle requires equal time in travelling both the distances be written as:

$$t = \frac{H}{V_s} = \frac{L}{V} \qquad \qquad ...(3.1)$$

By stokes law:

$$V_s = \frac{g\, d_p^2\, (\rho_p - \rho_a)}{18\, \mu} \qquad \qquad ...(3.2)$$

Substituting vs from Eq. 3.1 in to Eq. 3.2 the diameter of particle can be obtained by following expression:

$$t = \frac{H}{\dfrac{g\, d_p^2\, (\rho_p - \rho_a)}{18\, \mu}}$$

We know that $V_s = \dfrac{HV}{L}$ from Eq. 3.1.

$$d_p^2 = \frac{V_s\, 18\, \mu}{g\, (\rho_p - \rho_a)}$$

$$d_p = \frac{HV\, 18\, \mu}{L\, g\, (\rho_p - \rho_a)} \qquad \qquad ...(3.3)$$

Eq. 3.3 gives the main diameter of particles which can be collected in a gravitational settling chamber of given dimension L and H

where, L = Length of equipment

H = Height of equipment

The efficiency of gravitational settling chamber can be improved by arranging horizontal plates inside the chamber is shown in Fig. 3.8.

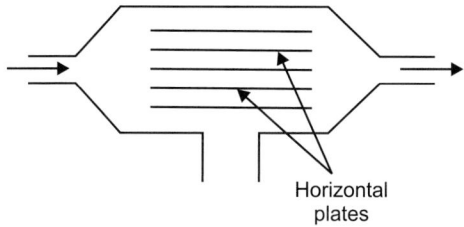

Horizontal
plates

Figure 3.8: Arrangement of plates inside chamber.

Advantages of gravitational settling chamber (GSC)

1. Simple construction and design.
2. No moving part.
3. No skilled labour is required.
4. By proper selection of material of construction any type of pollutant gas can be treated.

Disadvantage of GSC

The equipment is suitable for collection of particles with diameter more then 40 μm.

Uses of GSC

1. In cement industry.
2. In grain polishing.
3. In metal industry (where fumes are made).

Cyclone collector

A cyclone collector consists of cylindrical body attached to an inverted cone is shown in Fig. 3.9. The polluted gas enters tangentially from the top of the cyclone body mixing spirally downward resulting in to separation of particulates from the waste gas stream.

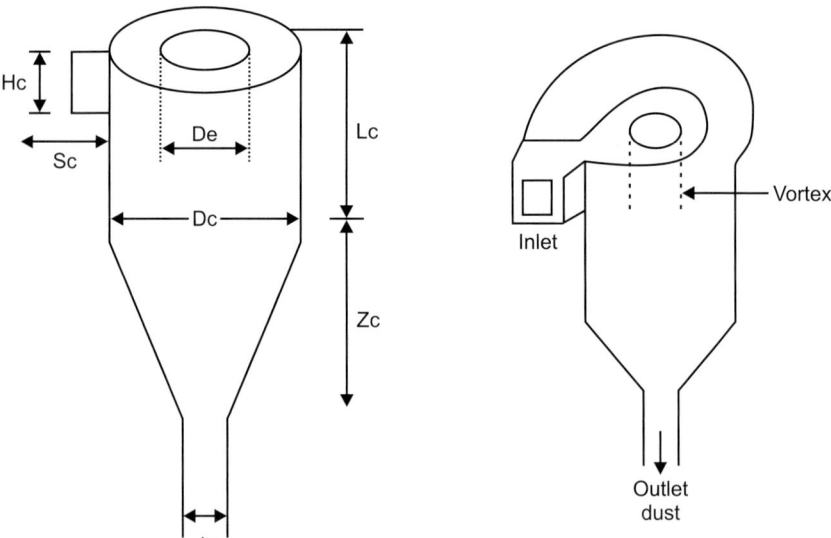

Figure 3.9: Cyclone collector.

As the particulars experience a centrifugal force. The particulates are thrown away towards the walls of the cyclone from where they slide in to the dust hopper. As the gas reaches near the end of the central part, it again starts rising upward making a second co-centric but smaller vortex.

Finally, the treated gas leaves from the top of the cyclone. A decrease in diameter of the cyclone and increase in particle density, gas inlet velocity, body length of cyclone, ratio of cyclone diameter to the exit diameter result in to increased collection efficiency of the cyclone. Collection efficiency for particles of < 5 μ ranges from 50–60%. For particles up to 20 μ, it ranges from 50–30% and for particles of 40 μ, is goes up to 95%. The minimum diameter of the particle which can be collected in a cyclone collector:

$$Dp_{min} = \left[\frac{9 \mu B}{\pi Nt V (\rho_p - \rho_a)} \right]^{\frac{1}{2}}$$

where, V = Inlet velocity

Nt = No of turns made by the gas

Advantages

1. Simple construction and operation.
2. No moving part.
3. Gases with high temperature and pressure can be treated by selection of suitable material of construction.
4. No skilled labour is required.

Disadvantages

1. High maintenance cost.
2. Large power requirement for high inlet gas velocity.
3. Used to separate particulates from fumes and fly ashes.

In these collectors, use of liquid (generally made to separate particulates from the polluted gas completes in following four steps.

1. Movement of particle towards liquid drops.
2. Collision between particle and liquid drop. (Water drops generally 10–1000 times larger than the particulates).
3. Adhesion of particle to the liquid drop: Depends upon surface characteristics, i.e., surface tension of liquid.
4. Precipitation of dust adhered to the liquid drop.

Different equipment designs of wet collectors are.

Spray tower

In this case, scrubbing liquid is sprayed over the rising polluted gas is shown in Fig. 3.10. Impingement and interception are the principle mechanisms responsible for separation of particulates.

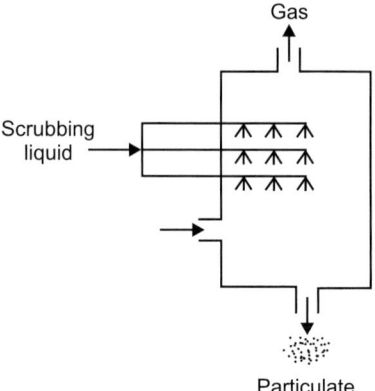

Figure 3.10: Spray tower.

A suitable packing material (e.g., glass fibres) is arranged in the column and the scrubbing liquid is sprayed over it. The particulate matter enters on the surface of the packing while the liquid simply acts as washing agent. Impaction and impingement are the principle mechanisms for removal of particulates. Packed columns are expensive to install, require high energy input. They can be used for removal of sub-micron particles and odours too.

Wet cyclone

Wet cyclone is shown in Fig. 3.11. The polluted gas enters tangentially at high velocity moving spirally upward resulting in to separation of particulates due to centrifugal force exerted on them. The scrubbing liquid is spread either from the side of the equipment towards the centre or from centrally located pipe towards the sides of the equipment. The dust separated from the gas stream is collected in to form of slurry. Impingement is the principle mechanism responsible for the separation of particulates.

Venturi scrubbers

The polluted gas is forced to pass through a narrow gap (Venturi throat) which is adjustable with the help of an adjustable screw. The throat velocity is maintained between 60–100 m/sec and the scrubbing liquid is spread is shown in the Fig. 3.12. Inertial impaction is principle mechanism responsible for separation of dust.

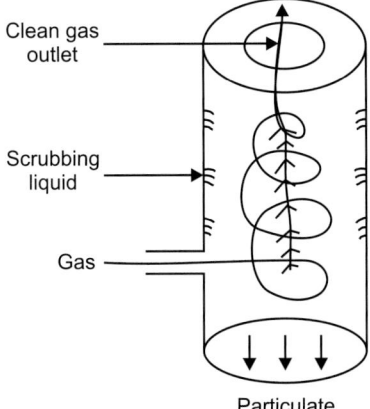

Figure 3.11: Wet cyclone.

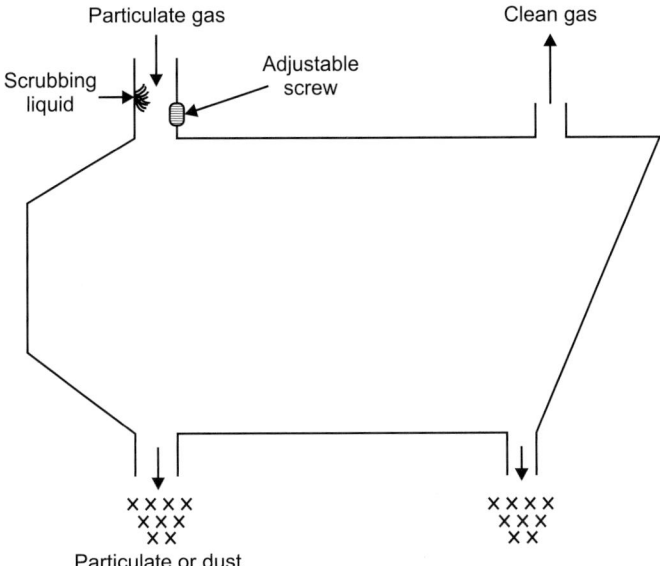

Figure 3.12: Venturi scrubber.

Common advantages of wet scrubber:

1. They are more efficient than dry collectors.
2. Problem of particle reentranment is eliminated.
3. Particulate matter as well as gaseous pollutants can be simultaneously removed by proper selection of suitable scrubber agent.
4. Generally cheap to install with sample construction.

Disadvantages of wet collectors:
1. High operational and maintenance cost.
2. High energy input is required to force the gas to move in upward direction.
3. Wet collectors dust which causes problems in handing and final disposal dust.

Electrostatic precipitator (ESP)

An electrostatic precipitator (Fig. 3.13) consists of discharge electrode (made up of tunguston or copper steel alloy) and collection electrode or plates 1–2 m wide and 3–6 m high with a spacing between plates 15–35 cm. The discharge electrode hangs between the plates with a suitable weight at their free end to keep them straight. A potential difference (60–100 kv) is maintained between the plates.

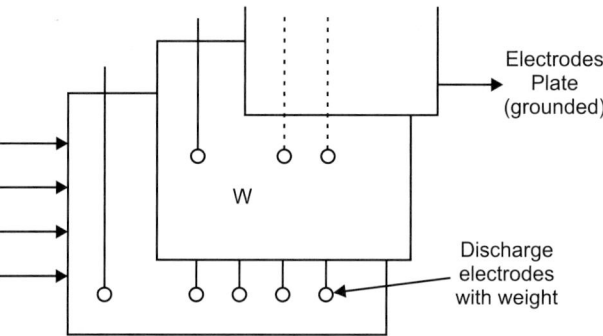

Figure 3.13: Electrostatic precipitator (longitudinal section).

As the polluted gas enters between the plates, the particles get charged and migrates towards oppositely charged collection electrodes. As soon as, a charged particle reaches at the collection electrode, it immediately looses its charge and falls in to the dust hopper. Electrostatic precipitator (plane section) is shown in Fig. 3.14.

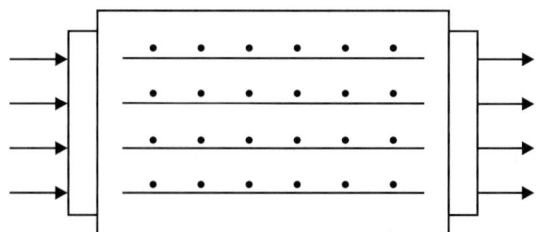

Figure 3.14: Electrostatic precipitator (plane section).

A resistively between 10^5–10^7 ohm-cm is required for efficient working. At low resistivity although particles acquire charge easily but also loose their charge rapidly and re-entering in to the gas stream. At high resistivity particles do not acquire charge easily resulting in to a poor collection efficiency of the equipment. The efficiency of ESP:

$$\eta = 1 - e^{\frac{Aut}{Q}}$$

A   =   Gross collection area of collection electrode.

Ut =   Migration velocity of particles towards collection electrode.

Q   =   Volumetir flow rate of gas.

Advantages

1. Highly efficient.
2. Any type of gas can be treated with exception of explosive gases.
3. Less time required (0.1–10 seconds).
4. Compact design.

Methods for removal of gaseous pollutants

Absorption: The polluted gas and suitable liquid are brought in to intimate contact using one of the following equipment:

1. Spray tower.
2. Bubble cap tower.
3. Sieve plate column.
4. Packed column.

The efficiency of pollutant gas removal depends upon:

1. Conc. of pollutant gas in the waste gas stream.
2. Conc. of absorbent.
3. Time of contact.
4. Reaction rate between pollutant gas and absorbent (if any).

Examples of some of the absorbent are shown in Table 3.2.

Table 3.2: Examples of some of the absorbent.

Gas	*Absorbent*
SO_2	Alkaline water $(NH_4)_2$, SO_4 solution, simple water, 1:1 mixture of xylidine and water.
NO_x	Water aquas HNO_3, HCl
HF	Water and NaOH
H_2S	3:2 mixture of phenol and NaOH, soda ash solution containing suspended iron oxide.

Adsorption: The polluted gas is passed through a porous bed of adsorbent and the liquid is allowed to flow counter currently.

The type of adsorbent, concentration of pollutant gas in waste affects the removal efficiency of packed tower, which needs high energy input to pass the gas through the packed bed due to the large pressure drop across the bed.

The system is useful for treatment of odours gases, explosive gases and flammable gases which can not be treated by other methods. Some of the absorbent used are shown in Table 3.3.

Table 3.3: Some of the absorbent used.

Gas	Absorbent
SO_2	Pulverised lime stone, alkalised alumina
NO_x	Zeolite, Silica gel
H_2S	Iron oxide pellets
HF	NaCl pellets
Organic vapour	Activated carbon

Some examples for treatment of gases:

1. In H_2SO_4 plants, SO_2 gas is removed by absorption methods using water.
2. In smelter units, the SO_2 containing polluted gas is passed over spheres (diameter 1.6 mm) of alkalised alumina which adsorbs SO_2. The spheres are then exposed to reducing gas (mixture of H_2 + CO) resulting in to formation of CO_2 and H_2S. Sulphur is recovered from for marketing from H_2S.
3. In power plants pulverised lime is directly injected in the furnace converting $CaCO_3$ in to reactive calcium oxide (CaO) under the heat effect. The exhaust gas from the furnace is passed through a water scrubber. This results in to formation of CaS and $CaSO_4$ slurry which is sent to salting tanks. The separated water is recycled to scrubber.
4. In HNO_3 plants, NO_x containing gas is passed over a zeolite bed resulting in to separation of oxides of nitrogen from the waste gas stream. The bed is then regenerated either by raising the temperature of the bed by hot air or by steam.

3.3.7 Noise pollution

Unwanted or undesirable sound is noise. It is harmful to human ears. Noise is increasingly becoming a major pollutant. As noise pollutes the air, noise pollution can in fact be included in air pollution. Just like smoke, dust, toxic fumes, etc. Noise is included as air pollutants in Environment Protection Act (EPA).

Measurements units

Measurement of sound is causing pollution is difficult as sound level at origin place is different to observer hearing it. The sound measured at the source is meaning less. There must be a distance at which the hearing process is taking place. This is because the sound becomes lesser and lesser as the source is further and further away. Therefore all measurements must also indicate the distance. It is always decibels (dB) along with distance. Decible is the unit of sound invented by the engineers of bell telephone laboratory.

Normal sound level

Soft whispers	40 dB
Residual area	45 dB
Laboratory and hospitals	50 dB
Hotel, schools	60 dB
City traffic	70–80 dB
Air craft	100–110 dB

Effects

Noise interferes with normal human activities affects noise level. High level of noise creates an adverse effect on the hearing ability. Continuous exposure to high level noise leads to physiological disorders or stress to living beings. Irritation, frustration, fatigue, headache, anxiety, hypertension, insomnia, hearing loss, mental depression are generally associated with exposure to high intensity of noise for shore durations or moderate levels for a prolonged periods. Uneasiness and lack of concentration causes by noise affect the workers efficiency and even lead to accidents. Sudden explosions create cracks in building walls and break window glass. High intensity sound can damage our physical as well as mental health. Blood pressure rises also rises due to intense sound level.

1. 80–85 dB sound causes discomfort.
2. 100–110 dB sound caused stress.
3. 120–130 dB sound caused dizziness, pain in the ear due to prolonged exposure.
4. >150 dB sound causes permanent damage to the hearing mechanism.

Sources of sound pollution

1. Industry sound (factories).
2. Vehicles sound (road and rail transport).
3. Music system (by party and in election).

4. Construction of building or things.

5. Space rockets.

3.3.8 Radioactive pollution

The radioactive pollution is defined as the physical pollution of living organisms and their environment as a result of release of radioactive substances into the environment during nuclear explosions and testing of nuclear weapons, nuclear weapon production and their use, mining of radioactive ores, handling and disposal of radioactive waste, and accidents at nuclear power plants. Nuclear power plants generates electricity and at the same time hazardous radioactive waste also. The proportion of radioactive pollution is 12–15% of the total energy of the explosion. Radioactive pollution is due to radioactive rays emitted from nuclear waste, which may cause mutation or destruction of nucleotides present in gene structure. Radionuclides are the main sources of pollution; they emit beta particles and gamma rays, radioactive substances.

An element is radioactive when it has an unstable nucleus that spontaneously releases energy. Radioactivity is a phenomenon related to unstable atomic nuclei with excess of energy and/or mass, which spontaneously decompose emitting ionising radiation in the form of electromagnetic waves (gamma rays) or streams of subatomic (alpha, beta, or neutron) particles. The activity of a particular radioactive substance is characterised by the constant decay rate and the half-life ($t_{1/2}$—time taken for the activity of a given quantity of a radioactive substance to decay to half of its initial value), and it is a general rule of thumb that ten half-lives are required for each radioisotope to be eliminated. Since the half-lives of various nuclei vary from seconds to billions of years, the time required for their total decay significantly differ as well.

Radioactive particles move through the air in the form of dust from both the mining of uranium and the wind moving over the tailings-mountains of uranium and thorium rich earth left on the ground after 3 to 4% of uranium or thorium is removed for processing. Extracting the usable uranium and thorium pollute the equipment used, the liquid that washes it, the vehicles that transport it, the clothing of the workers, the water they wash with, and the air with the radioactive gases that are routinely vented become polluted. Radioactive pollution continues at every step along the way without end; in the reactors, the submarines, the weapons manufacturing, stockpiling, storage, testing, use, and dismantling.

Sources of radioactive particles

Fast development of the nuclear power plant and the widespread use of radioactive isotopes, radioactive material has been released to the environment from various sources as a result of actions committed either on purpose or accidentally through negligence or simply ignorance. Regarding the global radiological consequences, expressed as the major contributors to environmental contamination were the nuclear weapons tests followed by the accidents of the nuclear fuel cycle in power plants.

Nuclear weapons testing sites and accidents: Nuclear energy released from reaction is called a nuclear explosion, and its effects can be both immediate and delayed but equally destructive. Its immediate effect is equivalent to multiple volumes of energy described as 'nuclear blast', and is powerful enough to blast and burn anything within its range (kilometers). Those who receive energy released by its explosion from farther distances of about 30 km radius, or become contaminated by the nuclear blast near the explosion site, will sustain the delayed effects, or the nuclear reactions, in their body. The volumes of emitted charged particles received by the body continue to react and in the process, create chemically reactive compounds called *free radicals* inside the human anatomy. The free radicals will subsequently destroy the human DNA and further disrupt the natural chemical compositions of the cells, often impairing the natural ability of cells to self-repair. The victims who received doses of radiation that went into a nuclear reaction inside their body have the potential to develop cancer, leukemia, mental defects, reproductive failure, and destruction of the immune system.

Solution or remedies to this problem: There are no solutions to close this pollution source; in as much as the Partial Test Ban Treaty of 1963 was ignored by many countries. Actually, these countries are regarded as racing against each other in their aim to gain recognition as supreme nuclear power. Recently, North Korea has joined the race.

Nuclear-power generating plants: Other sources of radioactive pollutants in the environment are received through the so-called 'controlled chain reactions for energy by nuclear-power generating plants'. These power plants do not release greenhouse gases but it appears that modern nuclear power plants release radioactive gases, like krypton 85, tritium-carbon and Carbon-14 in amounts that are traceable in the environment and form part of the atmospheric pollution.

Solutions and remedies to this problem: Current gaseous abatement techniques are being applied, which involves filtrating the release by way of dry, high-efficiency particulate aerosols to eliminate actinide aerosols. Actinide refers to the series of radioactive elements ranging from numbers 89 through 103.

To use of wet gas scrubbers to remove soluble fission products like the harmful Cesium 137 radioactive waste particles. However, the disposal of Cesium 137 waste is very expensive, and currently there have been recommendations to repurpose this nuclear waste substance. Suggestions offered are their use as irradiators to kill existing and remaining micro-organisms present in packed meat, as part of the food processing.

Adsorption technologies can be used to eradicate the unstable chemically reactive gases like iodine. Adsorption mechanisms in nuclear waste management are done by way of chemical reactions that aim to create chemical bonds between the adsorption compound and the harmful chemical emissions. The latter can be captured for disposal as a radioactive waste. Another term used to refer to this technique in eliminating the harmful gases in nuclear power plant releases, is 'ion exchange'.

Microbial Metabolism

4.1   Introduction

Biological waste treatment process is the process by which any waste can be treated biologically by using micro-organisms for final discharge with in the tolerance limit specified by National standards for waste discharge and World Health Organisation (WHO). Microbial metabolism is the process in which micro-organism metabolise the organic material present in the waste. Organic material is catabolised in to different end products through specific metabolic pathways, that micro-organism follow for waste degradation. For different substrate catalysis, different metabolic pathways are followed as enzyme used for catalysis of substrate material present in waste, is specific and produced by a certain micro-organism.

For example, starch is hydrolysed by amylase enzyme produced by *Bacillus amyloliquifaciens*, cellulose is hydrolysed by cellulase enzyme produced by *Trichoderma viride* and protein is hydrolysed by protease enzyme produced by *Bacillus subtilis*. The concept of substrate consumed by micro-organism, can be understood as hypothesis given by scientist 'PERT'.

4.2   PERT hypothesis for biological treatment

Scientist PERT has given a hypothesis for treatment of waste using micro-organism. According to that, waste water contains good amount of organic material. Micro-organisms either aerobic or anaerobic, feed upon that waste. Micro-organisms consume some amount of substrate (S_1) from total or initial substrate and it is used for growth and development of micro-organism and increase their count ($X_1, X_2, X_3...$). Remaining amount of organic material as substrate S_2 is utilised by micro-organism to convert it into valuable products ($P_1, P_2, P_3, ...$) during metabolic process. During this metabolism, if the biological process is driven by aerobic micro-organisms under aerobic condition then carbon present in organic material is converted in to CO_2, nitrogen is converted in to NO_2 and sulphur is converted in to SO_2. If the biological process is driven by anaerobic micro-organisms under anaerobic condition then carbon present in organic material is converted in to methane, nitrogen is converted in to NH_3 and sulphur is converted in to H_2S. PERT hypothesis for microbial metabolism is shown in Fig. 4.1.

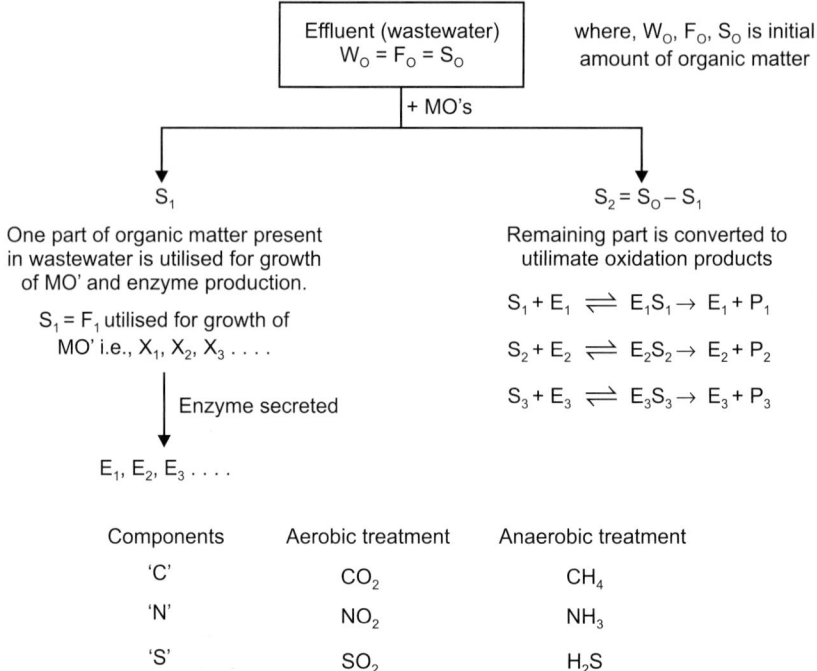

Figure 4.1: PERT hypothesis for microbial metabolism.

4.3 Microbial metabolic pathways

Biological degradation of recent biomass and organic chemicals during solid waste or wastewater treatment proceeds either aerobic (respiration), anaerobic (methanogenesis) and some time anoxic (denitrification). In aerobic process, organic compounds like carbohydrates, proteins, fats, or lipids are digested using aerobic bioreactors like activated sludge system, that leads to the formation of carbon dioxide, water, and a significant amount of surplus sludge. Oxygen in pure form or air must either be supplied by aeration or by injection in to the reactor.

Capacity for oxygen transfer and the stripping efficiency for carbon dioxide from respiration are two important factor in oxygen supply. It is stripping of CO_2 which is common process required to prevent a decrease value of pH and to remove heat energy. During respiration, denitrification process occurs in which chemically bound oxygen supplied in the form of nitrate or nitrite and yields dinitrogen anaerobic organisms, such as methanogenes or sulphate reducers use nitrate as bulk mass to reduce redox potential. If anaerobic zones are formed in sludge flocs of an activated sludge system, e.g., by limitation of the oxygen supply, methanogens and sulphate reducers may develop in the centre of sludge flocs and produce small amount of methane and hydrogen sulphide. Both aerobic and anaerobic micro-organisms are consuming the waste material as feed (carbon and energy source) and metabolise waste components in to valuable products by using different metabolic pathways.

4.3.1 Hydrolysis of cellulose by aerobic and anaerobic micro-organisms

Cellulose, hemicellulose and lignin are the major structural compounds of plants. Cellulose is the most abundant biopolymer on earth. Cellulose fibres are formed of linear chains of 120–1300 glucose units linked together by glycosidic bonds. These fibres are arranged in a matrix of hemicelluloses, pectin, or lignin. The hemicelluloses consist mainly of xylans or glucomannans, which have side chains of acetyl, gluconuryl, or arabinofuranosyl units. Hemicellulose and pectin or lignin make a cover and protect cellulose.

To make cellulose fibres available to micro-organisms, first of all hemicellulose, pectin, or lignin matrix must be degraded microbiologically or solubilised chemically. Cellulose degradation is naturally occurring in the presence of oxygen in soil and also in the absence of oxygen in the rumen of ruminants.

There are some microbial genera containing cellulolytic micro-organisms, e.g., genera of fungi; *Trichoderma, Phanaerochaete, Neocallimastix, Piromyces*, and genera bacteria, *Cellulomonas, Pseudomonas, Thermomonospora* (aerobic cellulose degraders) and *Clostridium, Fibrobacter, Bacteroides, Ruminococcus* (anaerobic cellulose degraders). The anaerobic digestion of cellulose can be done by following steps, such as hydrolytic, fermentative, acetogenic, and methanogenic steps which are shown in Fig. 4.2.

Hydrolysis and fermentation

Hydrolysis of cellulosic material is catalysed by the group of micro-organisms, used for fermentation also. The distinction of the two phases is of more theoretical than practical relevance. Hydrolysis is the rate limiting step for other steps followed by fermentation, as hydrolysed monomers will be substrate for fermentation process. Hemicellulose and pectin are hydrolysed ten times faster than lignin rich cellulose.

Acetogenesis and acidogenesis

In the acidification reaction vessel, hydrolysis of polymers to monomers is normally slower than fermentation of monomers to fatty acids and other fermentation products. Due to this, no sugar monomers can be detected as

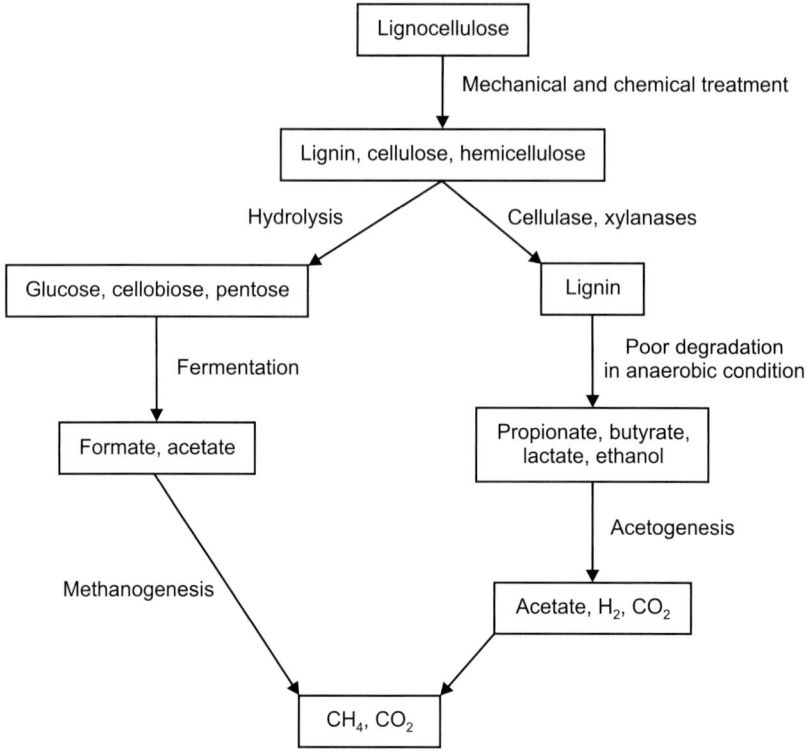

Figure 4.2: Anaerobic degradation of lignocellulose and cellulose to methane and CO_2.

residue during steady state operation. Oxidation of fatty acids like propionate or *n*-butyrate, is the rate-limiting step for methane forming step in reaction vessel. Fatty acid degradation is the slowest reaction overall in a two stage methane reactor fed with carbohydrate containing wastewater from sugar production and require larger reaction vessel size to hold fatty acid that contains part for long time.

Thus, the methane reactor has to be larger than the acidification reactor to permit longer hydraulic retention times.

The rate of cellulose degradation depends on the available form of the cellulose in the wastewater. If cellulose is strongly bonded with lignin, lignin prevents access of cellulases enzyme produced by micro-organism, to the cellulose fibres. If cellulose is in a crystalline form, cellulases enzyme can easily attach to it, and then hydrolysis can be done relatively fast.

Methanogenesis

In this step, produced acids are consumed by methanogenic micro-organisms to convert acids in to methane and CO_2. For methanogenesis process, acetogenesis became the rate-limiting process, leading to propionate and butyrate formation. Naturally plant material contains cellulose in form of lignin encrusted. Due to the highly restricted access to these complexes by cellulases, hydrolysis of cellulose is the rate-limiting step in its degradation to methane and CO_2.

4.3.2   Anaerobic degradation of starch

Carbohydrates are made up of homopolymers or heteropolymers of hexoses, pentoses, or sugar derivatives. They occur in either soluble form or as particles, forming grains or fibres of various sizes. Starch metabolism is done by hydrolysis, which is done by amylase enzyme produced by hydrolytic bacteria to form soluble monomers or dimmers after hydrolytic cleavage. Soluble substrates can be taken up and metabolised in to valuable products which are shown in Fig. 4.3.

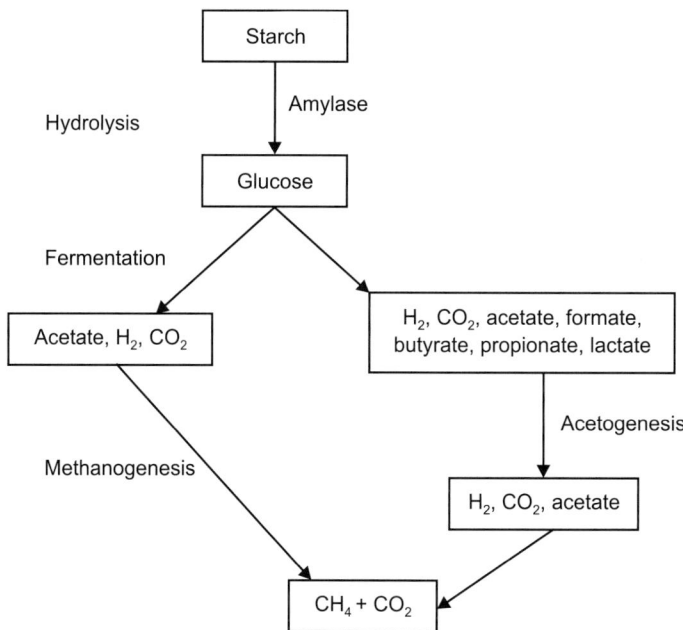

Figure 4.3: Anaerobic degradation of starch.

4.3.3 Anaerobic degradation of protein

Proteins are biological macromolecules, present in soluble and non-soluble form. When protein molecule is present outside the cell at an acidic pH, soluble proteins precipitate in presence of enzymes. For example, precipitation of casein by addition of rennet enzyme. Protein can also be converted in to biogas by methanogenesis. The metabolic steps for protein degradation in a methanogenic ecosystem are given in Fig. 4.4. Hydrolysis of protein is catalysed by several types of protases enzymes that cleave proteins in to amino acids, dipeptides, or oligopeptides. Hydrolysis of proteins requires a neutral or weakly alkaline pH compare to carbohydrate which required acidic pH. Acidification of protein containing wastewater proceeds optimally at pH values of 7 or higher. Acetogenesis of fatty acids from deamination of amino acids requires a low H_2 partial pressure for the same reasons as for carbohydrate degradation. This can be maintained by a syntrophic interaction of fermentative, protein-degrading bacteria and acetogenic and methanogenic or sulphate-reducing bacteria.

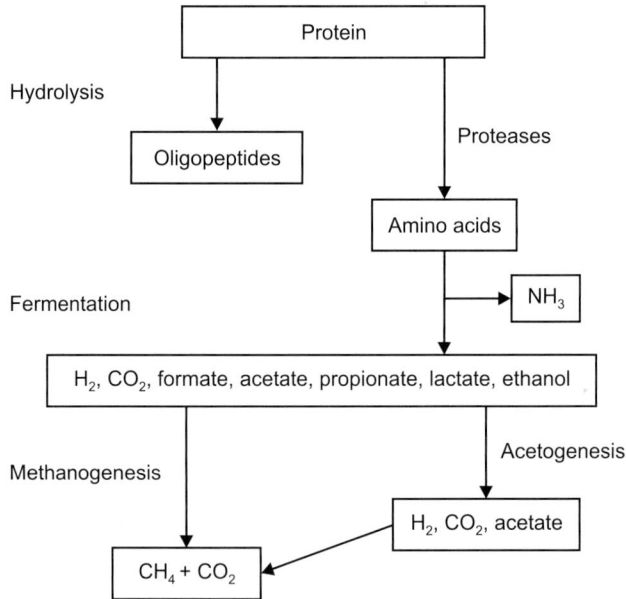

Figure 4.4: Anaerobic degradation of protein.

4.3.4 Anaerobic degradation of neutral fats and lipids

Fats and lipids are biopolymers that contribute significantly to the Chemical Oxygen Demand (COD) in sewage sludge, cattle and swine manures, and wastewater from the food processing industry, for example, slaughterhouses or potato chip factories. Hydrolysis is the process to convert fats and lipids in to simple form like fatty acids saturated and unsaturated by use of hydrolytic enzymes like lipases. To provide a maximum surface for hydrolytic cleavage by lipases or phospholipases, solid fats, lipids, or oils must be emulsified. Glycerol and saturated and unsaturated fatty acids like palmitic acid, linolic acid, linolenic acid and stearic acid are formed from neutral fats. Lipolysis of phospholipids generates fatty acids, glycerol, alcohols like serine, ethanolamine, choline, inositol and phosphate. Lipolysis of sphingolipids generates fatty acids and amino alcohols like sphingosine, and lipolysis of glycolipids generates fatty acids, amino alcohols, and hexoses such as glucose and galactose. Steps of anaerobic degradation for fats are shown in Fig. 4.5.

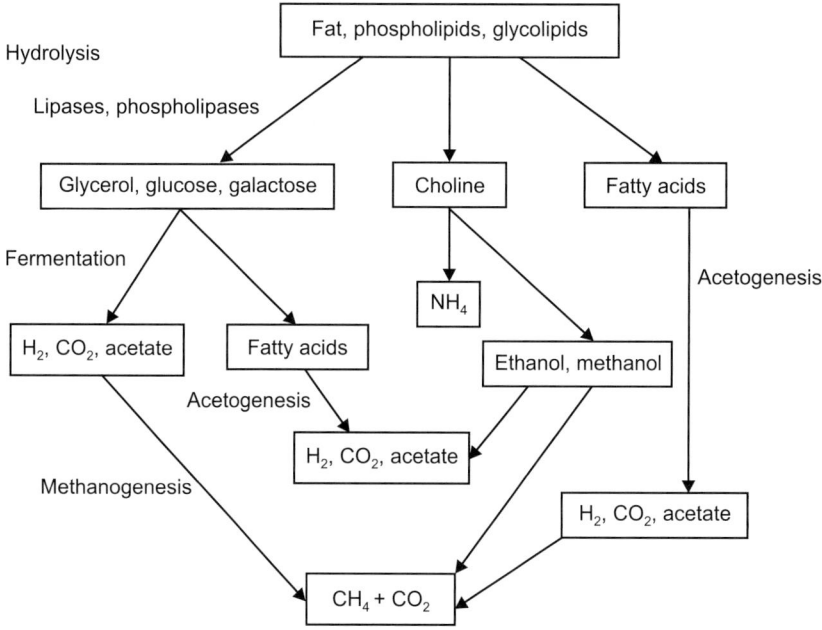

Figure 4.5: Anaerobic degradation of fats.

4.3.5 Metabolic pathway for ethanol production

Glucose is first converted in to pyruvic acid by the glycolysis pathway. Now pyruvate is converted in to ethanol molecules after following various steps and intermediate formation. Figure 4.6 shows the pathway of ethanol production. Ethanol is produced from glucose (sugar) in anaerobic condition, commonly used micro-organism is *Saccharomyces cerevisiae*.

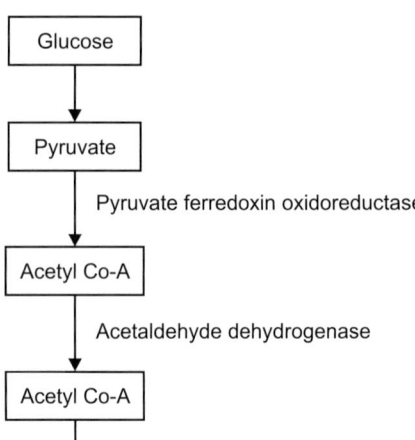

Figure 4.6: Metabolic pathway for ethanol production.

4.3.6   Metabolic pathway for acetate production

Acidic acid producing micro-organisms grow in ethyl alcohol converting ethanol in to acetate as shown in metabolic pathway (Fig. 4.7). This process can be used for commercial production of vinegar from alcohol (wine). *Acetobacter aceti* produces acetic acid in aerobic condition.

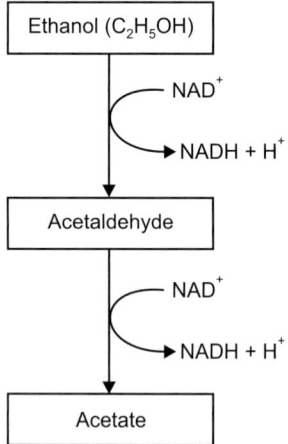

Figure 4.7: Metabolic pathway for acetate production.

Study on the anaerobic bacteria shows that some micro-organisms like *Clostridium thermoacetical, Clostridium thermoautotrophicum* etc., have the potential for the large scale production of acetate. One mole of glucose produces three moles of acetate. The flucose molecule is converted in to ethanol first in anaerobic process by *Saccharomyces cerevisiae.* Now this ethanol molecule is converted anaerobically in to acetate molecule. This conversion can be utilised for commercial production of acetate.

4.3.7   Metabolic pathway for mixed acid production

In mixed acid fermentation process the six carbon sugar, i.e., glucose is converted in to various organic acids and ethanol. The produced mixture having organic acids like succinic acid, fumaric acid, lactic acid, acitic acid, etc., and ethanol. Different products are produced in this pathway so it is called mixed pathway (Fig. 4.8).

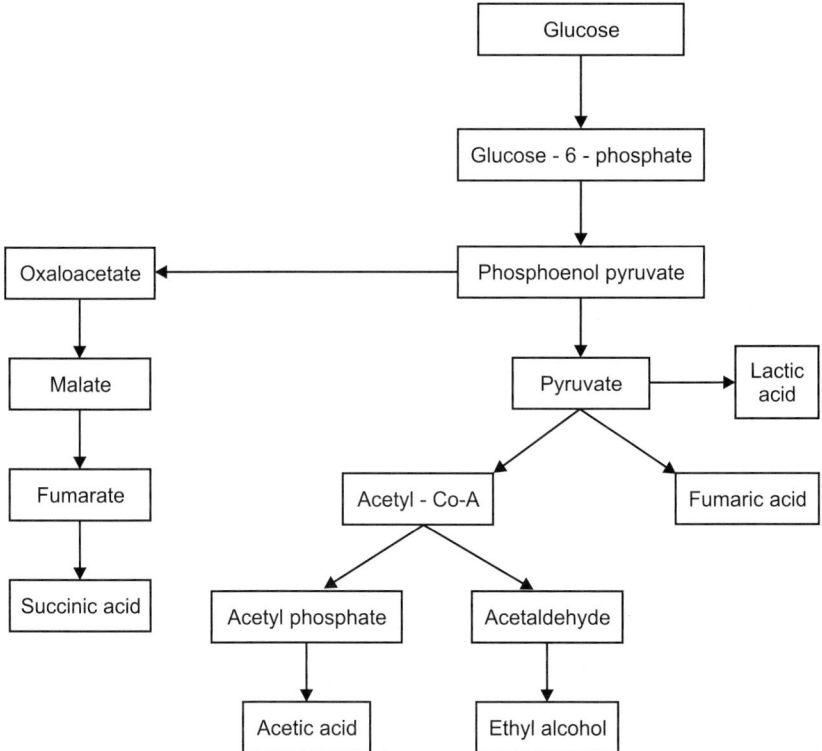

Figure 4.8: Metabolic pathway for mixed acid production.

4.3.8 Metabolic pathway for anaerobic fermentation

The pathway representing some valuable products synthesise during anaerobic digestion process. Various products like propionic acid, isopropyl alcohol, ethanol, butyric acid, butanol etc., as presented in the metabolic pathway. Butyric acid is a four carbon fatty acid which is formed in colon by bacterial anaerobic fermentation. Butyric acid can be found in most cultured dairy products, it can help to improve health of host gut and also help to control diabetes. Metabolic pathway for anaerobic fermentative products are shown in Fig. 4.9.

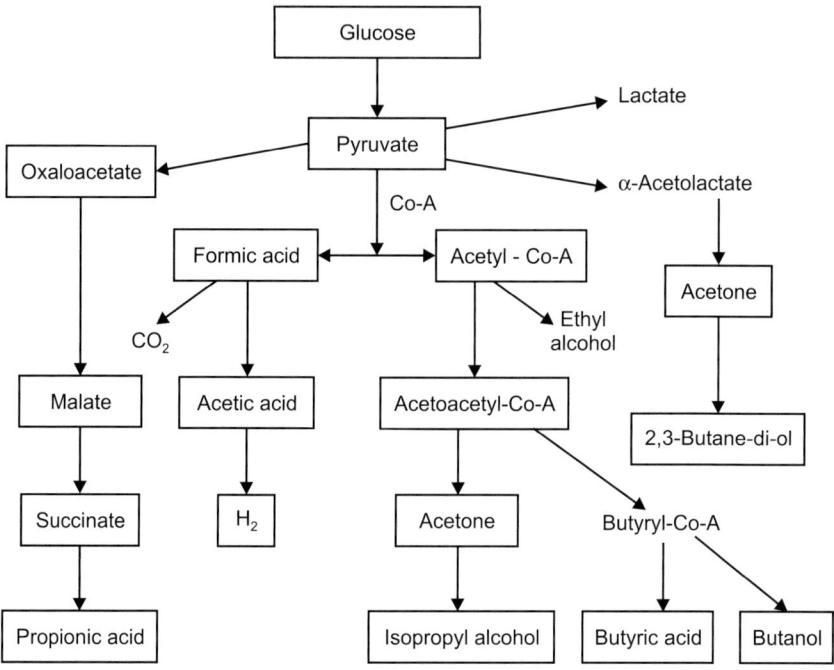

Figure 4.9: Metabolic pathway for anaerobic fermentative products.

4.3.9 Metabolic pathway for biofuel production

Biofuels like ethanol, Butanol and isopropanol can be produced from various source of raw materials like cellulose, starch, proteins and fats. Metabolic pathway for biofuel production are shown in Fig. 4.10. In first step, hydrolysis of these raw materials is done by use of various micro-organisms for different sources for example fungal species like *Trichderma viride*, *Trichoderma reesei* converts cellulosic raw materials in to glucose, *Bacillus amyloliquifaciens*

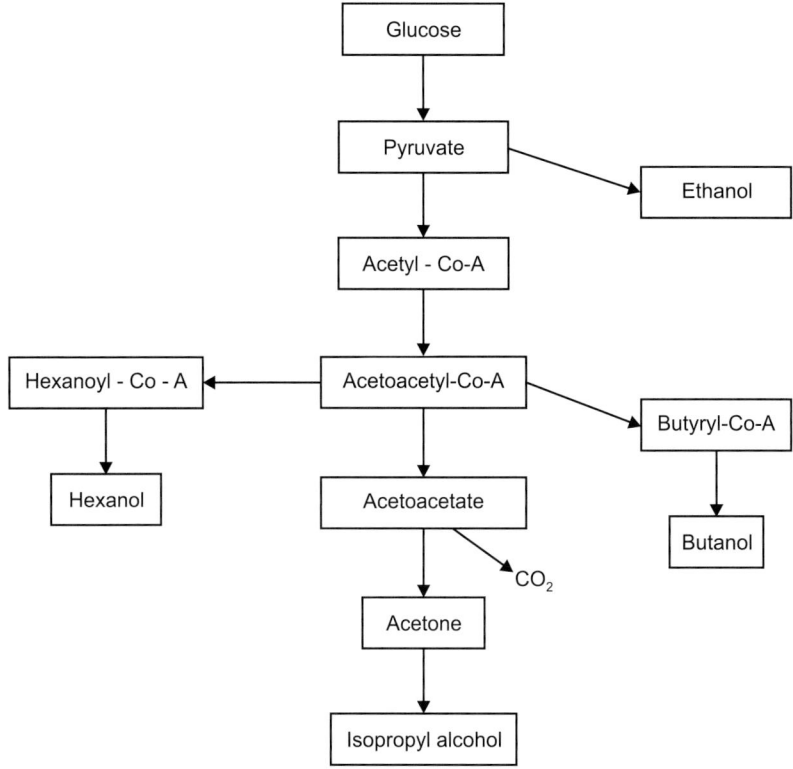

Figure 4.10: Metabolic pathway for biofuel production.

produces amylase enzyme that is necessary for the hydrolysis of starchy material, *Bacillus subtilis* produced protease which hydrolyses the protein molecules, *Bacillus cereus, Acinetobacter radioresistens*, etc., produces lipase enzyme that catalyses the fat molecules.

After hydrolysis of cellulose, starch, protein and fat, sugar is produced. This sugar or glucose is now finally converted in to ethanol by the use of *Saccharomyces cerevisiae* in anaerobic fermentation process. The produced ethanol can be utilised as fuel.

Analytical Techniques for Environmental Monitoring

5.1 Introduction

Depending upon type of waste and its characteristics, different environmental parameters are required for environmental monitoring. These parameters influence the efficiency of the different types of treatment methods. The nature and characteristics of the waste material depends on its source from where it is being generated. Biological Oxygen Demand (BOD) and Chemical Oxygen Demand (COD) are major parameters used for liquid waste monitoring. Values of BOD and COD of a liquid waste act as indicators of the level of pollution and these parameters have to be monitored. During the treatment process using physical, biological or chemical method, there will be reduction in these parameters. During treatment process of such waste, some valuable products like biohydrogen, biofertiliser, single cell protein, bioethenol, biodiesel is produced. According to regulatory authorities reduction of BOD and COD up to minimal national standards is required to discharge waste in open field. The process of biological treatment of waste required micro-organisms. These micro-organisms degrade complex organic material as waste in to simple compounds and consume some part of waste for their growth and development.

Growth of micro-organism during the treatment process is very important and that should be optimum for best performance of microbes. C/N Ratio of the waste materials is an important indicator of microbial growth during the process of waste treatment. Elements like sulphur and phosphorus should also be present in small amount along with carbon and nitrogen. Amount of this content must be known. For any microbial growth during the degradation process, pH is the most important parameter. The knowledge of various tools and techniques is required for effective monitoring of environmental pollution. These techniques are essential to determine the composition of waste material before the treatment and at the end of treatment process.

Knowledge of parameters and the techniques required to estimate, is prerequisite for selection and designing of treatment reactors. Few important parameters of the waste are total solid, volatile solid, organic materials such as hemicelluloses, cellulose, starch, reducing sugar and lignin, etc. In this chapter there will be discussion about different parameters and techniques that are used to determine the contents of waste materials.

5.2   Wastewater monitoring

5.2.1   Biological oxygen demand (BOD)

'BOD measures the requirement of oxygen by micro-organisms when a sample of water is treated at a temperature of 20°C for an elapsed period of five days'. If we have to determine the biochemical oxygen demand in given water sample then measurement of dissolved oxygen in the sample is required. To measure dissolve oxygen and further Biological oxygen demand, some instruments or apparatus and chemical reagents will be required as follows.

Apparatus/Instrument: BOD bottles having capacity of 250–300 ml, foil cap, incubator and titration apparatus are required for measurement of dissolved oxygen.

Reagents:

1. Manganous sulphate solution: To prepare this solution, dissolve 364 gm $MnSO_4.H_2O$ in water, filter it and make volume up to one liter. The $MnSO_4$ solution should not give a colour with starch when added to an acidified potassium iodide (KI) solution.

2. Alkali-iodide-azide reagents: For saturated or less than saturated sample- Dissolve 350 gm KOH and 75 gm KI in distilled water and dilute to 500 ml. Add 5 gm $NaNO_3$ dissolve in 40 ml distilled water. This reagent should not give a colour with starch solution when diluted and acidified.

3. Sulphuric acid: H_2SO_4 concentrate-1 ml is equivalent to about 3 ml alkali iodide Azide reagent.

4. Starch-soluble: Starch powder mixture (2% starch solution).

5. Standard sodium thio-sulphate titrant: Dissolve 6.205 gm $Na_2S_2O_3.5H_2O$ in distilled water. Add 0.4 gm solid NaOH and dilute to 1000 ml distilled water.

Procedure to measure BOD

1. Prepare the required dilution of sample as 10%, 20%, 30%, etc.

2. Add phosphate buffer, magnesium sulphate, calcium chloride and ferric chloride solution to each bottle (1ml/litre) maintain the pH 7.2.

3. Fill the BOD bottles up to overflow, there should not be any air bubble in the bottle.

4. Keep one bottle of the same sample and same dilution in BOD Incubator at 20°C for 5 days.

5. In second bottle, add 1 ml of $MnSo_4$ and 1 ml of Alakali Azide reagent in the bottle due to this yellow ppt forms. Let the ppt settle down upto the half of the bottle.

6. Add about 2 ml of concentrated sulphuric acid to dissolve the precipitate; solution becomes clear and golden in colour.
7. Take 201 ml of the above sample in 250 ml conical flask add 1 ml of freshly prepared stach indicator (solution become dark blue).
8. Titrate this 201 ml solution with standard sodium thio-sulphate solution; disappearance of colour will be the end-point.
9. Note the burette reading for calculation.

By performing above mentioned steps, we can findout burette reading of sodium thiosulphate in ml. Initial DO in mg/l and Final DO in mg/l.

Calculation: Now, as per data available we can calculate BOD by using following formula:

BOD mg/l in the given sample = Initial DO – Final DO ×Dilution factor

Dilution factor = Final volume of sample/initial volume of sample

While performing experiment to determine BOD, we should keep few points in mind that titration should be done carefully, apparatus should be washed and carefully measure the volume of reagents and sample.

5.2.2 Chemical oxygen demand (COD)

Recommended method to determine chemical oxygen demand is open reflux method. Organic matter present in sample is oxidised by a boiling mixture of chromic and sulphuric acids. A sample is refluxed in strongly acid solution with a known excess of potassium dichromate ($K_2Cr_2O_7$). After digestion, the residual unreduced $K_2Cr_2O_7$ is titrated with ferrous ammonium sulphate to determine the amount of $K_2Cr_2O_7$ consumed and the matter which can be oxidised, is calculated in terms of oxygen equivalent. Keep ratios of reagent weights, volumes, and strengths constant when sample volumes other than 50 ml are used. Some samples which have very low COD may need to be analysed in replicate to get most reliable data. Results are further enhanced by reacting a maximum quantity of dichromate, provided that some residual dichromate remains. For determining the chemical oxygen demand in given water sample, first of all measurement of dissolved oxygen in the sample is required.

To measure dissolve oxygen and further chemical oxygen demand, some instruments or apparatus and chemical reagents are required. To perform above activity, apparatus like reflux apparatus, blender and wide-bore pipette and chemical reagents will be required as follows:

1. Standard potassium dichromate solution: Dissolve 12.260 g $K_2Cr_2O_7$, primary standard grade, previously dried at 150°C for 2 h, in distilled water and dilute to 1000 ml. This reagent undergoes a six-electron

reduction reaction, the equivalent concentration is 6×0.04167 M or 0.2500 N.

2. Sulphuric acid reagent: To prepare this reagent add Ag_2SO_4, reagent or technical grade, crystals or powder, to concentrate H_2SO_4 at the rate of 5.5 g Ag_2SO_4/kg H_2SO_4. Leave it for 1 to 2 day to dissolve.

3. Ferroin indicator solution: Dissolve 1.485 g, 1,10-phenanthroline monohydrate and 695 mg $FeSO_4 \cdot 7H_2O$ in distilled water and make up volume to 100 ml. This indicator solution may be purchased from market as already prepared indicator solutions are available in market.

4. Standard ferrous ammonium sulphate (FAS) titran (0.25 M): Dissolve 98 g Fe $(NH_4)_2(SO_4)_2 \cdot 6H_2O$ in distilled water then add 20 ml concentrate H_2SO_4, cool, and make up volume up to 1000 ml by adding distilled water.

5. Mercuric sulphate: $HgSO_4$, crystals or powder.

6. Sulphonic acid: Used if the interference of nitrites is to be eliminated.

7. Potassium hydrogen phthalate (KHP) standard: $HOOCC_6H_4COOK$: Lightly crush and then dry KHP at $110°C$. Dissolve 425 mg in distilled water and make up volume up to 1000 ml. KHP has a theoretical COD of 1.176 mg O_2/mg and this solution has a theoretical COD of 500 μg O_2/ml. This solution is stable under low temperature. Observe development of visible biological growth if any. Weekly preparation of KHP is satisfactory.

Treatment of samples with COD of >50 mg O_2/l: Blend sample if required and pipette 50.00 ml into a 500-ml refluxing flask. For samples with a COD of >900 mg O_2/l, use a smaller portion diluted to 50.00 ml. Add 1 g $HgSO_4$, along with several glass beads, then very slowly add 5.0 ml sulphuric acid reagent and mix to dissolve $HgSO_4$. Mixing perform under low temperature to avoid possible loss of volatile materials. Add 25.00 ml 0.0417M $K_2Cr_2O_7$ solution and mix. Attach flask to condenser and turn on cooling water. Add remaining 70 ml sulphuric acid reagent through open end of condenser. Continue swirling and mixing while adding sulphuric acid reagent.

To prevent foreign material from entering refluxing mixture open end of condenser should cover with a small beaker and reflux for 2 h. Cool and wash down condenser with distilled water. Disconnect reflux condenser and make up volume of mixture up to about twice its volume with distilled water. Cool up to room temperature and titrate excess $K_2Cr_2O_7$ with FAS, using 2 to 3 drops ferroin indicator. The quantity of ferroin indicator is not critical; the same volume for all titrations can be used. Take as the end point of the titration the first sharp colour change from blue-green to reddish brown that persists for 1–2 min. Samples containing suspended solids or other components may require additional determinations. The blue-green colour may reappear. In the same manner, reflux and titrate a blank containing the reagents and a volume of distilled water equal to that of sample.

Alternate procedure for low-COD samples: Extreme care is required in this procedure because even a trace of organic matter on the glassware or from the atmosphere may create gross errors. If increased sensitivity is required then concentrate a larger volume of sample before digesting under reflux. In this process add all reagents to a sample larger than 50 ml and reduce total volume to 150 ml by boiling in the refluxing flask open to the atmosphere without the condenser attached. Calculate amount of $HgSO_4$ which is to be added on the basis of a weight ratio of 10:1, $HgSO_4$:Cl^- by using the amount of Cl^- present in the original volume of sample. Then carry a blank reagent through the same procedure. In this technique there is no loss of easily digested volatile materials. It has the advantage of concentrating the sample without lose of volatile materials.

Determination of standard solution: Evaluate the quality of reagents by conducting the test on a standard potassium hydrogen phthalate solution.

Calculation:

$$\text{COD as mg } O_2/l = \frac{(A - B) \times M \times 8000}{\text{ml sample}}$$

where, A   = ml FAS (ferrous ammonium sulphate) used for blank
       B   = ml FAS used for sample
       M   = molarity of FAS
      8000 = milli-equivalent weight of oxygen × 1000 ml/l

5.2.3   Estimation of TSS, TVS, TDS, ash content, lignin, cellulose, hemicellulose

Total, fixed, and volatile solids in water, solids, and biosolids
Total solids (A) = Total suspended solids (B) + Total dissolve solids (C) (B)
Total suspended solids:

Total solids: All solids present in water are denoted as total solids. Total solids are measured by evaporating all of the water out of a sample and weighing the solids which remain after evaporation of water.

Dissolved solids: Solids which are dissolved in the water and would pass through a filter are known as dissolved solids, examples, salt or sugar dissolved in water.

Suspended solids: Solids which are suspended in the water and would be retaining by surface of filter.

Types of suspended solids

There are three types of suspended solids.

1. Settleable solids.
2. Non-settleable solids.
3. Colloidal solids.

Some apparatus like desiccators, drying oven, for operation at 103°C to 105°C, analytical balance, capable of weighing to 0.1 mg, graduated cylinder, beaker, glass funnel, whatman filter paper, conical flask and porcelain dish (crucible), 25 ml to 100 ml capacity and filtration unit will be required for the determination of these suspended solids in a given sample, reagents of good quality are also required.

Procedure: To get best result, first of all dry the filter paper at 105°C in hot air oven for 1 hour, cool in dessicator and take weight as W1, Pour 50 ml water sample on the filter paper by arranging the paper on a clean conical flask. Now keep the filter paper in hot air oven for 1 hr. at 105°C and then cool the filter paper in dessicator and take weight as W2.

Take all the weights in Mg.

Initial weight of filter paper (W1) = ...

Final weight of filter paper (W2) = ...

Calculation:

Total suspended solids of sample mg/l = W2–W1 × 1000/ ml of sample.

Where, W1 = initial weight of filter paper (mg)

W2 = Final weight of filter paper (mg)

1000 = To covert the values as TSS in mg/l.

Total dissolve solids

Total solids: All type of solids present in water either dissolved or suspended considered as total solids. Total solids are measured by evaporating all of the water out of a sample and weighing the solids which remain after evaporation.

Type of solids: There are two types of solids.

1. Dissolved solids: Solids which are dissolved in the water and would pass through a filter.
2. Suspended solids: Solids which are suspended in the water and would be caught by a filter.

To determine total dissolve solids, apparatus like desiccators, drying oven, for operation at 103 to 105°C, analytical balance, capable of weighing to 0.1 mg, graduated cylinder, beaker, glass funnel, whatman filter paper, conical flask and porcelain dish (crucible), 25 ml to 100 m capacity, filtration unit and good quality reagents.

Procedure: First of all dry the porcelain dish at 105°C in hot air oven for 1 hr. then cool in dessicator and take weight as W1. Then pass 50 ml water sample from the filter paper by arranging the paper on a clean conical flask and collect the filtered water in pre weighted porcelain dish. Keep the Porcelain Dish (crucible) in hot air oven for 1 hr. at 105°C to evaporate water. The water should evaporate completely. At last cool the Porcelain Dish (crucible) in dessicator and take weight as W2. Take all the weights in mg.

Initial weight of porcelain dish (crucible) (W1) = ...

Final weight of porcelain dish (crucible) (W2) = ...

Calculation:

Total dissolve solids of the given water sample mg/l = W2 – W1 × 1000/ ml of sample

where, W1   =   Initial weight of porcelain dish (crucible) (mg)

W2   =   Final weight of porcelain dish (crucible) (mg)

1000   =   To covert the values as TDS in mg/l

Procedure for estimation of total solid

Preparation of evaporating dishes: If volatile solids are to be measured, treat clean evaporating dishes and watch glasses at 550°C for 1 hour in a muffle furnace. If only total solids are to be measured, heat dishes and watch glasses at 103°C to 105°C for 1 hour in an oven. Cool and store the dried glasswares in desiccators. Weigh each dish and watch glass prior to use (record combined weight as 'W_{dish}').

Preparation of samples

Fluid samples: If the sample contains enough moisture to flow readily, stir to homogenise, place a 25 to 50 g sample aliquot on a prepared evaporating dish. If the sample is to be analysed in duplicate, the mass of the two aliquots may not differ by more than 10%. Cover each sample with a watch glass, and weigh to the nearest 0.01 g (record weight as 'W_{sample}'). Spread each sample so that it is evenly distributed over the evaporating dish. Evaporate the samples to dryness on a steam bath.

Solid samples: If the sample contains pieces of solid material examples, dewatered sludge, take cores from each piece with a No. 7 cork borer or crush the entire sample coarsely on a clean surface by hand, use rubber gloves for the purpose. Place a 25 to 50 g aliquot of the crushed sample on a prepared evaporating dish. If the sample is to be analysed in duplicate, the mass of the two aliquots may not differ by more than 10%. Cover each sample with a watch glass, and weigh (record weight as 'W_{sample}'). Spread each sample so that it is evenly distributed over the evaporating dish. Dry the samples at 103°C to 105°C for 12 hours then cool to balance temperature in an individual desiccators containing fresh desiccant, and weigh. Cool the residue in a desiccator to balance the temperature. Weigh the residues. Repeat igniting (30 min), cooling, desiccating, and weighing steps until the weight change is less than 4% or 50 mg, whichever is less. Record the final weight as '$W_{volatile}$'.

Calculations:

1.
$$\% \text{ Total solids} = \frac{W_{total} - W_{dish}}{W_{sample} - W_{dish}} \times 100$$

Or

$$\frac{\text{Mg total solids}}{\text{Kg sludge}} = \frac{W_{total} - W_{dish}}{W_{sample} - W_{dish}} \times 1,000,000$$

where, W_{dish} = Weight of dish (mg)

W_{sample} = Weight of wet sample and dish (mg)

W_{total} = Weight of dried residue and dish (mg)

2.
$$\% \text{ Fixed solids} = \frac{W_{volatile} - W_{dish}}{W_{total} - W_{dish}} \times 100$$

Or

$$\frac{\text{Mg fixed solids}}{\text{Kg sludge}} = \frac{W_{volatile} - W_{dish}}{W_{total} - W_{dish}} \times 1,000,000$$

where, W_{dish} = Weight of dish (mg)

$W_{volatile}$ = Weight of wet sample and dish after ignition (mg)

W_{total} = Weight of dried residue and dish (mg)

3.
$$\% \text{ Volatile solids} = \frac{W_{total} - W_{volatile}}{W_{total} - W_{dish}} \times 100$$

Or

$$\frac{\text{Mg volatile solids}}{\text{Kg sludge}} = \frac{W_{total} - W_{volatile}}{W_{total} - W_{dish}} \times 1,000,000$$

where, W_{dish} = Weight of dish (mg)

      $W_{volatile}$ = Weight of residue and dish after ignition (mg)

      W_{total} = Weight of dried residue and dish (mg)

5.3   Estimation of lignin, hemicelluloses and cellulose

Agro-waste (crop residue) is composed of cellulose, hemicellulose and lignin as major components. For estimation of these crude fibres two components are required:

1. Acid detergent solution (ADS).
2. Acid detergent fibres (ADF).

ADS are prepared by dissolving 20 g cetyltrimethyl ammonium bromide in 1 litre of N sulphuric acid.

5.3.1   Preparation of ADF

Leaf material (0.5–2 g) is distilled with 50 ml ADS by boiling then content of beaker were transferred to glass plate. The residue was repeatedly washed with boiling water. The residue was sucked dry each time with 20 ml acetone and then dries. The crucibles were kept overnight in hot air oven at 100°C and then cool in desiccators and weighted. The residue which remained insoluble in hot ADS was the amount of ADF in given sample. The ADF content per gram dry matter was calculated on this basis.

Methods of estimation

There are two methods.

Method 1: Lignin estimation: ADF obtained as described above was used for the estimation of cellulose, lignin. Horizontal staining Jar containing ADF, were found suitable. Water was raised in Jar. 20 ml of freshly prepared buffered permanganate solution was stirred in with a glass rod. The crucibles were then transferred to filtration system. The crucibles were the kept in clean jars and level of water adjusted. 20 ml of buffered permanganate solution was poured in each crucible and allowed for 15 minutes and then sucked to dryness.

The crucible were placed in another set of jars and filled with 20 ml demineralising (DM) solution, after 5 minutes solution was sucked to dryness.

Crucible were again filled with 20 ml DM solution and allowed to react for 15 minutes then sucked dryness. The process is repeated 3 times to remove the oxidised lignin, formed as a result of reaction with buffered permanganate solution. Steps for lignin removal is shown in Fig. 5.1.

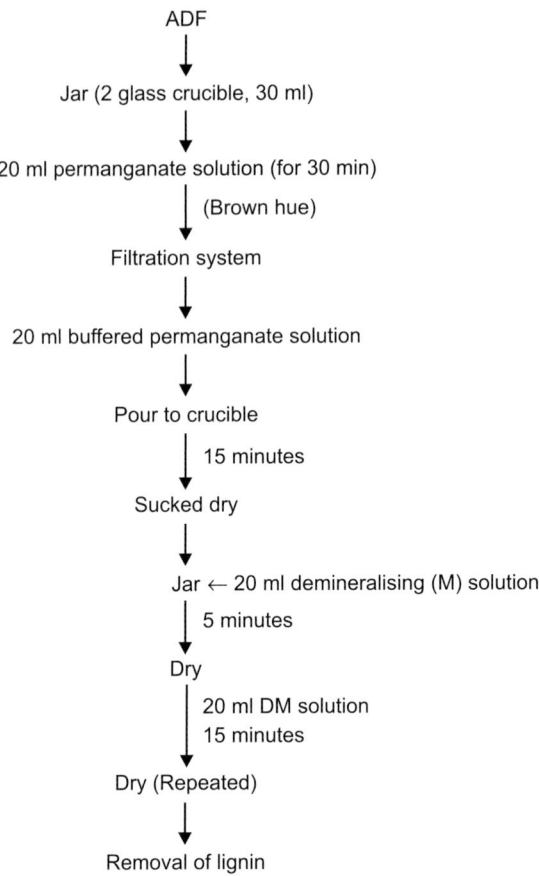

Figure 5.1: Steps for lignin removal.

Methods 2: Cellulose and hemicelluloses estimation.

Calculation: Once we obtain different fractions using above mentioned method we can calculate the amount of cellulose, hemicelluloses and lignin. It can be calculated by using following formulas.

Fraction B – C = Cellulose

Fraction A – B = Hemicellulose

C itself = Lignin

Determination of lignin

Lignin is a complex heteropolymer and one of the major component, examples cellulose, hemicelluloses and lignin. Lignin primarily consists of *p*-hydroxyphenyl (H), guaiacyl (G), and syringyl (S) units formed by the oxidative coupling of *p*-coumaryl, coniferyl, and sinapyl alcohols, respectively, which are products of the phenylpropanoid pathway. Steps for cellulose and hemicelluloses estimation is shown in Fig. 5.2.

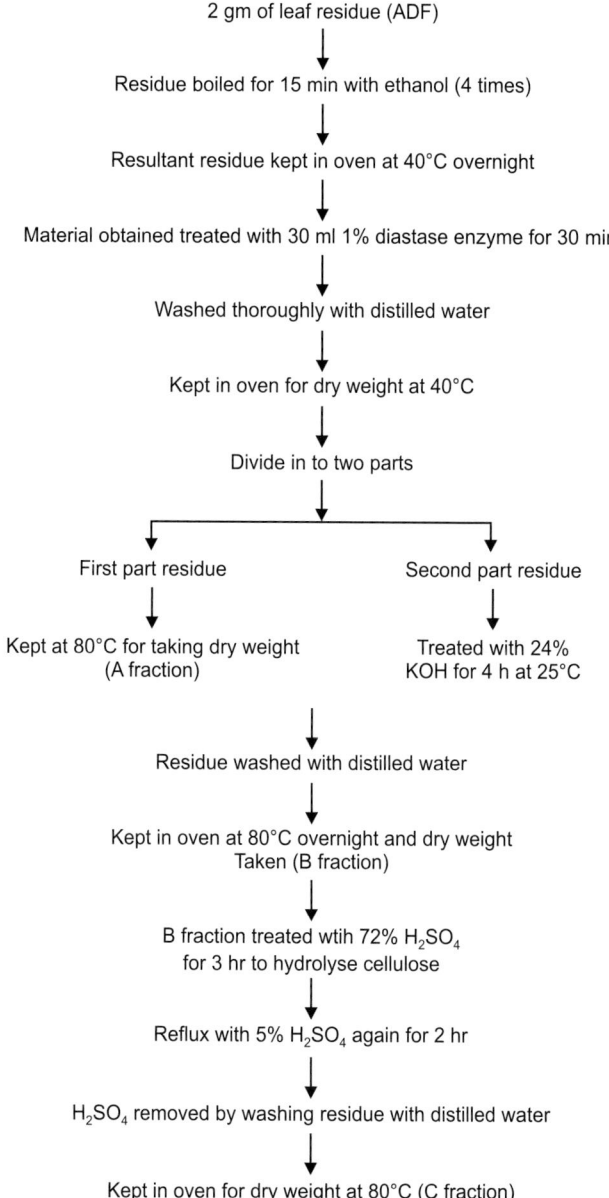

Figure 5.2: Steps for cellulose and hemicelluloses estimation.

Lignin completely deposited in the secondary cell wall, and provides a coating for cellulose-hemicellulose microfibrils, thus ensuring stiffness, strength, and impermeability for the lignified tissues. These properties of lignin protect the energetic polysaccharides against attack from pathogens and herbivores.

Lignin is also important for water transport in plants, mechanical resistance of grains, the textile and paper industries, and as a major hindrance in the generation of bioethanol there is a growing interest in improving the assays used for its quantification. Several methods have been described to measure the presence of lignin in biomass samples. However, there is no universal method to determine lignin. This is a major drawback because each technique can give different results for a same sample.

Acetyl bromide and thioglycolic acid method for lignin estimation

The acetyl bromide, thioglycolic acid are the more common methods used to quantify lignin. These methods are based on solubilisation of lignin and determination of absorbance values spectroscopically at 280 nm. This method was initially developed to provide a sensitive method for analysing small samples of forage plants. Acetyl bromide protocol is based on the formation of acetyl derivatives in non substituted OH groups and bromide replacement of the á-carbon OH groups to produce a complete solubilisation of lignin under acidic conditions. It is an indirect method, the lignin content may be overestimated and may occur due to the oxidative degradation of structural polysaccharides (e.g., xylans) during the exposure of the cell wall with the acidic solution. By its time, thioglycolic acid method is based in the formation of thioethers of benzyl alcohol groups found into the lignin, resulting in solubilisation of this polymer under alkaline conditions. The thioglycolic acid method can underestimate the lignin content due to the specificity of the reaction with ether bond types of lignin. In addition, during the precipitation steps, a fraction of soluble lignin can remain in solution, thereby resulting in an underestimation of the total lignin content.

Klason method for lignin estimation

For the direct quantification of lignin the Klason method can be used. It is a gravimetric assay. In this method, an insoluble lignin fraction is extracted from the plant tissues after digestion with 72% sulphuric acid followed by partial solubilisation of cell wall polysaccharides. The compounds such as proteins and non-extracted polysaccharides can also be measured together with lignin that results an overestimation of the lignin content. On the other hand, a considerable fraction of soluble lignin cannot be measured resulting in underestimation of lignin. Despite of the inconsistencies reported these methodologies are quite consolidated for use in wood biomasses. However, in herbaceous plants where the amount of lignin might be quite lower and sugar content quite higher than in wood, these inconsistencies among the methods might be amplified. Furthermore, choosing the most suited method to determine lignin in a specific test is still a challenge. Therefore, we compared the total lignin content in sugarcane bagasse, soyabean root, and soyabean seed coat using the acetyl bromide, thioglycolic acid and Klason methods. We also evaluated the monomeric composition of lignin in the contrasting tissues, as well as the production of furfurals to analyse the causes of inconsistencies observed among the methods.

We compared the amount of lignin as determined by the three most traditional methods for lignin measurement in three different tissues as sugarcane bagasse, soyabean roots and soyabean seed coat, contrasting for lignin content and composition. The amount of lignin determined by thioglycolic acid method was severely lower than that provided by the other methods in all tissues analysed. Klason method was quite similar to acetyl bromide in tissues containing higher amounts of lignin, but expressed lower recovery of lignin in the less lignified tissue. To determine the reason of the inconsistencies observed, we determined the monomer composition of all plant materials, but found no correlation among them. We found that the low recovery of lignin presented by the thioglycolic acid method were due losses of lignin in the residues disposed throughout the procedures. The furfurals production by acetyl bromide method does not express the differences observed. The acetyl bromide method is the simplest and quick among the methods evaluated presenting similar or best recovery of lignin in all the tissues analysed.

5.3.2   Bacteriological examination of wastewater

Multiple tube fermentation method

This method determines the bacteriological quality of water which has been developed to prevent transmission of water born diseases of fecal origin. In this method presence of indicator organisms is used to detect fecal contamination of water. Coliforms bacteria are the most frequently used indicator organisms. Coliforms are gram-negative non-endospore forming, rod shaped bacteria that ferment lactose with acid and gas formation within 40 hours at 35°C. Normally, coliforms are not pathogenic, but some time they can cause opportunistic infections.

Most probable number (MPN) test

By use of this method, most accurate number of coliform bacteria is obtained by testing a large sample of water. Determination of MPN is shown in Fig. 5.3.

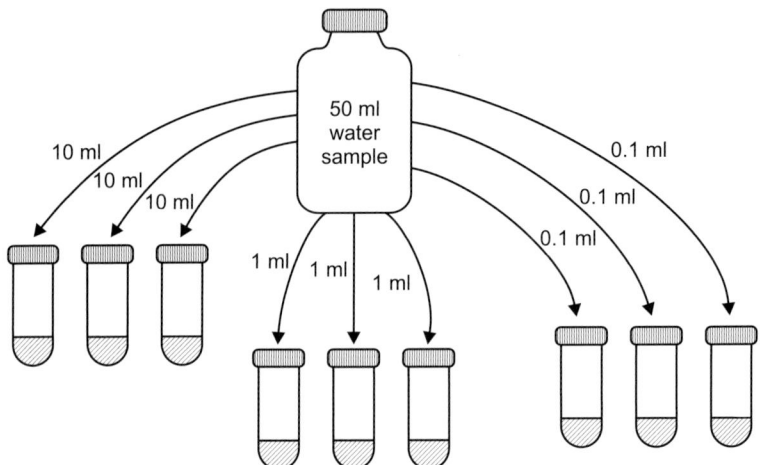

(Most probable number dilution series:
Three set of tubes containing 10 ml, 1 ml and 0.1 ml sample each)

General formula for determining the MPN value

MPN / 100 ml = MPN value (Table 5.1) 5 (10 / largest volume tested)

Figure 5.3: Determination of MPN.

Total coliform can be detected and enumerated in the multiple tube fermentation technique.

This technique will be completed in two stages.

1. Presumptive test.
2. Confirmed test.

Presumptive test: In the presumptive test, dilutions from the water sample are added to lactose fermentation tubes. The lactose broth can be made selective for gram-negative bacteria by adding 'Lauryl sulphate' or 'Brilliant green' and bile.

Fermentation of lactose to gas is positive reaction:

$$\text{Water sample} + \frac{\text{Lactose broth}}{\text{(Lauryl sulphate)}} \xrightarrow[\text{24–48 hours}]{\text{Fermentation}} \boxed{\text{Gas + Acid}}$$

Sample tubes containing gas and acid shows indication of presence of coliform bacteria.

Confirmed test: A confirmed test can be done on MUG agar (Methylumbeliferon glucuronide). Almost all strains of *E. coli* produce enzymes glucuronidase (GUD). It *E. coli* is added to a nutrient medium containing 4-methylumbelliferone glucuronide (MUG), GUD converts MUG to a fluorescent compound that is visible with an ultraviolet lamp. Steps of presumptive and confirmed test is shown in Fig. 5.4

1. Presumptive test:

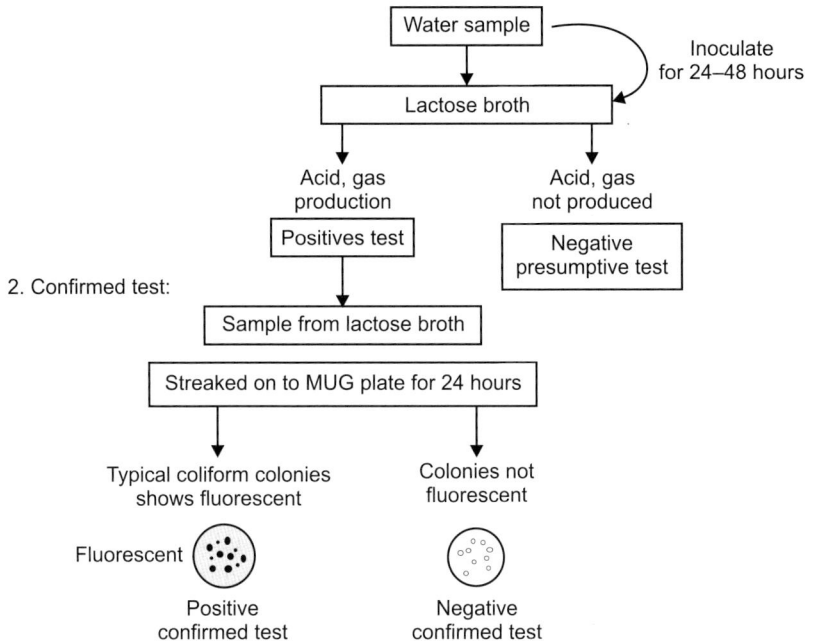

2. Confirmed test:

Figure 5.4: Steps of presumptive and confirmed test.

The number of coliforms is determined by a statistical estimation called the Most Probable Number (MPN) methods. In the presumptive test, tubes of lactose broth are inoculated with samples of water being tested. A count of number of tubes showing acid and gas is then taken, and then is compared to a statistical MPN table. The MPN is the most probable number of coliforms per 100 ml of water. Most probable number dilution series. Three set of tubes containing 10 ml, 1 ml, 0.1 ml sample each.

General formula for determining the MPN value:

MPN/100 ml = MPN value (Table 5.1) × (10/largest volume tested)

To determine the MPN, record the number of positive tubes (gas formed), then look up the number on the chart.

Usually dilution series will consist of aliquots of 10 ml, 1.0 ml, and 0.1 ml, if all 3 tubes of 10 ml tubes turn positive (presence of gas), 2 of 1 ml, and 1 of 0.1 ml tubes are positive this is reported as 3-2-1. This gives a MPN value of 17 from the MPN calculation chart is shown in Table 5.1.

Table 5.1: MPN calculation chart positive tubes value.

0-0-0	<2	3-0-0	8	5-0-0	23	5-3-3	170
0-0-1	2	3-0-1	11	5-0-1	30	5-4-0	130
0-1-0	2	3-1-0	11	5-0-2	40	5-4-1	170
0-2-0	4	3-1-1	14	5-1-0	30	5-4-2	220
		3-2-0	14	5-1-1	50	5-4-3	280
1-0-0	2	3-2-1	17	5-1-2	60	5-4-4	350
1-0-1	4			5-2-0	50	5-5-0	240
1-1-0	4	4-0-0	13	5-2-1	70	5-5-1	300
1-1-1	6	4-0-1	17	5-2-2	90	5-5-2	500
1-2-0	6	4-1-0	17	5-3-0	80	5-5-3	900
		4-1-1	21	5-3-1	110	5-5-4	1600
2-0-0	4	4-1-2	26	5-3-2	140	5-5-5	1600
2-0-1	7	4-2-0	22	0	<1.1	5	6.9
2-1-0	7	4-2-1	26	1	1.1	6	9.2
2-1-1	9	4-3-0	27	2	2.2	7	12.0
2-2-0	9	4-3-1	33	3	3.6	8	16.1
2-3-0	12	4-4-0	34	4	5.1	9	23.0
						10	23.0

Other detection methods of bacteria

Detection of bacteria is important in many industries to protect food products, air, and water from microbial contamination or to identify the source of infection in a clinic. A traditional method of bacterial detection is culture collection. This method is effective but can take hours or days to show results and may miss most types of bacteria. There are some new methods; these are more rapid methods of bacterial detection being developed to streamline the process and increase rates of detection. Some of these methods are as follows:

1. Polymerase chain reaction (PCR).
2. Infrared devices that detect bacteria in food, and rapid scans that detect bacterial contamination in blood platelets.
3. Biosensor-based methods.
4. Immunological-based methods.

Most of these methods detect bacteria by measuring oxygen levels or by generating electrical disturbances that indicate the presence of bacteria. The traditional technique of bacterial detection is bacterial counting for which take a sample, grow a bacteria culture, and count the bacteria that grow. This method is commonly used in clinics or pathology labs. Since platelet products must be stored at room temperature, they are at a high risk for bacterial contamination.

Traditional culture techniques based on detection of changes in oxygen levels that indicate the presence of bacteria, but results can take seven days.

Therefore, advance rapid methods are the need of the day to detect bacteria, like solid-phase cytometry, which detects and counts all fluorescently labelled bacteria within three minutes. FACS (Fluorescence Assisted Cell Shorter) and MACS (Magnet Assisted Cell Shorter) are devices to count microbes very quickly. Like the methods used to detect bacteria in platelet products, bacterial detection in water or air typically requires platelet counts, where water is placed on an agar surface and a culture is allowed to grow. After sufficient time to allow bacteria to multiply, bacterial colonies are counted. Another way to identify bacteria in water is to use a virus to infect bacteria with fluorescent reporter molecules that can be identified by fluorescence spectroscopy.

Sensor is a new method of bacterial detection that has potential for a wide range of applications. Sensor is coated with bacterial antibodies that have an electric current passed through it. When this sensor comes into contact with bacteria, the sensor detects changes in the frequency that indicates bacterial presence. This technology has been used to improve detection of *E. coli* bacteria in meat-processing facilities as well as detecting microcystin-LR (MC-LR) toxin in drinking water. This technology detects bacteria in minutes, whereas the older culture method takes hours to days.

Polymerase Chain Reaction (PCR) is a molecular technique of bacterial identification that has several advantages over other methods of bacterial detection. Some estimates state that more than 99% of all the bacteria in the human body cannot be cultured, making traditional techniques inadequate for many applications. PCR method has the potential to detect low amounts of bacteria very quickly using RNA and DNA amplification techniques.

Nucleic acid-based methods

These methods are operated by detecting specific DNA or RNA sequences in the target pathogen. This can be done by hybridising the target nucleic acid sequence to a synthetic oligonucleotide (probes or primers) which is complementary to the target sequence. There are many bacterial pathogens such as *Clostridium botulinum, Vibrio cholerae, Staphylococcus aureus*, and *Escherichia coli* O157 which produced toxins that caused foodborne diseases. The toxin-related genes in these pathogens can be detected by nucleic acid-based methods. Nucleic-acid based methods detect the specific genes in the target pathogens, therefore preventing ambiguous or wrongly interpreted results. The recent nucleic acid-based methods described are simple polymerase chain reaction (PCR), multiplex polymerase chain reaction (mPCR), real-time/quantitative polymerase chain reaction (qPCR), NASBA, loop-mediated isothermal amplification (LAMP) and microarray technology.

Nucleic acid sequence-based amplification (NASBA)

NASBA technique was developed in 1991 by Compton. In this technique amplification of nucleic acids occurs under isothermal conditions, unlike PCR which requires thermocycling system. NASBA is normally used for the amplification of RNA whereby the single-stranded RNA template is converted into complementary DNA (cDNA) by the reverse transcriptase during the reaction. This reaction occurs at around 41°C, two specific primers and three enzymes: Avian Myeloblastosis Virus (AMV) reverse transcriptase, T7 RNA polymerase and RNase H take part in reaction. The NASBA amplicons can be detected by agarose gel electrophoresis. This leads to the development of a novel real-time NASBA which uses fluorescently labelled probes which are molecular markers to detect the single-stranded RNA amplicons, thus, producing a homogenous NASBA assay Real-time NASBA has been used for the detection of various foodborne pathogens such as *Salmonella enterica*, *Vibrio cholerae, Staphylococcus aureus, Campylobacter jejuni*, and *Campylobacter coli*.

Real-time NASBA is capable to detect viable micro-organisms that present in food samples through mRNA amplification and the detection of RNA targets which will indicate the presence of viable cells. Real-time NASBA has been used to differentiate viable from non-viable bacterial cells. RNase treatment is basically required to degrade target mRNA from dead cells. Before nucleic acid extraction or treating the samples with RNase-free DNase is required prior to performing the NASBA assay.

Biosensor-based methods

Biosensor based methods can also be used for microbial count. Biosensor is an electronic analytical device that consists of two main components, one is transducer and another is bioreceptor. The bioreceptor recognise the target analyte. Following material can be used as bioreceptor:

1. Biological material: Examples are enzymes, antibodies, nucleic acids and cell receptors.
2. Biologically derived material: Examples are aptamers and recombinant antibodies.
3. Biomimic: Examples are imprinted polymers and synthetic catalysts.

The transducer that converts the biological interactions into a measurable electrical signal. There are different type of transducers depending upon reaction, examples are optical, electrochemical, mass-based, thermometric, micro-mechanical or magnetic. Biosensors are easy to operate and they do not require sample pretreatment, unlike nucleic-acid based methods and immuno-logical methods which require sample pretreatment for concentrating the pathogens before detection. Optical, electrochemical and mass-based biosensors are commonly used for the detection of foodborne pathogens.

Immunological-based methods

Immunological methods for detection of foodborne pathogens are based on antibody-antigen interactions, whereby a particular antibody will interact and attached to its specific antigen. The binding capacity of a particular antibody to its respective antigen determines the sensitivity and specificity of immunological based methods. Immunological based methods involve the use of polyclonal and monoclonal antibodies. Enzyme-linked Immunosorbent Assay (ELISA) and lateral flow immunoassay is best methods which recently used for the detection of foodborne pathogens.

5.4 Air quality monitoring

5.4.1 Particulate matter, $PM_{2.5}$, PM_{10}

Air quality index

Every living system requires good quality air, food and water for their servival. Due to huge industrialisation and mismanagement of waste disposal, air of surroundings is going to be polluted. To monitor the quality of air a index has been developed that is known as Air Quality Index (AQI). The AQI is an index for reporting air quality on daily basis. It tells about the quality of air, how clean or polluted air is? It also indicate the health problems according to level of air quality. The AQI focuses on health effects you may experience within a few hours or days after breathing polluted air. Environmental Protection Act determines the AQI for five major air pollutants regulated by the Clean Air Act, these are ground-level ozone, particle pollution (particulate matter), CO, SO_2, and NO_2. For each of these pollutants, EPA has established minimal national standards for air quality to protect public health. Air quality index levels is shown in Table 5.2.

Working of AQI

The range of AQI is from 0 to 500. In AQI index, if the AQI value is high, the greater the level of air pollution and the greater the health problem. For example, an AQI value of 50 represents good air quality with little potential to affect public health and an AQI value over 300 represents hazardous air quality. An AQI value of 100 is considered as the national air quality standard for the pollutant, the EPA has set level of AQI to protect public health. AQI values below 100 are generally thought of as satisfactory. When AQI values are above 100, air quality is considered to be unhealthy-at first for certain sensitive groups

Table 5.2: Air quality index levels.

Air quality index levels of health concern	Numerical value (range)	Meaning
Good	0 to 50	Air quality is considered satisfactory, and air pollution may cause little or no risk.
Moderate	51 to 100	Air quality is acceptable; however, for some pollutants there may be a moderate health concern for a very small number of people who are unusually sensitive to air pollution like children and old people.
Unhealthy for sensitive Groups	101 to 150	Members of sensitive groups may experience health effects. The general public is not likely to be affected.
Unhealthy	151 to 200	Everyone may begin to experience health effects; members of sensitive groups may experience more serious health effects.
Very unhealthy	201 to 300	Health alert: everyone may experience more serious health effects.
Hazardous	301 to 500	Health warnings of alarming conditions. The whole population is more likely to be affected.

of people, then for everyone as AQI values get higher. The purpose of the AQI is helping people to understand what local air quality can affect to your health. For better understanding, the AQI is divided into six categories. Each category represent a different level of health concern.

AQI colours

Environmental Protection Act has assigned a specific colour to each AQI category to make it easier for people to understand quickly whether air pollution is reaching unhealthy levels in their surroundings. For example, the colour orange means that conditions are 'unhealthy for sensitive groups,' while red means that conditions may be 'unhealthy for everyone,' and so on.

5.5   Sound monitoring

Definition and measurement: Any unpleasant, damaging or irritating noise that has the potential to harm people, wildlife or the environment is called as noise pollution.

Unit for measurement of sound: The unit used to measure the intensity or loudness of sounds is decibel (dB). A sound can also be measured by its pitch, which is the frequency of sound vibrations per second. For example, a low pitch produced by a deep voice, makes fewer vibrations per second than a high voice. Sounds with higher pitch, such as a sound from a violin, have a high rate of vibrations. Sound is generally recorded with a microphone. Sound sensor can also be used to measure sound level. Sound sensors work like microphones but these are more accurate. Examples of average decibel (dB) levels are as per Table 5.3.

Table 5.3: Sources of sound and sound levels.

S. No.	Source	Noise levels in decibels (Db)
1.	Volcano eruption	190
2.	Thunder	120
3.	Jet plane	120
4.	Factory boiler	110
5.	Trains	110
6.	Car and bikes	90
7.	Noisy class, gymnasium, alarm clock, police whistle	80
8.	Type writing	50
9.	Average residence	40
10.	Whispering	15

Sources of noise pollution: Major source of unwanted sounds are made by transportation vehicles such as airplanes, trains, cars, trucks, buses, motorcycles and construction site equipment such as pneumatic hammers, air compressors, bulldozers, loaders, dump trucks and pavement breakers. Noise can also come from household appliances such as music and television sets, air conditioner, refrigerator, lawn mowers, leaf blowers, loudly talking neighbours or a gathering of people.

Health hazard: According to the World Health Organisation (WHO), exposure of sound level above 50 dB can be hazardous to hearing and has the risk of contributing to high blood pressure, strokes and even heart attacks. When the body is exposed to high levels of noise, it reacts by releasing stress hormones and keeping the body in a perpetual level of tension. Long time exposure to loud sounds may result in side-effects such as irritation and anger, lack of concentration, interrupted sleep and hearing-related damage. The human ear feels pain at 120-140 decibels, and for that reason, we are tend to protect our ears with our hands when listening to sounds above this decibel range.

Environmental threat: Plants also require peaceful environments for their better growth and good crop quality. Due to noise pollution growth of plants affected and causes poor crop quality. Noise creates adverse effects on trees.

The adverse effect appears up to decades, even after the source of the noise goes away. It has been seen that birds and other animals change their behaviours in response to human noise, traffic or machinery noise. Noise creates sound waves that indirectly weaken the strength of buildings, bridges and monuments, and most of the time it can put buildings in dangerous condition.

Controls: Due to the increasing focus on noise pollution, engineering controls are designed to eliminate or reduce the level of noise produced. It would be good to isolate work stations exposed to excessive noise or insulate noisy work areas. For example, noisy equipment and machinery are replaced with improved models that are isolated in separate rooms equipped with sound-absorbent materials, dampers, mufflers, silencers or barriers. These materials are used in construction to keep outside noise from coming into homes and classrooms. Now days, most vehicles are equipped with mufflers, aircraft engines are designed to make less noise, and modern subway systems are less noisy.

5.6   Radioactive monitoring

It is very difficult to measure radioactive contamination in the field. Particles such as alpha and low-energy beta radiation are significantly affected by minute amounts of overburden, e.g., dust or precipitation. Therefore, detection rather than measurement is more realistic for alpha-beta monitoring. Particles having higher penetrating power, such as gamma and higher energy X-rays, are affected less by such overburden.

Although uranium and plutonium, both are alpha emitters, field survey of uranium can be done by measuring beta emissions from the thorium. For plutonium, the best technique is to detect the accompanying contaminant Am-241, which emits a gamma ray. If we know the original assay and the age of the weapon, the ratio of plutonium to americium may be computed accurately and the total plutonium contamination determined. Many of the factors that may not be controlled in a field environment may be managed in a mobile laboratory that may be brought to an accident site. The laboratory capabilities include gamma spectroscopy, low background counting for very thin alpha- and beta-emitting samples, and liquid scintillation counters for extremely low-energy beta emitters such as tritium.

5.6.1   Laboratory techniques

It is mandatory to follow laboratory procedures to quantitatively measure radiation contamination. Due to this, mobile laboratories are available within the department of defense and national security agencies for deployment to an accident site.

Following laboratory techniques are required for measurement of radiation.

1. Gamma and X-ray spectroscopy.
2. Alpha-beta counting.
3. Liquid scintillation

Gamma and X-ray spectroscopy

The major tools are detectors used in gamma and X-ray spectroscopy. These are a reasonably high-resolution gamma, X-ray detector (such as a High Purity Germanium or selectively high resolution NaI) and a multi-channel analyser. This equipment makes it possible to accurately determine the energies of the gamma and X-rays emitted by a contaminated sample. Usually, spectroscopic techniques are not used for absolute measurements of amount of contamination in a sample; but by adjusting for the energy dependency of detection efficiencies and using standard spectral unfolding techniques, the amounts of various isotopes present in the contaminant may be determined accurately. For example, spectroscopy facilitates for determination of the relative abundance of Am-241 to Pu-239. It provides accurate calibration of the most sensitive survey techniques like FIDLER.

Alpha and beta counting

Alpha and beta counting provide reasonably accurate determination of the absolute amount of contamination in a sample. Two types of counters are common and both are based on simple principle. In one, a reasonably sensitive alpha and beta detector, such as a thin layer of ZnS mated to a photomultiplier tube, is mounted in a chamber that is shielded to remove background radiation. The sample should be made very thin to reduce self-absorption. It is inserted into the chamber under the detector. To reduce the air absorption of the radiation in the chamber, air should be evacuated from the chamber. The count rate is then measured. Knowing the geometry of the experiment that allows translating the count rate to an absolute evaluation of sample activity.

Another alpha and beta technique involves gas-flow proportional counters. In this technique, a sample is placed into the chamber of a proportional counter. Emitted radiation causes ionisation of the gas in the counter that is electronically amplified and counted. Sample preparation is very difficult part of the experiment in both types of alpha and beta counters. To achieve best measurements of activity, radiation absorption must be reduced by the overburden caused by the sample itself. To perform this, few techniques are used including dissolving the sample onto a sample holder; evaporation of the solvent leaves a very thin, negligibly absorbing sample. Quantitative alpha and beta counting is a difficult and time-consuming process.

Liquid scintillation

The energy of the radiation is very low in detecting beta radiation from tritium. The resultant absorption is very high, that solid samples may not be used for quantitative analysis. In this situation, the contaminant may dissolve in a scintillating liquid. Glass vials of such liquid may then be placed in a dark chamber and the resulting scintillation light pulses counted using photo-multipliers. There is major difficulty of sample preparation with this process. Scintillation liquids are extremely sensitive to most impurities that may change the output of light pulses. To avoid this problem, it would be better to wipe a fixed area of a hard surface in the contaminated area with a small piece of filter paper. The cloth may then be immersed totally in scintillation liquid in such a way that subsequent light emission shall be visible to one of the photo-multipliers in the analysis chamber. In alternate method, the filter paper may be replaced by a special plastic material that dissolves in scintillation liquid without significantly quenching light output. The technique works best when the contamination is gathered without large amounts of local dirt, oil, etc.

Detection of uranium and plutonium

Uranium and Plutonium are alpha emitters, they also emit X-rays; therefore scintillation detector can be used for detecting these elements. Detection of uranium contamination is fairly straightforward. Among the radiations emitted in the decay of U-235 is an 80-keV X-ray. The 185.7-keV X-ray is one of the most easily detectable photons from highly-enriched uranium, and has better penetrating power for the entrance windows of scintillators than low-energy X-rays. Instrument setup and field calibration of the detector, permits the measurement of the X-ray activity per square meter and thus evaluation of the uranium contamination.

Plutonium detection is more complicated compare to uranium. Pu-239 emits a 17-keV X-ray that may be detected with a FIDLER detector. However, absorption of that relatively low-energy X-ray by overburden and also with interference by background signals in the same range as the desired X-ray makes measuring the 17 keV a highly uncertain technique. Plutonium contamination may be determined more accurately through indirect techniques.

Indirect technique for plutonium detection

Good quality plutonium contains several isotopes like Pu-241, Pu-239. Pu-241 beta decays, with a half-life of 14.35 years, to Am-241. Am-241 subsequently decays with the emission of a 60 keV X-ray which is like the 80-keV X-ray of uranium. It is relatively easy to detect under field conditions. Thus, a most sensitive technique for detecting weapons grade plutonium is to detect the contaminant Am-241. One thing is important that, this technique requires more information than the direct detection of radiation from the most plentiful isotope. These informations are such as knowledge of the age and original assay of the weapon material; however, decay times, weapon age, and assay are known or controllable quantities, while overburden and its effect on alpha and low-energy X-rays are not.

5.7 Minimal national standards for waste disposal

Minimal national standards for wastewater disposal (according to environment protection amendment rule 3A). Parameters and standard values for disposal of wastewater are shown in Table 5.4.

Table 5.4: Parameters and standard values for disposal of wastewater.

Parameter (mg/l)	Standards			
Suspended solids	Inland surface water	Public sewers	Land for irrigation	Marine coasted area
	100	600	200	100
Dissolved solid	2100	–	2100	100
pH value	5.5–9	5.5–9	5.5–9	5.5–9
BOD	30	350	10	100
Total residual chlorine	1.0	–	1.0	
Ammonical nitrogen	50	50	–	50
Kjeldahl nitrogen	100	–	110	100
Free ammonium	5.0	6.7	–	100
Dissolved phosphate	5.0	–	5.8	–
Sulphate	1000	1000	1000	–
Sulphide	2.0	–	–	0.5
Fluoride	2.0	15	–	15
Chloride	1000	1000	600	–
Total chromium	2.0	2.0	–	2.0
Led	0.1	1.0	–	2.0
COD	250	0.01	–	250
Mercury	0.01	0.01	–	0.01
Nitrate nitrogen	10	–	14	20
Cadmium	2.0	1.0	1.6	2.0

5.7.1 Load based standards

Table 5.5 shows parameters and load based standards and Table 5.6 shows maximum permissible concentration limit (ppm).

Table 5.5: Parameters and load based standards.

Oil refinery industry	
Parameter	*Quantum in kg/1000 T of crude processed*
Oil and grease	10.3
Phenol	0.70
BOD	10.50
Suspended solids	13.5
Sulphide	0.37

Pulp and paper industry	
Parameter	*Quantum in kg/ T*
Total organic chloride	2 kg/T of product
Tanneries	28 m³/T of raw hide
Dairy	2.8 m³/T or kL of milk

Table 5.6: Maximum permissible concentration limit (ppm).

Parameter	*Synthetic fibre industry*	*Breweries*	*Oil refineries*	*Sugar industry*	*Wooden industry*	*Fertiliser industry*
BOD	30	30	12–15	35–100	100	–
TSS	100	100	13–20	32–100	100	100
pH	6.5–8	–	6–8.5	6.5–8	–	6.5–8
Oil and grease	–	–	8–10	10	10	–
Phenol	–	–	0.7–1	–	5	–
Sulphides	–	–	0.35–0.5	–	2	–
Chromium	–	–	–	–	2	2
Ammonical nitrogen	–	–	–	–	–	50
Free ammonia	–	–	–	–	–	4
Nitrogen as nitrate	–	–	–	–	–	10
Arsenic	–	–	–	–	–	0.2
Vanadium	–	–	–	–	–	0.2
Total kjeldahl nitrogen	–	–	–	–	–	100

6

Management and Treatment of Waste

6.1   Introduction

Solid waste is the unwanted solid matter or useless solid materials which are generated by various commercial activities in a given area and residential areas. Solid waste can be classified according to site of origin (industrial, commercial, construction, domestic, or institutional and research laboratories); according to its constituents (organic material, metal, plastic, glass, paper, etc.), or according to hazard nature (toxic, non-toxin, radioactive, infectious, flammable, etc). Solid waste management reduces or eliminates adverse impacts on the environment, ecology, human health, supports economic development and improved quality of life. Solid waste can be managed by number of different processes which are involved in waste for a municipality. These include surveying, monitoring, collection, transport, processing, recycling, reusing and disposal.

6.2   Types of waste

Wastes divided on the basis of state are of three types:
1. Solid wastes.
2. Liquid wastes
3. Gaseous wastes.

6.2.1   Classification of solid wastes

Municipal solid waste

Solid waste of municipal contains construction, demolition debris, sanitation residue, domestic waste and waste from streets. This waste is mainly from residential apartments, shopping malls and commercial complexes. These may be further categories as:

Garbage: Garbage refers to the organic matter which is biodegradable solid wastes constituents produced during the preparation of food using meat, fruit, vegetable, etc. A lot of garbage is generated from agro-based industries or during crop harvesting practices.

Rubbish: Rubbish refers as non-biodegradable solid waste that having either combustible or non-combustible materials. The combustible waste includes paper, wood scrap, rubber, plastic, leather, etc., while non-combustible waste are mainly metals, glass, ceramics, etc. Rubbish wastes contain about 25% moisture.

Hospital waste

Hospital waste is generated during the process of diagnosis, treatment of diseases, vaccination of human beings, animals, waste generated in research activities in these fields, waste of the production and biological tastings. It may include wastes like knife, blade, other sharps, solid waste, disposables, anatomical waste, culture, slides, disposable syringes, swabs, bandages, and human excreta, non recyclable petry plates, etc. The hospital waste contains moisture content about 85% and there are up to 5% non-combustible solids. This type of waste is highly infectious and can be serious threat to human health if not managed in a scientific and discriminate manner.

Industrial waste

Industrial waste includes chemicals, paints, oils, fats, pulps, flash, etc. Manufacturing industry produces waste which is solid, semi-solid and liquid. This waste can be biodegradable, self igniting, explosive, toxic or radioactive. The chemical processes based industries generate a variety of waste, both organic and inorganic which are mixed solutions or mixture with wide range of component concentration.

Agricultural waste

Agriculture waste includes farm animal excreta and crop residue, etc. Animal, fruit and vegetable waste contains valuable minerals and nutrients. Human waste, agricultural farm waste and animal farm contains nitrogen, phosphorus, potash and trace elements. This type of waste plays vital role to increase the fertility of the soil results solid and optimum plant growth. After burning of waste as fuel in the conventional manner makes poor use due to loss of valuable nutrients. In India 2 kg/person agricultural waste is generated per day.

Effects of solids wastes

1. Effects on human health and animals.
2. Effect on monuments.
3. Effect on vegetation.
4. Effects on environment (soil, water, air).

Management of solid waste

Major methods of waste reduction, waste reuse and recycling are the preferential options when managing waste. There are many environmental benefits that can be further derived from the use of these methods. These methods can reduce or prevent green house gas emissions, reduce or minimise the release of pollutants, conserve resources, reduce energy consumption and reduce the cost for waste treatment technology and landfill space.

Therefore it is recommended that these methods can be adopted and incorporated as part of the waste management plan. Type of solid waste and their contribution in total waste is shown in Fig. 6.1.

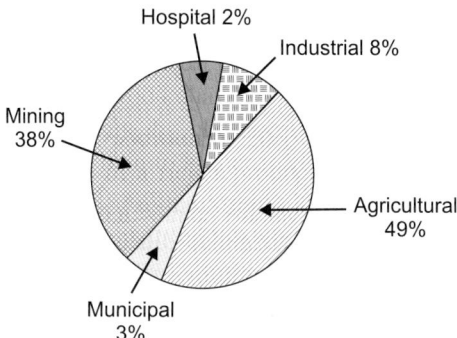

Figure 6.1: Type of solid waste and their contribution in total waste.

Waste reduction and reuse

The waste reduction and reuse of products are preventive methods of waste management. These can eliminate the production of waste at the source of usual generation and reduce the demands for large scale treatment and disposal facilities. The Methods of waste reduction also include manufacturing of products with less packaging, encouraging customers to bring their own reusable or biodegradable bags for packaging, encouraging the public to choose reusable products such as vessels, cloths, napkins and reusable plastic and glass containers, backyard composting and sharing and donating any unwanted materials rather than discarding them. All of the methods of waste prevention mentioned require public participation. Such type of practices should be promoted by public and private organisations like educational institutions should aware their students and society about these techniques so that everyone can contribute in waste reduction and recycle.

In order to get the public onboard, training and educational programmes need to be undertaken to educate the public about their role in the process. Government may need to regulate the types and amount of packaging used by manufacturers and make the reuse of shopping bags mandatory. Zero discharge industries should be promoted, motivated and awarded for performing their work honestly.

Four R's to be followed for solid waste management:

1. Refuse: Instead of buying new containers, carry bags, cans, bottles, etc., from market, use the ones that are in the house. Refuse to buy new items.

2. Reuse: Do not throw away the containers, bottles, cans and poly bag but these should be utilised to keep small things.

3. Recycle: The waste materials should be collected separately. Collect the recyclable waste for recycling. Recycling refers to the removal of items from the waste stream to be used as raw materials in the manufacture of new valuable products. Now this definition recycling occurs in three stages: first the waste is sorted and recyclables collected, the recyclables are used to create raw materials. These raw materials are then used in the production of new useful products. The sorting of recyclables may be done at the source (i.e., within the offices, hotels, household, etc.), for selective collection by the municipality or to be dropped off by the waste producer at a recycling centres.

4. Reduce: The waste reduction process is also very effective for waste management. To control the generation of unnecessary waste, e.g., carries your own shopping bag when you go to market and keep this things in it.

6.2.2 Waste collection

Solid waste control sanitation

Solid waste collection*:* The major part of overall solid waste management programme is effective collection and transportation. The basic mode of collection is from communal storage point. The waste is delivered to fixed storage bins usually built from concrete blocks to the location from where the collection vehicle will ultimately transport it to the side of disposal. Daily collection is essential because the organic matter degrades or putrefies fast. The pre-sorting at the primary source requires public participation which may not be forthcoming if there are no benefits to be derived. A system of selective collection by the government may be costly. It would require more frequent circulation of trucks within a neighbourhood or the importation of more vehicles to facilitate the collection. Another option is to mix the recyclables with the general waste stream for collection and then sorting and recovery of the recyclable materials can be performed by the municipality at a suitable site.

Waste sorting by the municipality has the advantage of eliminating the dependence on the public and ensuring that the recycling does occur. The major disadvantage however, is that the value of the recyclable materials is reduced since being mixed in and compacted with other garbage can have adverse effects on the quality of the recyclable material. The waste treatment techniques requires transform the waste into a form that is more valuable products, manageable, reduce the volume or reduce the toxicity of the waste thus making the waste easier to dispose of. The Treatment techniques are selected based on the composition, quantity, quality and form of the waste material. Some waste treatment methods being used now a days include subjecting the waste to extremely high temperatures, dumping on land or land filling and use of biological processes to treat the waste. It should be noted that treatment and disposal options are chosen as a last but management strategies reducing, reusing and recycling of waste should be given reference.

Solid waste disposal: The area of barren land is shrinking day by day and population is increasing rapidly that increases urbanisation. The solid waste discharge becomes a problem. Different methods for the waste disposal are as following:

1. Open dumping: The Open dumps process refers to uncovered area that is used to dump solid wastes of various types. The waste is untreated, unprocessed, uncovered and not screened. The rain water peculates from the dumps contaminates nearby land and water, spreading diseases. In developed nations open dumps are being phase out.

2. Land filling: Land filling is generally located in the barren lands which are on the outskirts of the urban areas where a large amount of generated waste is dumped. The differences between open dumping and land filling is that, it is a pit or ditch that is dug in the ground. The garbage is dumped in to the pit, which is then covered, every day a layer of soil is scattered on top of it and some mechanism, usually earth-moving equipment is used to compress the garbage, which now forms a cell-likewise, everyday the garbage is dumped and forms a cell. After the landfill is full, the area is covered with a thick layer of mud. It has some disadvantages like ground water pollution. Biogas is piped out for energy generation.

3. Sanitary land filling: Sanitary land filling is alternative to landfills, which will solve the problem of leaching to some extent. It is more hygienic and built methodically. Constructing sanitary land filling is expensive and it also has its own disadvantage.

Sanitary landfills are designed to greatly reduce or eliminate the risks that waste disposal may pose to the public health and environmental quality. These processes are usually placed in areas where land features act as natural buffers between the landfilling and the environment. For example, the area may be comprised of clay soil which is fairly impermeable due to its tightly packed particles, or the area may be characterised by a low water table and an absence of surface water bodies thus preventing the threat of water contamination.

The strategic placement of the landfill other protective measures are introduced into its design. The bottom and sides of landfills are lined with layers of clay, concrete or plastic to keep the liquid waste, known as leachate, from escaping into the soil. The leachate is collected and pumped to the surface for treatment. Boreholes or monitoring wells are dug in the vicinity of the landfill to monitor groundwater quality.

Landfilling is divided into a series of individual sections and only a few sections of the site are continuous filled with trash. This minimises exposure to wind and rain. The daily waste is loaded and compacted to reduce the volume, a cover is then applied to reduce odours and keep out pests. When the landfill has reached its capacity it is capped with an impermeable seal which is typically made up of clay soil.

In some sanitary landfills energy is being recovered. The natural anaerobic decomposition of the waste in the landfill produces gases which include carbon dioxide, methane and traces of other gases. Methane can be used as an energy source to produce heat or electricity. Thus some landfills are fitted with landfill gas collection systems to capitalise on the methane being produced. The process of generating gas is very slow, for the energy recovery system to be successful there needs to be large volumes of wastes. These landfills exhibits the least environmental and health risk and the records kept can be a good source of information for future use in waste management, however, the cost of establishing these sanitary landfills are high when compared to the other land disposal methods.

The advantages of sanitary land fill over an open dump are:

1. Public health problems are minimised because flies, rats and other pests are unable to bread in the covered refuse.
2. There is no air pollution.
3. Fires hazardous are minimal in sanitary landfill.
4. There is no ground water pollution.

Controlled dumps: Controlled dumps are waste disposal sites which consist most of the requirements for a sanitary landfill but usually have one deficiency. They may have a planned capacity but no cell planning, there may be partial leachate management, partial or no gas management, regular cover, compaction in some cases, basic record keeping and they are fenced or enclosed. These dumps have a reduced risk of environmental contamination, the initial costs are low and the operational costs are moderate. While there is controlled access and use, they are still accessible by scavengers and so there is some recovery of materials through this practice.

Bioreactor landfills: Modern technological advancement have lead to the development of the bioreactor landfill. Enhanced microbial processes are being used in bioreactor landfills to accelerate the decomposition of waste. The major controlling factor is the constant addition of liquid to maintain optimum moisture for microbial digestion. This liquid is usually added by re- circulating the landfill leachate. If produced leachate in not enough, water or other liquid waste such as sewage sludge can be used. The landfill may use either anaerobic or aerobic microbial digestion or it may be designed to combine the both. The enhanced microbial processes have the advantage of rapidly reducing the volume of the waste creating more space for additional waste, they also maximise the production and capture of methane for energy recovery systems and they reduce the costs related with leachate management. For bioreactor landfills to be successful the waste should be comprised predominantly of organic matter and should be produced in large volumes. Main features of a modern landfil is shown in Fig. 6.2.

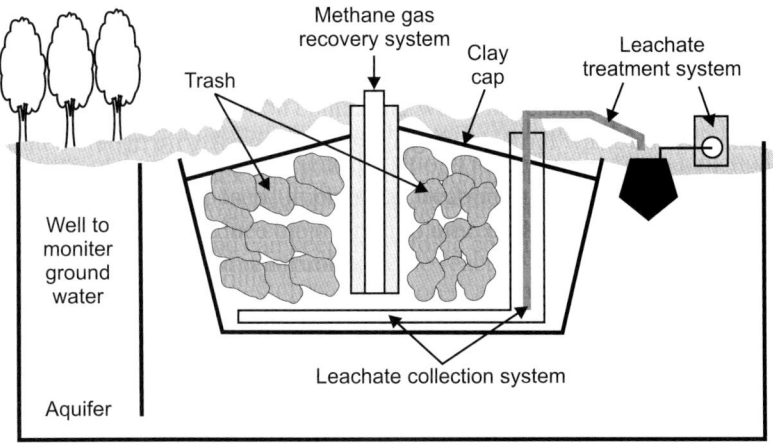

Figure 6.2: Main features of a modern landfil.

6.3   Type of waste treatment

6.3.1   Thermal treatment

Thermal treatment is a process that involves the use of heat to treat waste. Descriptions of some commonly utilised thermal treatment processes are listed below:

Open burning (uncontrolled burning): In the open burning method, burning of solid waste materials in a manner that causes smoke and other emissions to be released directly into the air without passing through a chimney or stack. This process includes the burning of outdoor piles, burning in a burn barrel and the use of incinerators which have no pollution control devices and as such release the gaseous by products directly into the atmosphere. Open-burning has been practiced by a number of urban centres because it reduces the volume of refuse received at the dump and therefore extends the life of their dumpsite. Garbage may be burnt because of the ease and convenience of the method or because of the cheapness of the method. In countries where house holders are required to pay for garbage disposal, burning of waste in the backyard allows the householder to avoid paying the costs associated with collecting, hauling and dumping the waste.

Open burning has many adverse effects on all living beings, monuments and the environment. This uncontrolled burning of garbage releases many pollutants into the atmosphere. These include dioxins, particulate matter, polycyclic aromatic compounds, volatile organic compounds, carbon monoxide, hexachlorobenzene and ash. The harmful effects of open burning are also felt by the environment. This process releases acidic gases such as the halo-hydrides; it also may release the oxides of carbon, sulphur and nitrogen. Oxides of sulphur and nitrogen contribute to acid rain, ozone depletion, smog and global warming. In addition to being a green house gas carbon monoxide reacts with sunlight to produce ozone which can be harmful. The particulate matter creates smoke and haze which contribute to air pollution.

Incineration: Incineration is the process in which the burning of solid waste is takes place in large furnace. In this process recyclable material is segregated and the non-recyclable material is burnt. At the end of the process ash is left, some ash flies out with the hot air. This is called fly ash. The remaining ash has high concentration of dangerous toxins such as toxins of heavy metals. Disposing this ash poses a problem. At present incineration is considered the last resort and is used mainly for treating hospital (infections waste). Incineration is the most common thermal treatment process which takes place at high temperature. This is the combustion of waste in the presence of oxygen. After incineration, the wastes are converted to carbon dioxide, water vapour and ash. This method may be used as a means of recovering energy to be used in heating or the supply of electricity. In addition to supplying energy, incineration technologies have the advantage of reducing the volume of the waste, rendering it harmless, reducing transportation costs and reducing the production of the green house gas methane.

Plasma arc furnaces: Plasma arc furnaces are used for incineration of hazardous waste. High temperature is applied in plasma arc, these are electrically neutral, stream in gaseous form consisting of positively charged particles, by the electron beam to this. Pressure of this plasma arc is responsible for its temperature, transport properties and permitting the distractive capacity. The temperature rises to 10000°C. The waste gets decomposed within milliseconds at extremely high temperature. The major advantage of this technique for decomposition of waste material is without generation of secondary combustion products, the produced flue gases cleanup easily.

Wet oxidation: In this technique of waste degradation wet oxidation is applied at high temperature. The principle of this process is that any waste material that can burn and also can be oxidised in the presence of water at 250°C–700°C. Produced sludge is exposed at high temperature and pressure in a reaction chamber (260°C, 1000–1700 psi). After increase in pressure (1000–1700 psi) the air is injected in presence of water to enhance oxidation. Solid waste reacts with the oxygen and the products in solid form can be separated from liquid by using grit removal, precipitation, settling, vacuum filtration or concentrate by dehydration.

6.3.2   Thermochemical conversion methods

Thermochemical conversion methods consist of as per following:

1. Pyrolysis
2. Thermal liquifaction
3. Carbonisation
4. Torrefaction

Pyrolysis

Pyrolysis is the process in which thermal degradation of solid waste (wood) in the absence of oxygen. It enables biomass to be converted to a combination of solid char, gas and a liquid bio-oil. Pyrolysis process is of two types on the basis of time and temperature utilised in the process. They can be commonly categorised as 'fast pyrolysis' and 'slow pyrolysis'. The products of pyrolysis are generated in roughly equal proportions with slow pyrolysis. Bio-oil is the yield of fast pyrolysis, can be as high as 80 per cent of the product on a dry fuel basis. Bio-oil can act as a liquid fuel or as a feedstock for chemical production. Different bio-oils production processes are under development, including fluid bed reactors, ablative pyrolysis, entrained flow reactors, rotating cone reactors, and vacuum pyrolysis.

Any solid waste is heated at high temperature in the absence of oxygen can be degraded. Word 'biomass pyrolysis' is generally associated with the processes involving bio-oils and liquid chemical fuel production. The steps involved in thermal conversion of waste, are briefly mentioned as in Fig. 6.3.

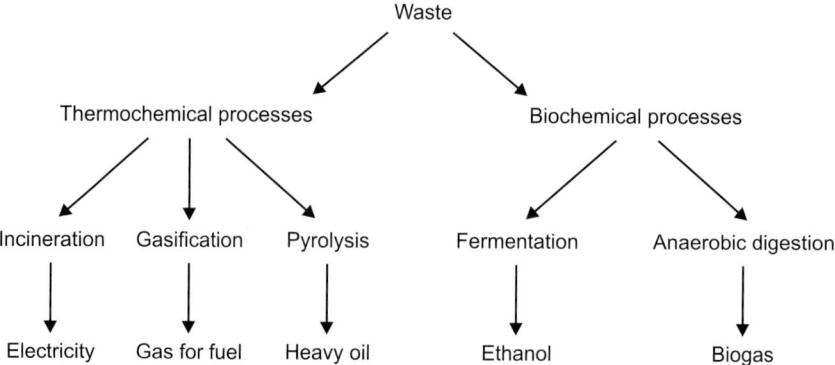

Figure 6.3: Thermal conversion processes of waste in to valuable products.

Fast/flash pyrolysis is performed at high temperature (400–600°C) for very short time (0.6–3.5 seconds). The shorter time exposure of high temperature to the organic matter (e.g.,waste) in fast/flash pyrolysis process results in increased significance of heat and mass transfer, and phase transition along with chemical reaction kinetics. Long residence times (few minutes to hours) and lower temperature range (205–360°C) favour charcoal formation. In this process reactors like fluidised bed reactors use smaller particle size and high temperature to achieve very fast heat transfer, leading to minimised char formation. The low thermal conductivity of biomass particles is very well exploited in such reactors where pellets of biomass are pressed against heated surface, resulting formation of vapour as well as exposing unaffected inner surface. Dry biomass, small particle size, short residence times, moderate-to-high temperatures, and rapid quenching of pyrolysed vapour will favour fast pyrolysis. The lack of predictive kinetic constants for fast pyrolysis is due to its unsteady state nature as the biomass complexity requires multistage thermal decomposition with production of substantial quantities of highly unstable compounds. These factors have great impact on the design of a fast pyrolysis system which should rapidly heat biomass to desired temperature as well as quickly quench down the products.

Thermal liquefaction

Thermal liquefaction is very much similar to pyrolysis process in simplified comparisons. Both processes differ in operating parameters, requirement of catalyst, and final products. Liquefaction produces mainly liquid and some amounts of gaseous components at temperature and pressure ranges of 250–350°C and 700–3000 psi, respectively, in the presence of alkali metal salts as catalyst. To facilitate the overall process, liquefaction may require supplemental CO and

H_2 as reactants. The mechanisms of liquefaction reactions lack sufficient description about role of catalysts. The catalysts hydrolyse the cellulose, hemicelluloses, and lignin macromolecules into smaller micellar-like fragments, which are further degraded to smaller compounds. In such type of degradation reactions like dehydration, dehydrogenation, deoxygenation, and decarboxylation takes place.

In comparison to torrefaction/carbonisation, thermal liquefaction can provide liquid fuels in line with petroleum products along with several high value chemicals. In biomass thermochemical conversion, liquefaction, could not be successful at commercial scale. The possible factors that limit the liquefaction commercialisation could be the lower overall yield of oil (between 20–55% w/w) compared to contemporary options like pyrolysis, inferior oil quality (heavy tar like liquid), higher reaction temperature, pressure, requirements of catalysts and other reactants (CO, propanol, butanol, and glycerine).

Carbonisation and torrefaction

Carbonisation is used for biochar formation whereas, Torrefaction is a thermal treatment to convert biomass into more efficient form of energy source containing less moisture and high fixed carbon, for the purpose to produce chemical feedstock which reduces the associated transportation costs, and torrefaction are closely related processes. In carbonisation, the biomass is thermochemically treated at the temperature range between 200°C to 318°C in the absence of oxygen. There will be complete conversion of biomass into biochar in this carbonisation process.

Thus, the product gains much higher energy density than the raw biomass, which lowers the transportation cost of the carbonised biomass due to reduction in volume of biomass (waste). In the case of torrefaction, there is partial degradation of the biomass (particularly the hemicellulose), giving off various types of volatiles resulting in brittle, dried and more volatile free solid product.

Carbonised or torrefied biomass has favourable characteristics such as, hydrophobic nature, similar to properties as coal, easy to crush, grind or pulverise. The end-products contains condensable gases such as water vapour, formic acid, acetic acid, furfural, methanol, lactic acid, and phenol. Non-condensable gases such as carbon dioxide, carbon monoxide and small amounts of hydrogen and methane are also obtained.

Thus, carbonisation and torrefaction processes are used for the conversion of biomass into more promising forms of energy source and to reduce the associated transportation costs. Although it is efficient form of energy, still it is not in competition with petroleum fuels in transport sector.

Gasification

Concept and principle: Gasification is the process of converting fuels from solid in nature to gaseous fuel. It is very similar to pyrolysis but It is not simply pyrolysis. Pyrolysis is only one of the steps in the conversion process. Combustion with air and reduction of the product of combustion, (water vapour and carbon dioxide) into combustible gases, (carbon monoxide, hydrogen, methane, some higher hydrocarbons) and inert, (carbon dioxide and nitrogen) are other steps of this process. The process leads to generation of a gas with some fine dust particles and condensable compounds termed as tar, if this produced gas is to be used in internal combustion engines, particle size must be restricted to less than about 100 ppm each.

Gasification is a complete thermal breakdown of the biomass particles into a combustible gas, volatiles and ash in an enclosed reactor known as gasifier, in the presence of any externally supplied oxidising agent (air, O_2, H_2O, CO_2, etc.). Amount of oxidising agents is depends on stoichiometric amount of oxidising agent. Stoichiometric amount is the theoretical amount of air or any other oxidising agent required to burn the fuel completely.

Gasification is a two-step, endothermic process. It is an intermediate step between pyrolysis and combustion. During the first step the volatile components of the fuel are vaporised at temperatures below 600°C by a group of complex reactions. In this step of the process, no oxygen is needed. Volatile vapours include hydrocarbon gases, hydrogen, carbon monoxide, carbon dioxide, tar and water vapour. Char and ash are the by-products of the process which are not vaporised. Char is made up of fixed carbon. In the second step, char is gasified through the reactions with oxygen, steam and hydrogen. Residual unburned char is combusted to release the heat needed for the endothermic gasification reactions.

Gas, char, and tars are the main gasification products. Gasification products, their composition and amount are strongly influenced by gasification agent, temperature, and pressure, heating rate and fuel characteristics. These fuel characteristics are composition of fuel, water content and granulometry. Gaseous products formed during the gasification may be further used for heating or electricity production. The main gas components are CO_2, CO, H_2O, CH_4, H_2 and other hydrocarbons.

Combustible gas, produced during gasification can be cleaned and used for the synthesis of special chemical products or for the generation of heat and/or electricity. Specific hydrogen – carbon monoxide mixtures are known as water gas, cracked gas, and methanol synthesis gas or oxo-synthesis gas.

Gasification is a unique technology that can even convert waste (from MSW to agricultural or crop residues, like coconut shells, rice husks, straw, wood residues, bagasse, etc.), to a useful and high quality energy source. It is known how complicated the disposal of any kind of waste is, now-a-days due to environmental regulations and legislations. Separation of the noxious substances from the fuel gas is the advantage of the gasification process prior to the combustion.

Biomass gasification technology

Biomass has been considered as a major energy source, prior to the discovery of fossil fuels like coal and petroleum. It is widely used in rural communities of the developing countries for their energy needs in terms of cooking and limited industrial use. Even it is not currently popular in developed countries. Biomass, which is in solid form, can be converted into gaseous form through gasification process. Biomass gasification has also received much attention in recent times. The solid biomass is converted to simplified products like CO and H_2, in the optimised concentrations of oxygen and H_2O at temperatures 800°C which is completely distinct from gasification, via., anaerobic digestion. The final products are syngas, CO_2, NO_x, SO_x, and ash/metal slag (quantity will depend upon the type of the waste: municipal, agricultural, or wood biomass). CO and H_2 mixture is known as syngas. It has multiple applications such as fuel cells, synthetic fuel, and chemical feedstock. As for as technology is concern, gasification is an excellent method of extracting bioenergy free from N, P, S, Cl and metals contamination from diverse biomass types without further treatment or upgrading.

6.3.3   Biological waste treatment

Composting

Composting is the decomposition of organic matter under controlled aerobic conditions by the action of micro organisms and small invertebrates. There are a number of composting techniques being used now days. These techniques include: in vessel composting, windrow composting, vermicomposting and static pile composting. The composting process is controlled by making the environmental conditions optimum for the micro-organisms involved in decomposition of waste. The rate of compost formation is controlled by the composition and constituents of the materials, i.e., their Carbon/Nitrogen (C/N) ratio, the temperature, the moisture content and the amount of air. It is natural process of decomposition of organic waste and yield manure or compost which is rich in nutrients. Composting is a biological process in which micro-organisms like fungi and bacteria convert degradable organic waste in to humus like substance. This humus is rich in carbon and nitrogen content and it is a best medium for growing plants. Municipal solid waste (MSW) contains 32–40% organic matter in India. This waste can be recycled by compositing. This method is clean, safe and can significantly reduce the amount of disposable garbage. Organic fertilisers have advantages over chemical fertilisers as they increase the ability of the soil to hold water, making it easier to cultivate. Vermicompost also contains good amount of nutrient. For the growth of micro-organisms require carbon as an energy source and nitrogen for the synthesis of some proteins. If the correct C/N ration is not achieved, then application of the compost with either a high or low C/N ratio can have adverse effects on both the soil and the plants. A high C/N ratio can be maintained by dehydrated mud and a low ratio corrected by addition of cellulose.

Moisture content present in waste is greatly influences the composting process. The micro-organisms require the moisture content to perform their metabolic functions. If the waste becomes too dry the composting is not good. If there is too much moisture then it is possible that it may displace the air in the compost heap depriving the organisms of oxygen and drowning them.

In this process high temperature is required for the elimination of pathogenic organisms. However, if temperature is too high, as >75°C then the organisms will not survive, those are necessary to complete the composting process. Optimum temperatures for the composting process are in the range of 50–60°C. Aeration is another a very important factor and the quantity of air need to be properly controlled during this process of composting. If oxygen is not sufficient, the aerobic micro-organisms will begin to die and will be replaced by anaerobes. The anaerobes are undesirable since they will slowdown this process, produce odours and also produce the highly flammable methane gas. In this process, aeration can be done by churning the compost.

Anaerobic digestion

Anaerobic digestion uses biological processes to decompose organic waste. However, where composting can use a variety of aerobic micro-organisms, which must require air, anaerobic digestion uses anaerobic bacteria to decompose the waste. Aerobic respiration, typical of composting, results in the formation of CO_2 and H_2O. While the anaerobic respiration results in the formation of CO_2 and CH_4. In addition to generating the humus which is used as a soil conditioner, anaerobic digestion is also used as a method of producing biogas which can be used to generate electricity. This process require nutrients such as nitrogen, phosphorous and potassium, also requires the pH be maintained around 7 and the alkalinity be appropriate to buffer pH changes, temperature should also be controlled.

Integrated solid waste management

Integrated solid waste management is an overall approach to create sustainable systems that are economically affordable, socially acceptable and environmentally effective. This integrated solid waste management system requires the use of a range of different treatment methods. Collection and sorting of the waste is the key to the functioning of such a system. It is important to note that no one single treatment method can manage all the waste materials in an environmentally effective way. Thus all the available treatment and disposal options must be evaluated equally and the best combination of the available options suited to the particular community chosen. Effective management plans are needed to operate in such a ways which best meet current social, economic, and environmental conditions of the municipality.

6.4   Solid waste management by vermiculture

Vermiculture is a modern concept of developing an ecosystem for effective utilisation of organic residuals with the help of invertebrates like earthworms. Earthworms have been defined as the invertebrates, belonging to phylum annelida, order oligochaeta, class clitellata, which live in soil. Earthworms require moist soil to live. The colour of earthworms is red or pink, long, cylindrical and divided into segments. Earthworms play a key role in soil biology by serving as natural bioreactor to effectively utilise the beneficial soil microflora and destroy soil pathogens, thus converting organic wastes into valuable products such as biofertlisers, biopesticides, vitamins, enzymes, antibiotics and proteinaceous worm biomass.

Earthworms have importance because they farm bacteria which produce the plant growth factors. The role of earthworms in agriculture was known to farmers since long ago, but their role in waste treatment is a new area. A good number of earthworm species have been identified from different places. The worms which are active on surface litter are the only worms to play a role in organic matter degradation. Irrespective of soil types, availability of moisture, quality and quanity of humus, pH of the soil, earthworms adapted to varied conditions are found distributed in the soils. When the conditions are favourable to these soil dwelling worms, they remain active in the soil and help in the distribution of humus to soil layers. Earth worm activity improves the porosity in soil, thus facilitating free entry of air and capillary flow of water. The secreted materials from eartworm body wall activate the soil microbial population.

Major components from compostable organic solid waste can be formed that enters the land fills and causes air, water and soil pollution apart from spoiling the aesthetics of the surroundings. To solve this problem we should start creating awareness among the public about its safe handling. The waste that is segregated can be subjected to biological activity through microbes and earthworms. Day by day, waste generated in the cities is increasing, natural method of microbial composting will not be sufficient for solid waste management. Micro-organism are primary decomposers; there are other higher levels of organisms as decomposer. These higher levels of organisms are recognised as secondary decomposers. Earthworms form one of the major group of organisms included under secondary decomposers, decompose waste very quickly. These earthworms have short life cycle, prolific breeding and high rate of food consumption. They feed upon and partially decomposed organic matter with minimum of 78–80% moisture content. They can be acclimatised to feed on any organic waste of plant and animal origin except poultry droppings.

Earthworms have advantages for waste management, lies in minimising the time of composting and composting of any substance to degrade organic waste. Due to mixing of secretions from earthworms with the composted material increases the water holding capacity of the compost apart from having stimulatory effect on plant growth. When earthworms feed on partially degraded organic waste, they draw into their mouth fine bits of food particles. This food material undergoes further digested by the enzymatic activity in their gut and finally the mucus coated excreta (vermicast) is released from the body. Thus, organic waste exposed to earthworm activity undergoes physical and biochemical breakdown.

Due to this digestion process, the surface area will increase in this kind of material and due to further biochemical degradation, it forms more suitable substratum for microbial activity. Loose porous structure favours good aeration in to the soil. Thus, earthworms cast encourage the establishment of microbial populations to use in the process of decomposition.

6.4.1 Vermicompost as organic manure

To study the importance of vermicompost as organic manure, trails at field level, in pot mixes and in nursery beds has been tested to study the effect on various crops. It was found that the load on the organic manure and chemical fertiliser application is almost reduced by 30 to 50 per cent on application of vermicompost. The efficiency of biofertilisers improved by application to crop along with vermicompost. Vermicompost has stimulatory effect on seedling development and in different stages of vegetative propagation of plants. This is related to the earthworm exudates and metabolites of the microbes associated with vermicompost. Vermicomposting of urban organic solid waste, helps in minimising the use of chemicals in agriculture. Many of the farmers involved in organic farming practices, have the opinion that the repeated use of vermicompost to fields have brought down the incidence of diseases in crops.

Range of nutrients in vermicompost are given in Table 6.1 that highlights the physicochemical analysis of vermicompost.

Table 6.1: Range of nutrients in vermicompost.

Nutrient	Range
Organic carbon (%)	9.25–18.98
Total nitrogen (%)	0.60–1.50
Available phosphorus (%)	0.12–0.30
Available potassium (%)	0.15–0.60
Available sodium (%)	0.05–0.30
Calcium and magnesium (MEQ/100 g)	22.60–47.70
Copper (ppm)	2.00–9.70
Iron (ppm)	2.00–9.40
Zinc (ppm)	5.75–11.60

6.4.2 Earthworms in agriculture

In agriculture system, earthworms play a very important role, as they improve the soil texture, enrich the soil, and enhance the nutrients in the crops. They also act as powerful biopesticide and protect the useful microflora of the soil. Earthworms eat soil and grit particles as grinding medium for waste organic residues. Soil excreted by the earthworms has a natural acidity or basicity (pH) and contains balanced plant nutrients in available form. Plant takes these nutrients by the process of ion exchange and make them available to the roots when required, but preventing their leaching to the groundwater. By this means they protect their losses and consequent groundwater pollution. They accelerate the decomposition process of crop residues and convert them into balanced plant nutrients, H_2O and CO_2. These are produced and effectively utilised in a slow release manner.

Living soil

The soil produced by the earthworms is known as living soil that has an enhanced ability to absorb the atmospheric moisture. This soil is structurally stable. The beneficial micro-organisms which are present in this soil use agro waste to fix atmospheric nitrogen, stabilise the fixed soil phosphorus, make potassium, calcium, magnesium, sulphur and essential micronutrients available, produce vitamins, antibiotics and plant growth hormones. Excess micro-organisms are digested by the earthworms as their food. They also eliminate soil pathogens and ineffective micro-organisms by selective predation. It has been reported by agricultural researchers that by introducing large number of earthworms into agricultural soil doubles the yield of wheat, increases the yield of grass four times and multiplies clover yields tenfold. Experiments also proved that addition of live earthworms increased yields much more than the addition of dead worms did, showing that it is the action of live earthworms that enhances the soil productivity. The castings of earthworms, which consists largely of digested soil and particles of organic matter, is more chemically neutral then the surrounding soil. So by consuming soil, processing it and excreting the remainder known as castings. Sufficient numbers of earthworms help to keep a field closer to the neutral pH range. Soil that is excessively acidic or basic can inhibit the growth of plants and microbes both.

Proper utilisation of organic residues

Earthworms ensure proper utilisation of organic residues generated through farming practices as agro waste such as sugarcane trash, banana stems, paddy and wheat straw, coir waste and weeds. These agro wastes are being neglected by the farmers. Earthworms use these residues at the rate of 10 T per hectare. Their fertiliser value is as good as other composts, which would need 200 T of raw organic waste to produce the same amount. With the use of vermicomposting, the cost of application of chemical fertilisers and pesticides is saved, labour in tilling the ground is not required and also crops require less water for irrigation purpose.

6.4.3   Designing of vermifilters for sewage and faecal matter

Solid organic residues

Solid organic waste is generated as sewage waste in city but open defection is quite prevalent in our villages as well as in urban slums. This sort of human excreta is nothing but solid organic residual. Vermiculture package to be harnessed in such cases involves addition of vermicasting. The biofertiliser produced with vermiculture is known as vermicasting. Vermicasting along with a bedding of cellulosic organics such as paddy husk, straw, sugarcane bagasse, will be required for this purpose. When such bedding is provided, it is removed periodically. A basal dose of vermicasting of 1.5–2 kg/m^2 has been found quite effective in odour and fly control, bioindicating health and sanitation. Animals performance and their health can be improved if they kept on such bio-sanitised bedding with a given food consumption. The spent bedding has been found to be odour-free and has at least 5 times higher resource value for use in agriculture. When marketed, it also fetches higher value.

Animal manures

The handling of animal manures can be improved without dilution with a water stream if we sprinkle vermicatings to sanitise them. Vermicastings have an immobilised culture of beneficial bacteria. As a result the animal manure which was creating pollution, now converted into a resource for agriculture. Daily sprinkling of about 0.1 kg/m^2 of vermicastings has been found quite effective for this purpose. This technique has been found to be quite effective in management of all the organic residuals such as garbage (kitchen or food waste) that produce odour and flies.

Rock dust

To control the bio-acidity, addition of 20–30% of rock dust is desirable in mixture. This also results in a richer product with higher quantity of plant nutrients. Moisture is applied to have about 50–60% moisture in the material being processed. For better results cellulosic residues can be mixed with. This Stabilised material is used in agriculture and for bio-sanitation.

6.4.4   Parameters to design vermifilter

Vermifilter provides a solid residence time upto one year, even though the hydraulic residence time (HRT) may be quite short (few minutes to an hour). Vermifilter can utilise total organics and nutrients and not just the simple organics. Vermifilter produces clean water with a low residual BOD, COD and nutrients as well. Two parameters-organic loading and hydraulic loading are very important to design vermifilters. This type of design is common for dilute or strong waste-water, slurries, sludges, as well as solid organic residuals. This design basis is also common for small as well as large communities and also for agro processing units, food and biotech industries that produce diverse nontoxic organic residuals solid as well as liquid. The performance of vermifilters are promising and very well for variety of wastes all within the limits of an natural oxygen delivery of 0.25 kg O_2/m^2/day. Hydraulic loading of 0.03 m/hr. is satisfactory. It has been recommended that vermifilters should be built in pair so that one of the systems could be rested to allow the ecology to recover from extended period of stress.

6.4.5   Operating procedure of vermifilter

Vermifilter is planted with water-tolerent plants such as banana, canna, arum, lily, etc. After the vermifilter is commissioned it is operated and maintained by noting the natural indicators of overloading and taking the appropriate steps. A healthy vermifilter is bioindicated by lush green and healthy vegetation.

6.4.6   Benefits of vermiculture

Benefits of vermiculture are given below:

1. Vermiculture technology is unique because it can utilise organic residues that cannot be utilised by any other bioconversion technology.
2. It offers a high solids retention time, even upto 8–12 months. This is achieved without any increase in hydraulic retention time and bioreactor size.
3. Vermiculture is a mixed culture of beneficial soil bacteria as the most diverse and productive bioprocessing agents.
4. Vermiculture is self controlled process.
5. It has a productivity of 1 kg/m^2/day for a 0.33 m thick bioreactor.
6. In vermiculture volumetric productivity is 3 kg/m^3/day. This is achieved without wastage of substrate and there is no further residue that needs to be tackled.
7. Bacteria are the prime bioconversion agents in vermiculture. These are selected by earthworms depending upon the changing substrate and demand on end product. Earthworms also carry out continuous upgradation of bacterial culture while they are doing their job.
8. Vermicasting favour farmers to have all the known and unknown beneficial micro-organisms in the field.
10. Vermicasting acts as a sustainable biofertilisers.

Biological Waste Treatment

7.1   Introduction

Industry is making the satisfactory collection, treatment and disposal of liquid effluents a formidable problem with serious implications for public health in developing countries. The water utilisation for municipal, agricultural and industrial purposes is increasing considerably, with a resultant increase not only in the volume of wastewater, but also in the concentration of the pollutants it contains. The rise in discharge of this wastewater into streams that are already diminishing in flow, because of increased withdrawals, makes it no longer possible to rely as much as in the past on the self purifying capacity of receiving bodies of waste. The decreasing available dilution for wastes, the increasing need for reuse of water and increasing public interest in the maintenance of clean streams compound the problem of liquid effluent treatment and disposal.

Thus, new and improved processes must be developed so that a higher percentage of the pollutants can be removed. Due to rapid growth in urban population production of waste is increased in the developing countries, the per capita contribution of wastewater is also increasing. Such increases in per capita production of wastewater result from the increased availability of piped water supplies and improved standards of living. Mechanised way of using water such as washing machines and garbage grinders has a significant effect on household water consumption. Due to this the volume of wastewater very large, its content of organic and mineral pollutants is also large. The concentration of polluting substances and organisms must be reduced during treatment of liquid effluents. Wide variety of processes to achieve such reduction of pollution is now available. The selected process for treatment must be appropriate to the pollution situation; however, conditions in developing countries frequently impose limitations on the choice of such treatment processes.

7.2   Objectives of wastewater treatment

Due to rapid change in industrialisation, huge volume of liquid effluent is generating which is a matter of concern. Liquid effluent treatment methods were developed in response to the concern for public health and the adverse conditions caused by the discharge of liquid effluents to the environment. To accelerate the forces of nature under controlled conditions in such facilities of comparatively small size that was the purpose of treatment of such waste. There is a wide range of biological treatment systems in use presently for the purification of liquid effluents based on the apparently simple processes by which mixed populations of micro-organisms degrade organic material, using it as a source of nutrients.

Biological waste treatment process is the process by which any waste treated biologically includes micro-organism for final discharge within the permissible limit specified by World Health Organisation (WHO). The minimum and maximum concentration of waste constituents are listed in Table 7.1.

Table 7.1: Concentration of major waste constituents.

S. No.	Constituents (mg/litre)	Minimum concentration	Maximum concentration
1	Total organic carbon (TOC)	82	163
2	Total nitrogen	22	44
3	Organic nitrogen	10	15
4	BOD 5 days at 20°C	112	225
5	COD	250	500
6	Free ammonia	10	25
7	Total phosphorus	5	8
8	Oil and grease	50	100
9	Total solid	350	730
10	Suspended solid	103	250
11	Settleable solid	5	11

7.3   Characteristics of liquid effluents

Sewage wastewater or municipal wastewater is liquid discharges from residences, business buildings and institutions. Industrial waste is discharged from manufacturing units. The volume of wastewater from residential areas varies from 210 to 390 litres per person per day depending on the type of dwellings. Largest volume of waste flows come from single-family houses that have multiple bathrooms, automatic washing machines and other water-using appliances. Stages of wastewater treatment are shown in Fig. 7.1.

Sewage or municipal wastewater is a complex mixture containing minerals and organic matter in many forms, including:

1. As component of sewage water large and small particles of solid matter floating and in suspension are present.

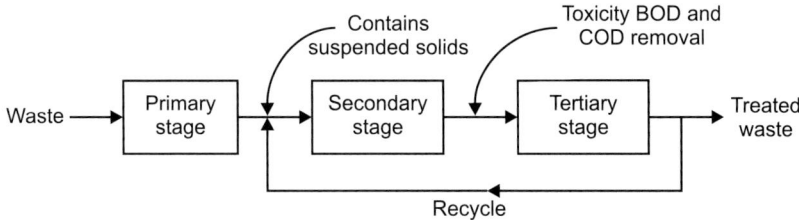

Figure 7.1: Stages of wastewater treatment.

2. Colloidal and pseudo-colloidal dispersion will be available.

3. Sewage also contains living micro-organisms, especially bacteria, viruses and protozoa; it acts as an excellent medium for the development of bacteria, some of which may be pathogenic.

Thus overall process of wastewater treatment divides in to three stages/steps:

1. Primary treatment stage.

2. Secondary treatment stage.

3. Tertiary treatment stage.

7.3.1   Primary treatment stage

It is essentially composed of physical treatment. The purpose of primary treatment stage is to reduce the overall volume of the waste to reduce the size of reactor used for treatment process.

Physical treatment steps are as follows:

1. Screening

2. Filtration

3. Equalisation in tank

4. Addition of alum and other coagulants

5. Sedimentation

7.3.2   Secondary treatment stage

Secondary treatment is composed of biological treatment using different type of reactors. Both aerobic and anaerobic reactors can be used as per nature of waste either simple or complex. In term of Biological Oxygen Demand (BOD) waste may be simple and complex. Waste having low BOD, considered as simple waste and high BOD containing waste called complex waste. Simple waste can be treated by using aerobic treatment process with help of aerobic microbes and anaerobic process for complex waste using anaerobic microbes.

7.3.3   Tertiary treatment stage

After biological treatment of liquid waste in secondary treatment process, BOD of waste will be reduced but pathogens and other nutrients components will be present. Tertiary stage may include removal of N_2 and P, virus removal and denitrification of treated waste. It is also known as polishing stage. Chlorination may also be involved as chemical treatment. Chlorine is acting as disinfectant to nutralise pathogenic microbes present in the treated liquid waste.

Two type of waste: solid and liquid

1. In case of solid waste primary treatment involved aggregation and separation of inorganic substances from organic one.
2. The separation of such contaminants is necessary to reduce the volume of reactor required for secondary treatment and organic matter can be used for landfill.
3. Primary treatment can eliminate more than 80% of suspended solids and 80% BOD and COD removal.

Advantage of biological treatment over other conventional waste treatment process:

1. Biological waste treatment process removes a wide variety of pollutants in single step, this makes process more cost effective.
2. This process requires less energy for treatment.
3. Risks of explosion, corrosion, toxic gas leakage, etc., are minimal.
4. We also get useful product like biogas during treatment process.
5. Less complex designed equipment is required, investment capital is less for treatment using this biological process.

Disadvantage: It requires large space and more processing time compare to traditional treatment processes.

Examples: Sewage treatment plant, effluent treatment plant.

7.4   Type of biological treatment

There are three basic categories of biological waste treatment:

1. Aerobic
2. Anaerobic
3. Anoxic

7.4.1   Aerobic treatment process

Aerobic treatment may follow some form of pretreatment such as oil removal, involves contacting wastewater with microbes and oxygen in a reactor to optimise the growth and efficiency of the biomass.

The micro-organism act to catalyse the oxidation of biodegradable organics and other contaminants such as NH_3, generating CO_2, H_2O and excess biomass. This excess biomass is known as sludge.

7.4.2   Anaerobic (without oxygen) and anoxic (oxygen deficient) treatment process

Anaerobic (without oxygen) and anoxic (oxygen deficient) treatments are similar to aerobic treatment, but use of micro-organism that do not require the addition of oxygen these micro-organisms use the compounds other than oxygen to catalyse the oxidation of biodegradable organics and other contaminants.

Bioreactor is accomplished in one of two general ways:

1. Fixed film process: In fixed film process micro-organisms are held on a surface of film, the fixed film, which may be mobile or stationary with wastewater flowing past the surface of film media. This process is designed to actively contact the biofilm with the wastewater and is mixed with oxygen when needed. Fixed film based treatment processes are biotowers (trickling filters), rotating biological contactors, and submerged biological contactors.

2. Suspended growth process: Suspended growth process is the process in which biomass is freely suspended in the wastewater. In this process, components of liquid are properly mixed and can be aerated by number of devices that transfer oxygen to the bioreactor contents.

   Different aeration methods can be used in this growth process. Aeration methods for suspended growth processes are diffused aeration, surface aeration.

7.4.3   Comparison of anaerobic and aerobic treatment process

Comparison of anaerobic and aerobic treatment processes are shown in Table 7.2.

Table 7.2: Comparison of anaerobic and aerobic treatment processes.

Characteristic	Anaerobic	Aerobic
Phases	Solid, liquid	Liquid gas solid
Degradation rate	Upto 80% volatile solid	Upto 50% volatile solids
Energy	Excess produced	Demands input
Duration of process	1–4 weeks (Only anaerobic stage)	4–16 weeks (Depending on the process)
Post treatment	Necessary	No
Odour emission	Low	High
Suitability of wastes	Wide (wet and dry)	Narrow (dry waste)
Biomass	Low	High

7.4.4   Micro-organisms involved in aerobic digestion process

Different types of aerobic micro-organisms are involved in this biological treatment process.

These are as follows:

Bacteria

Bacteria are the most common type of micro-organisms and their number may be more than 10^{12} cell/ml. They are responsible for the removal of about 85–90% of the BOD remaining after primary treatment of liquid waste.

1. Bacterium 'Zoogloea ramigera' secretes a mucous like polysaccharide which is involved in the attachment of various bacterial species to the filter or disc surface. They degrade carbohydrates, proteins, lipids in to CO_2, NO_3^-, SO_4^{-2} and PO_4^{-3}.

2. Many heterotrophic bacteria are also responsible for aerobic oxidation: Saricina, Pseudomonas, Eschorichia, Stophylococaes, Streptococcus, Aerobactor, Shigella Salmonella.

3. Ammonium released from protein is toxic to fish if present in river water. Nitrifying bacteria – Nitrosomonas and Nitrobactor convert toxicity (NH_4^+ NO_3^-) present in wastewater.

Fungi

Fungi usually applicable on surface of biofilm in filter beds. They may help in removal of nitrogen and phosphorus present in wastewater.

Protozoa

These are represented in wastewater by flagellates, ciliates and amoebae forms. The ciliate 'vorticella' is often used in activated sludge process.

7.4.5   Micro-organisms in anaerobic treatment process

Bacteria responsible for anaerobic digestion may be divided in to three groups.

Group I - Hydrolytic bacteria

This group of bacteria is responsible for hydrolytic degradation process of macromolecules in to soluble products such as sugars, amino acids, and fatty acids. These bacteria belong to genera – *Actinonyces, Aerobactorbacter, Escherichia, Klebsiell, Lactobacillus, Pseudomonos, Streptococcus, Streptomyces*, etc.

These bacteria degrade polymeric substrates by use of enzymes such as amylases, cellulases, lipases, pectinases and proteases. These are responsible for hydrolysis process of proteins, lipids and polysaccharides.

Group II – Acetogenic bacteria

In the second group the acetogenic bacteria ferment the end products of the first stage butyrate, propionate, caproate, glucose, amino acids, acetate, H_2 and CO_2.

1. Soluble carbohydrates, starch are fermented by micro-organism like species of *'Clostridium'* resulting in the formation of acetic acid, butyric acid, CO_2 and H_2.
2. Glucose is utilised by other *clostridium* species like *'Clostridium thermoaceticum'* and produce acetate.
3. Homoacetogenic bacteria are unique in that they can convert 1 mol of glucose to 3 mols of acetate. Out of these 3 mols, 2 mols are formed by fermentation of glucose and one mole is formed by fixation of CO_2.

$$2\ CO_2 + 4H_2 \rightarrow CH_3COOH + 2\ H_2O$$
$$4\ CO + 2H_2O \rightarrow CH_3COOH + 2CO_2$$

4. Methanol fermentation also take place by these organisms as follows:

$$CH_3OH + H_2O \rightarrow CO_2 + 6H^+ + 6e^-$$
$$3CO_2 + 6H^+ + 6e^- \rightarrow 3CO + 3H_2O$$
$$3CH_3OH + 3CO \rightarrow 3CH_3COOH$$

Net reaction:

$$3CH_3OH + 2CO_2 \rightarrow 3CH_3COOH + 2H_2O$$

Group III – Methanogenic bacteria

Methanogenic bacteria are involved in the third stage of bioconversion of organic substrates in to methane. These belong to group *'Archaebacteria'*.

They are found in water logged soils, guts of animals, sewage sludge rotting vegetable and aquatic sediments.

These orders of strict obligate methanogens have been recognised as these are the methane bacteria including some species of *Methanobacterium* and *Methanomicroblates* including species of *Methanomicrobium, Methanoganium Methanospirillum* and *Methanosarcina.*

1. Methanogenes are non motile and strict anaerobe.
2. Substrates such as CO_2 and H_2 have proved to be most ideal for the growth of methanogens.
3. Energy for their growth is derived from the reduction of CO_2 to methane.

Some examples of methanogenic bacteria are: *Methanobacterium bryantii, M. formicicum, M. Sochngenii, M. Thermoautotrophicum, Methanococcu vannielii, Methanococcus voltae, Methanogenium aggregans, Methanogenium marisnigri, Methanomicrobium mobile, Methanosarcina barkeri, Methano-brevibacter smithii* (Gut of human).

The two best described pathways involve the use of CO_2 and CH_3COOH as terminal electron acceptors and convert CO_2 and CH_3COOH in to CH_4.

$$CO_2 + 4H_2 \quad \rightarrow \quad CH_4 + 2H_2O$$

$$CH_3COOH \quad \rightarrow \quad CH_4 + CO_2$$

7.4.6 Principle of biological treatment

In general the principle of biological treatment of waste is shown in Fig. 7.2.

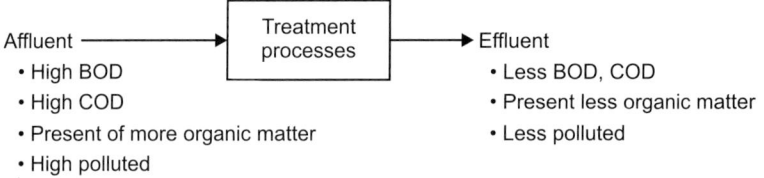

Figure 7.2: Biological waste treatment principle.

Basic principle behind the biological treatment process is that, waste containing complex organic material which having high BOD and COD and considered as highly polluted will be converted in to simple waste. By using selective biological treatment process, high BOD and COD will be reduced and complex organic material will be simplified in presence of micro-organisms.

Different components as carbon source, nitrogen source and sulphur present in wastewater, will be converted in to respective products depending upon methods used for treatment either aerobic or anaerobic. The conversion is shown in Table 7.3.

Table 7.3: Conversion of C,N,S during different treatment processes

Components	Aerobic treatment	Anaerobic treatment
C	CO_2	CH_4
N	NO_2	NH_3
S	SO_2	H_2S

7.4.7   Aerobic digestion/treatment process

Aerobic digestion (Fig. 7.3) of waste is the natural biological degradation and purification process in which bacteria in presence of oxygen, breaks down and digested the waste. During oxidation process, pollutants are broken down in the CO_2, H_2O, nitrates, sulphates and biomass (micro-organisms). By operating the oxygen supply with aerators, the process can be significantly accelerated. It is most widespread process is used throughout the world.

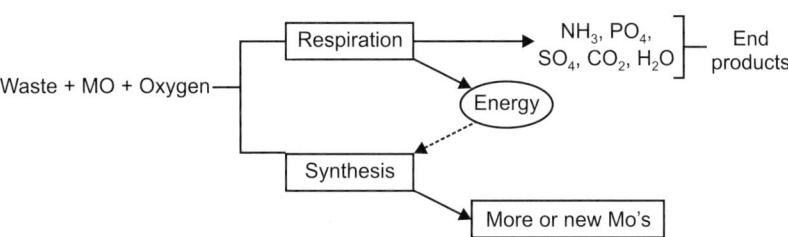

Figure 7.3: Path of aerobic digestion.

7.4.8   Anaerobic treatment/digestion process

Anaerobic digestion is a complex biochemical reaction carried out in a number of steps using several types of micro-organisms that require little or no oxygen to survive. CH_4 and CO_2 are produced as end product during this process.

Aerobic digestion proceeds in 4 steps:

1. Hydrolysis: Complex organic matter is decomposed in to simple soluble organic molecules using water to split the chemical bonds between the substances (Fig. 7.4).

2. Acidogenesis: The decomposition of carbohydrate by enzymes, bacteria, yeasts or molds in the absence of oxygen.

3. Acetogenesis: The fermentative products are converted in to acetate, hydrogen and CO_2 by acetogenic bacteria.

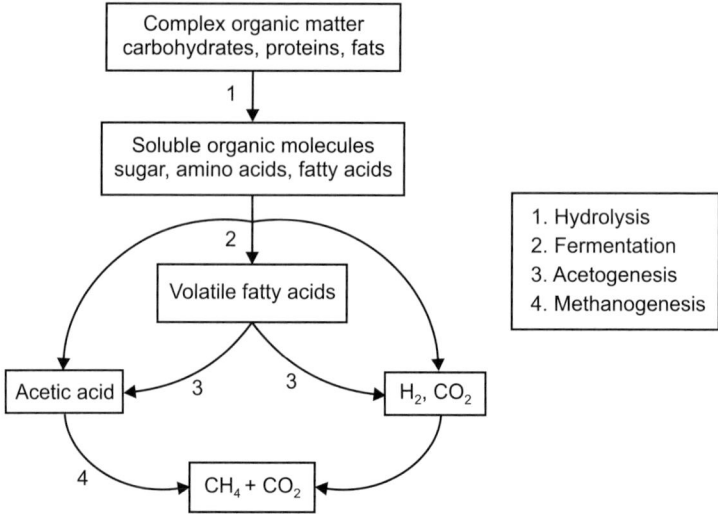

Figure 7.4: Metabolic pathway for complex organic material.

4. Methanogenesis: CH_4 is formed from acetate and hydrogen/CO_2 by methogenic bacteria

Hydrolysis

Complex materials such as lipids, proteins, and carbohydrates are primarily hydrolysed by extracellular, hydrolases, excreted by microbes present in stage-1 (Fig. 7.5). Hydrolytic enzymes, (lipases, proteases, cellulases, amylases, etc.), hydrolyse their respective polymers into smaller molecules, primarily monomeric units, which are then consumed by microbes. In methane fermentation of wastewaters containing high concentrations of organic polymers, the hydrolytic activity relevant to each polymer is of paramount significance, in that polymer hydrolysis may become a rate-limiting step for the production of simpler bacterial substrates to be used in subsequent degradation steps.

Acidogenesis

In this step, lipids will be to long-chain fatty acids using lipase enzyme. Population of lipase producing micro-organism should be in appropriate number. A population density of $10^4 - 10^5$ lipolytic bacteria per ml of digester fluid has been reported. Clostridia and the micrococci appear to be potent extracellular lipase producers. The long-chain fatty acids present are further degraded by p-oxidation to produce acetyl CoA.

Protease enzyme hydrolyses proteins to amino acids. Micro-organisms like *Bacteroides, Butyrivibrio, Clostridium, Fusobacterium, Selenomonas,* and

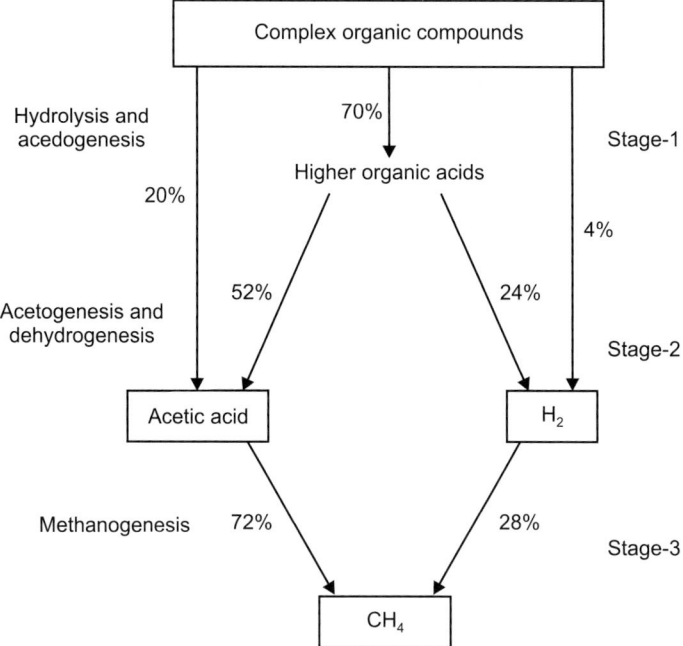

Figure 7.5: Stages of methane fermentation.

Streptococcus may be used for availability of protease enzyme. The amino acids produced during these steps are then degraded to fatty acids such as acetate, propionate, and butyrate.

Another component of the feed is polysaccharide such as cellulose, starch, and pectin. These polysaccharides are hydrolysed by cellulases, amylases, and pectinases enzymes. The cellulases are of three types: (i) endo-glucanases, (ii) exo-glucanases, (iii) cellobiase or *p*-glucosidase. These three enzymes act simultaneously on cellulose and hydrolysing its crystal structure, to produce glucose.

Microbial hydrolysis of starch requires amylolytic activity, which consist of five type amylase enzymes: (i) α-amylases, (ii) *p*-amylases, (iii) amylo-glucosidases, (iv) debranching enzymes, and (v) maltase that acts on maltose liberating glucose.

Pectinase enzyme is required for pectin degradation. These includes pectinesterases and depolymerases. Five carbon sugar and six carbon sugars will be converted to C_2 and C_3 intermediates and to reduce electron carriers (e.g., NADH), via., common pathways. Most anaerobic bacteria undergo hexose metabolism, via., the Emden-Meyerhof-Parnas pathway that produces pyruvate as an intermediate product along with NADH. The pyruvate and

NADH are transformed into fermentation end products such as lactate, propionate, acetate, and ethanol by other enzymatic activities produced microbial species.

Acetogenesis and dehydrogenation

Acetate and H_2 are directly produced by acidogenic fermentation of sugars, and amino acids, both products are primarily derived from the acetogenesis and dehydrogenation of higher volatile fatty acids. H_2-producing acetogenic bacteria are potent to produce acetate and H_2 from higher fatty acids. These are obligate micro-organisms. The use of co-culture techniques incorporating H_2 consumers such as methanogens and sulphate-reducing bacteria may therefore facilitate elucidation of the biochemical breakdown of fatty acids. The overall breakdown reactions for long-chain fatty acids are presented in (Table 7.4).

Table 7.4: Proposed reactions involved in fatty acid catabolism.

Fatty acids	Reaction
Even-numbered	
$CH_3CH_2CH_2COO^- + 2\ H_2O$	$\rightarrow$ $2\ CH_3COO^- + 2H_2 + H^+$
$CH_3CH_2CH_2CH_2CH_2COO^- + 4\ H_2O$	$\rightarrow$ $3\ CH_3COO^- + 4H_2 + 2H^+$
Odd-numbered	
$CH_3CH_2CH_2CH_2COO^- + 1\ H_2O$	$\rightarrow$ $CH_3CH_2COO^- + CH_3COO^- + 2\ H_2 + H^+$
$CH_3CH_2CH_2CH_2CH_2CH_2COO^- + 4\ H_2$	$\rightarrow$ $CH_3CH_2COO^- + 2\ CH_3COO^- + 4\ H_2 + 2H^+$

Due to high free energy requirements, H_2 production using acetogens is generally energetically unfavourable. Co-culture systems provide favourable conditions for the decomposition of fatty acids to acetate and CH_4 or H_2S. In addition to the decomposition of long-chain fatty acids, ethanol and lactate are also converted to acetate and H_2 by acetogenic bacteria along with *Clostridium formicoaceticum*. This produced hydrogen creats pressure in reaction vessel. The effect of the partial pressure of H_2 will be on the free energy associated with the conversion of ethanol, propionate, acetate, and hydrogen or carbon dioxide during methane fermentation. Low partial pressure of H_2 (10^{-5} atm) appears to be a significant factor in propionate degradation to CH_4.

Methanogenesis

Methanogens are physiologically united as methane producers in anaerobic digestion. In this anaerobic digestion, acetate and H_2 or CO_2 are the major substrates present in the natural environment. There are other substrate like formate, methanol, methylamines, and CO. These are also converted to CH_4 (Table 7.5).

Table 7.5: Reactions involving anaerobic oxidation in pure cultures or in co-cultures with H_2-utilising methanogens.

1. Proton-reducing (H_2-producing) acetogenic bacteria:

$$CH_3CH_2CH_2COO^- + 2H_2O \rightarrow 2\,CH_3COO^- + 2H_2 + H^+$$

$$CH_3CH_2COO^- + 3H_2O \rightarrow CH_3COO^- + HCO_3^- + H^+ + 3H_2$$

2. H_2-using methanogens and desulphovibrios

$$4H_2 + HCO_3^- + H^+ \rightarrow CH_4 + 3\,H_2O$$

$$4H_2 + SO_4^{2-} + H^+ \rightarrow HS^- + 4\,H_2O$$

3. Co-culture of 1 and 2

$$A + C\ 2\,CH_3CH_2CH_2COO^- + HCO_3^- + H_2O \rightarrow 4\,CH_3COO^- + H^+ + CH_4$$

$$A + D\ 2\,CH_3CH_2CH_2COO^- + SO_4^{2-} \rightarrow 4\,CH_3COO^- + H^+ + HS^-$$

$$B + C\ 4\,CH_3CH_2COO^- + 12\,H_2 \rightarrow 4\,CH_3COO^- + HCO_3^- + H^+ + 3\,CH_4$$

$$B + D\ 4\,CH_3CH_2COO^- + 3\,SO_4^{2-} \rightarrow 4\,CH_3COO^- + 4\,HCO_3^- + H^+ + 3\,HS^-$$

Methanogenic micro-organisms are obligate anaerobes and they require a redox potential of less than -300 mV for their growth. Isolation and cultivation of these microbes are tough task due to technical difficulties encountered in handling them under completely O_2-free conditions. By using improved methanogen isolation techniques more than 40 strains of pure methanogens have now been isolated. There are two major groups of methanogens: (i) H_2 and CO_2 consumers, and (ii) acetate consumers.

Some of the H_2 and CO_2 consumers are also capable of utilising formate. Limited number of strains can consume acetate, such as *Methanosarcina* species and *Methanothrix* species. These are not capable of consuming formate. As a large quantity of acetate is produced in the natural environment, *Methanosarcina* and *Methanothrix* play an important role in completion of anaerobic digestion and in accumulating H_2, which inhibits acetogens and methanogens. H_2-consuming methanogens are also important to reduce the levels of atmospheric H_2. Methanogens reduce CO_2 as an electron acceptor after consumption of H_2 and CO_2, via., the formyl, methenyl, and methyl levels through association with unusual coenzymes, to finally produce CH_4. The overall reaction can be expressed as:

$$CH_3COOH \rightarrow CH_4 + CO_2$$

In this reaction, a small part of the CO_2 is also formed from carbon derived from the methyl group; it is suspected that the reduced potential produced from the methyl group may reduce CO_2 to CH_4.

Microbiological and biochemical aspects of anaerobic digestion: The degradation of organic matter to produce methane is based on the complex interaction of several different groups of bacteria(consortia). For best performance of digester operation, it is require that these bacterial groups be in dynamic and harmonious equilibrium in the reaction vessel or digester. Changes in environmental conditions can affect this equilibrium and result in the synthesis of intermediates which may affect the overall digestion process. It is important to understand the basic microbiological and biochemical pathways, in order to maximise digestion and production of biogas. Anaerobic digestion of complex organic material is summarised hereafter.

Fermentations of complex materials occurred through oxidation reduction reactions to produce hydrogen, carbon dioxide and acetic acid. It has been reported the formation of methane from hydrogen and carbon dioxide:

$$4H_2 + CO_2 = CH_4 + 2H_2O$$

In above mentioned reaction, hydrogen reacted with carbon dioxide to form methane. It has been also assumed that the acetic acid produced was simply decarboxylated to form methane and carbon dioxide. Today the importance of maintaining a correct balance between the two phases is well recognised, and the two-phase concept is widely used in the control of the anaerobic process.

The four metabolic groups of micro-organisms, involved in anaerobic digestion include:

1. Hydrolytic and fermentative bacteria: These bacterial groups digest and convert a variety of complex organic molecules (i.e., polysacharides, lipid and proteins) into acetic acid, H_2 or CO_2, monocarbon compounds, organic fatty acids larger than acetic, and neutral compounds larger than methanol, a broad spectrum of end products (Fig. 7.6).

2. Hydrogen-producing acetogenic bacteria: This group of bacteria includes both obligate and facultative species that can convert the products of the first group bacteria. For example, the organic acids larger than acetic acid (e.g., butyrate, propionate) and neutral compounds larger than methanol (e.g., ethanol, propanol) to hydrogen and acetate are the products.

3. Homoacetogenic bacteria: This group of bacteria can convert very wide spectrum of multi or monocarbon compounds to acetic acid.

4. Methanogenic bacteria: Methanogenic bacteria convert H_2 or CO_2, monocarbon compounds (i.e., methanol, CO, methylamine) and acetate into methane. These are also involved in decarboxylation of acetate and form methane.

7.4.9   Microbial metabolism in anaerobic digestion

Biodegradation of organic wastes into methane (Fig. 7.7) using mixed culture requires the co-ordinated metabolic activities of different microbial populations.

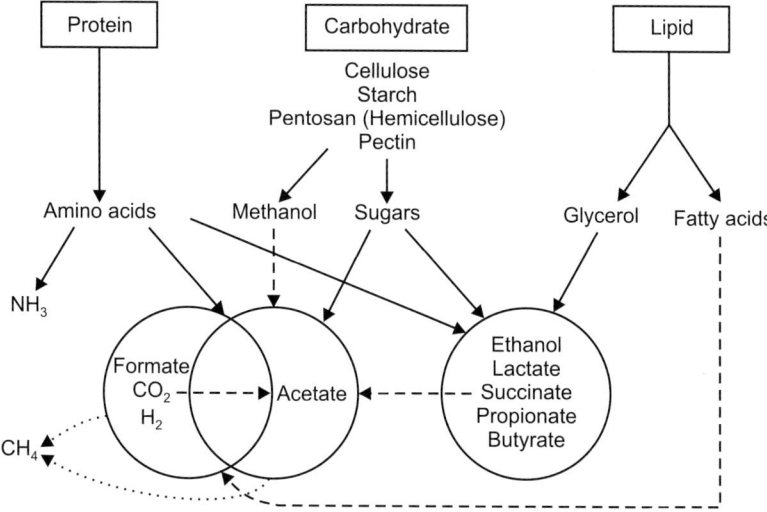

Figure 7.6: Pathway of protein, carbohydrate and lipid metabolism.

The key control parameters should be under control which influences the rate of organic degradation, the yield of reduced metabolites, and thermodynamic efficiency in the anaerobic digestion process. Effective digestion of organic matter requires the combined and co-ordinated metabolism of different kinds of carbon catabolising, anaerobic bacteria. Four different types of bacteria group have been identified and isolated from anaerobic digesters and their function in anaerobic digestion. The methanogenic bacteria perform an important role in anaerobic digestion because their unique metabolism controls the rate of organic degradation. They also direct the flow of carbon and electrons, by removing toxic intermediary metabolites, and by enhancing thermodynamic efficiency of interspecies metabolism.

In order to understand the intermediate metabolism of anaerobic digestion, examination is needed of the metabolic factors. These metabolic factors control the rate of organic degradation, the flow of carbon and electrons, thermodynamic efficiency in pure and mixed culture, and the bacteria associated with biogas production. This fundamental examination also helps to identifies several control parameters that can be engineered to improve methanogenesis and anaerobic digestion processes.

7.4.10 Effluent reuse

Water shortages are becoming a serious problem in the developing countries due to rapid growth of population, urbanisation and industrialisation coupled

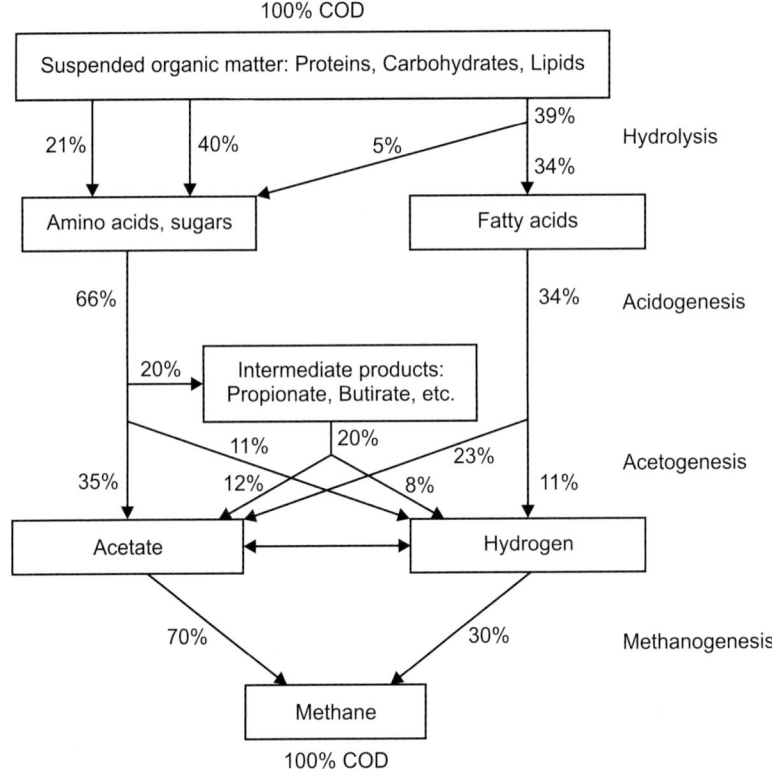

100% COD

Figure 7.7: Layout presentation of the decomposition of organic waste to produce methane.

with the introduction of modern intensive agricultural techniques causing increasingly heavy demand on water resources. Thus, the reuse of wastewater has become an attractive option for increasing water resources. Effluents from biological wastewater treatment plants may lack the characteristics required for direct reuse.

However, the most important uses of the reclaimed water are agricultural irrigation, fish rearing and ground-water recharge. The design of biological treatment facilities must ensure that the characteristics of the effluent are those required for reuse. Effluent will more often than not fail to meet these stringent standards and would require upgrading before reuse.

However, it should be noted that, for many places, these standards will be unnecessarily restrictive and they should be relaxed wherever feasible. Moreover, many effluent quality improvement methods are not appropriate for use in developing countries and are too costly.

Agricultural irrigation

The reuse of wastewater for agricultural purposes is an age-old and common practice. The quality of the reuse water is important both for the health of the workers and for the particular application for which it is used. Trace elements toxic to crops may be a problem; for example, boron, a component of many commercial laundry powders and one that is not removed by conventional treatment process, is well known as a toxicant in citrus fruit crops.

Fish rearing

Effluent from biological treatment plants has been used for rearing of fish. The most popular fish which have been successfully reared in effluents include carp and tilapia. The silver carp and the big head are capable of direct feeding on the plankton. The carp's popularity is largely due to its rapid growth rate and consequently high productivity under pond condition. In Europe carp productivities from sewage-fed ponds are reported to range from 400 to 900 kg/ha year whereas through careful feeding and mixing of fish species, productivities as high as 5000–7000 kg/ha/year have been achieved. Pond productivities of about 1000 kg/ha year are not uncommon in Asia where night soil is applied and the pond is well maintained. Industrial wastes have also been used in fish culture.

Groundwater recharge

Effluents can also be used for the purposeful recharge of groundwater. Such effluents should be free from heavy metals, with nitrogen and phosphorus contents of less than 50 and 10 mg/litre respectively and faecal coliforms always less than 1000/100 ml.

Hydroponics and aquaculture

Domestic wastewater, fully treated in WSPs, has been successfully used in growing vegetables in gravels rather than soil according to the horticultural practice known as hydroponics. While fish and ducks are reared in the fish ponds, the overflow from these ponds is used for hydroponics and finally the overflow from the hydroponics basin is allowed to seep into the soil. Such an arrangement is worth following in rural areas of developing countries. Hydroponics have a great future in countries like the Gulf and the Middle East where water is scarce and demand for vegetables can be met through hydroponics.

Municipal uses

In municipal practice the effluent can be reused for road washing, arboriculture (along roads) and watering of lawns and parks. Effluents to be used for watering golf courses, street flushing, lawns, etc., should be chlorinated to keep the coliform count below 1000/100 ml.

Water hyacinth

Water hyacinth has been used successfully to upgrade effluents, particularly for the removal of algae. Water hyacinth is able to take up large amounts of nutrients, i.e., nitrogen and phosphorus and heavy metals. At the same time its roots provide support for a gelatinous biomass which further stabilise organic matter, producing CO_2, inorganic substances and other materials. Bacteria and other organisms adhere to the gelatin-covered paste. When the hyacinth is harvested, all these substances are removed from the water. Hyacinth grows very rapidly in hot climates, doubling its mass in about 6 days.

One hectare of a hyacinth-covered pond can produce more than 4 T wet weight of plants or 200 kg of dry solids per day, production of more than 290 kg/ha/day has been reported. Reductions of 80 per cent nitrogen and 44 per cent total phosphorus have been achieved by 0.55 ha of a hyacinth pond 0.6 m deep with a detention time of 24–48 hours. and fed with 1000 m^3/day of facultative WSPs. Very low concentrations of ammonia nitrogen are present in water hyacinth ponds, which is important for fish rearing and clear, low-BOD effluents are produced.

8

Bioreactors for Waste Treatment

8.1   Introduction

The aim of biotechnology should be to develop such processes and products which minimise the damage to the environment and at the same time compatible with a high quality of life. This chapter covers all these aspects and exposes the reader to a variety of bioreactors, which are being used now-a-days.

The objective of the biological treatment of wastewater is to coagulate and remove the non-settleable colloidal solids and to stabilise the organic matter. The removal of carbonaceous organic matter in the wastewater which is measured as Biological Oxygen Demand (BOD) or Chemical Oxygen Demand (COD) or Total Organic Carbon (TOC), nitrification, denitrification and stabilisation are the purposes of biological treatment systems.

Bioreactors to treat carbon containing waste have undergone changes from activated sludge process and filter systems. Industrial wastewaters which are variable in their complex nature, volume and loading rate needs to develop a variety of bioreactors to get perfection in their treatment. Membrane bioreactors are newly developed and can keep away toxic chemicals during tackling other degradable waste materials.

This chapter also provides knowledge of principles and design aspects of various waste treatments methods. Several types of reactors may be used in biological treatment of wastewater. The design of biological system requires an understanding of the biological principles, kinetics of metabolism and physical operations necessary to control the environment in the reactors.

8.2   Biological waste treatment reactors

A bioreactor can be defined as a vessel in which biological reactions are carried out by micro-organisms or enzymes contained within the reactor itself. In hazardous, municipal, or industrial waste treatment, bioreactors are used primarily to reduce the concentration of contaminants in incoming wastewater to acceptably low levels. In particular, biological treatment appears to be especially versatile and cost effective when the concentration of pollutants in the wastewater is relatively low and the volumes to treat are large, thus making the use of other treatment alternatives (such as incineration) unattractive.

Wastewater typically contains a number of contaminants that should be removed, or at least significantly reduced in concentration.

These contaminants can be classified as follows:

1. Immiscible floating materials (e.g., oils, floating solids).
2. Suspended solids.
3. Soluble non-hazardous organic materials.
4. Soluble hazardous materials.
5. Soluble inorganic materials (e.g., ammonia and nitrates, phosphorus).
6. Volatile materials.

The choice of the possible sequence of specific treatments depends on the type and concentration of contaminants. In general, it is common practice to classify wastewater treatment processes in three categories, i.e., primary, secondary and tertiary treatment (see Fig. 7.1).

Wastewaters can be treated by aerobically and anaerobically, on this basis there are various type of reactors and treatment systems which are being used in very effective manner as shown in Fig. 8.1.

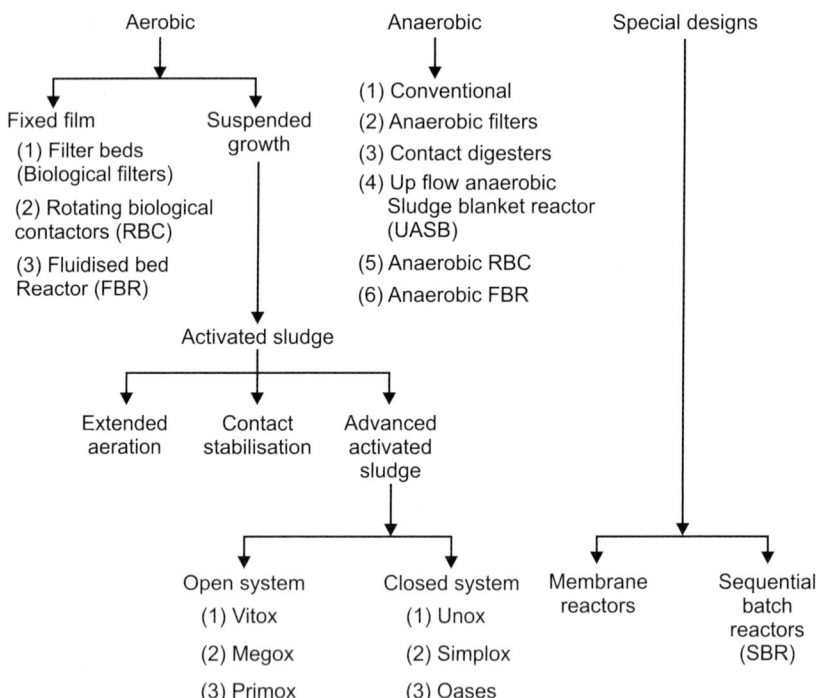

Figure 8.1: Classification of wastewater treatment systems and bioreactors.

8.2.1   Anaerobic vs aerobic reactors

Anaerobic reactors differ from aerobic reactors primarily because the former must be closed in order to exclude oxygen from the system, since this could interfere with anaerobic metabolism. A noticeable exception is constituted by anaerobic ponds and the bottom of facultative ponds, in which anaerobic conditions are established as a result of stratification and oxygen depletion in the lower part of the pond. An additional reason to require closed anaerobic reactors is the odours associated with anaerobic fermentation. An anaerobic reactor must also be provided with an appropriate vent or collection system to remove the gases (mainly methane and carbon dioxide) produced during anaerobiosis.

Conversely, aerobic reactors containing suspended biomass almost invariably require the use of an air-sparging or bubbling system to provide the micro-organisms with oxygen. One of the main drawbacks of oxygen as a key substrate is its low solubility in water (about 10 ppm at room temperature) as opposed to most other substrates, (e.g., glucose, nitrates), which have much higher saturation concentrations. In addition, because of the low oxygen concentration gradient (equal, under the most favourable circumstances, to the difference between the saturation concentration and the actual concentration in the water), the driving force for the mass transfer of oxygen from the air bubbles to the water is quite small. Therefore, a large air-water interface must be generated in order to supply enough oxygen to the system. Typically, this is accomplished by the use of one or more impellers which break up large air bubbles and disperse them in the liquid, with significant expenditure of energy.

The vast majority of existing biological treatment plants are aerobic. The reasons for this preference over anaerobic systems are the greater range of wastewaters that can be treated, easier control and greater stability of the process and more significant degree of removal of BOD, nitrogen and phosphorus. Because of the slower metabolism, anaerobic systems require a longer residence time of the waste in the reactor. This translates into a larger reactor volume to treat the same amount of waste. The slow metabolism also implies that a longer period of time is required for anaerobes to colonise the reactor. This, in turn, means that start-up time can be significant and that a longer period of time is required to bring the reactor back to full operation in case the bacterial population is lost because of a process upset. Anaerobes also require a more precise control of the operating parameters such as temperature or pH.

Whereas aerobic degradation is typically carried out by many organisms operating by and large independently and in parallel, anaerobes live in consortia in which different classes of organisms are responsible for carrying out single steps of the degradation process. This makes anaerobic reactors more prone to failures. The reasons for this can be traced back to hydraulic, organic, or toxic overloading of the reactor. Hydraulic overloading in continuous reactors is produced when the microbial population is washed out of the reactor as a result of too high a flow rate. This occurs especially when the population reproduces slowly, as in the case of anaerobes. This problem can be minimised by the use of immobilisation, as described below in greater detail. Organic overload is produced when the wastewater contains a higher concentration of organic compounds. This results in the rapid production of a significant amount of volatile acids by one of the intermediate classes of anaerobic organisms in the consortium (the acetogenic bacteria) and in the inhibition of the methanogens (the last organisms to act in a methanogenic consortium), with consequent failure of the reactor. Toxic compounds can also inhibit the activity of the methanogens or cause their washout with resulting reactor failure.

However, anaerobic processes have advantages of their own. They are typically capable of tolerating higher loading rates, do not require high mechanical energy input for air dispersion (as in the aerobic case) and produce less biomass per unit of waste degraded.

8.2.2   Aerobic treatment system

Fixed film system (biological filters)

Fixed film system employ reactors in which waste is contacted with microbial films attached to surface. Surface area of biofilm growth is very important, so surface area of biofilm growth is increased by plain a porous medium in the reactor. Rotating biological contactor (RBC), fluidised bed reactor (FBR), trickling filter and biological filters are being used in present prospective of waste treatment systems.

Biology of fixed film system

The biological organisms that attach themselves to the solid surface of the medium come from essentially the same groups as those in activated – sludge systesm. Heterotrophic organism with facultative bacteria being predominatnt. Fungi, protozoa, rotifers, insect larvae and sludge worms may also use. These micro-organisms attach to the medium as dense viscous films.

Facultative bacteria life: *Adcaligenes, Achromobacter, Flavobacterium, Pseudomonas, Sphaerotilus natuns, Baggiatoa, Nitrosomonas, Nitrobacter* are commonly used to grow as biofilm.

Growth of the film will be outward from the solid surface. Anaerobic and endogeneous metabolism occur at the biofilm medium surface interface. The rate of food removal in growth system of micro-organism on biofilm depends on wastewater flow rate, organic loading rate, rate of diffusivity of food and oxygen into biofilm.

Wastewater passes over this biofilm with dissolved organics passing in to the biofilm due to concentration gradients. Suspended particles and colloids are decomposed in to soluble products. Oxygen from the wastewater and from the air in the void space of the medium provides oxygen for aerobic reactions at the biofilm surface. These processes are represented in Fig. 8.2.

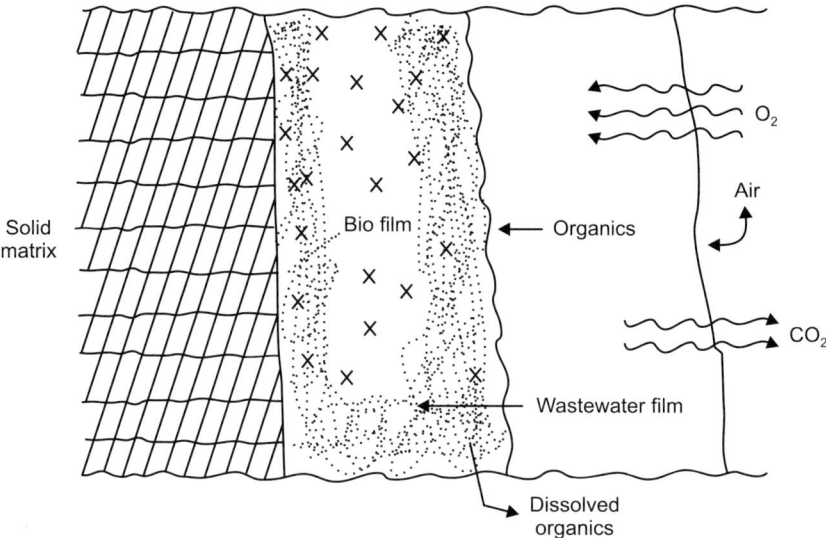

Figure 8.2: Biology of fixed or attached growth system.

Trickling filters are being used to a reactor in which irregular solid bed forms provide surface area for growth of biofilm. The system should have equipment for distribution of wastewater over the medium and for separating effluent.

Principles: The organic materials dissolved in wastewaters come in contact with the biofilm and are aerobically degraded by micro-organims. Settled sewage is distributed mechanically over the filter surface from where it trickles down the filter. Sorption and subsequent biological oxidation are the primary means of food removal.

Structural configuration

Filter medium: Medium is composed of crushed stone. These materials provide hardness, durability and chemically resistant surface for biofilm growth.

Size: Size of the material will be in the range of 45–100 mm, this size will provide specific surface area of 48 to 63 m²/m³. The porosities of particles will be about 40 to 55 per cent for specific application and perfect results. Plastic media may be used with advantages in specific surface area and porosity. Area up to 180 m²/m³ and porosities of 93 per cent are available with loose-bulk packing material.

Working: The loading of wastewater is accomplished by rotating distribution system. This distribution is based on the characteristics of the jet action of nozzles. This arrangement provides chances for air rotor for variable flow of loading wastewater. The under drain system is designed by concrete, tile etc., to carry treated wastewater and the biomass filters placed in series increase the depth of filter and increase the efficiency.

Affecting factors: Most important factors that affect the operation of trickling filter are organic loading, hydraulic flow rates, and temperature of the water and air. If the growth rate is rapid the organic loading rate will be high. If the growth is happening in excess amount then the chances of plugging of pores will increase and increasing the rate of hydraulic loading will lead to the sloughing and helps to keep the bed open. Temperature of wastewater and air determine the direction of air flow through the medium. Extreme cold may result in ice formation in the biofilm that lead the destruction of the biofilm. Trickling filters have played an important role in wastewater treatment.

Advantages of trickling filter

Trickling filter (Fig. 8.3) is very simple and has very low operating cost. It can be used for small communities in warmer climates. Multistage high rate filters can also be used. All factors that are taking part have been well controlled. The efficiency of trickling filter is good enough for treatment of wastewater.

Biotowers: Biotowers (Fig. 8.4) are deep trickling filters. These are designed for high flow rate of wastewater.

Structure: Biotower are made up of lightweight, modular media. This media is formed by arrangement of flat polyvinyl chloride sheets together in alternating patterns. This pattern of arrangement provides structural rigidity without excessive weight. The height of the arrangement up to 12 m to provide large volume in small containment structure. Sometimes wooden sheets in alternating patterns are used in place of plastic medium.

Medium such as river rock of nominal size 25 to 120 mm, Blast-furnace slag of 50 to 125 mm and plastic of high specific surface are being used now-a-days. Supply of wastewater by a rotating distributor like in trickling filter under drain systems are similar as trickling filter.

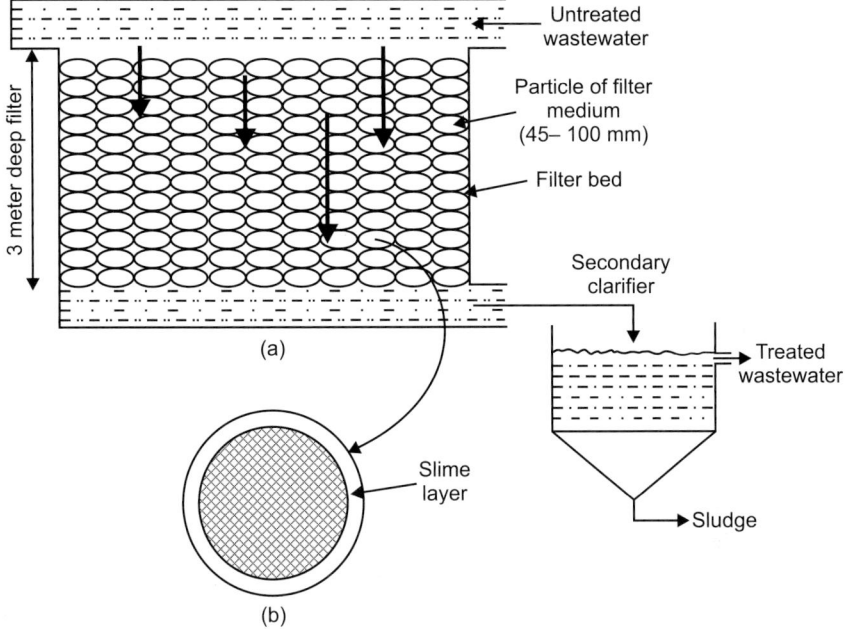

Figure 8.3: (a) Trickling filter and (b) single particle of filter medium.

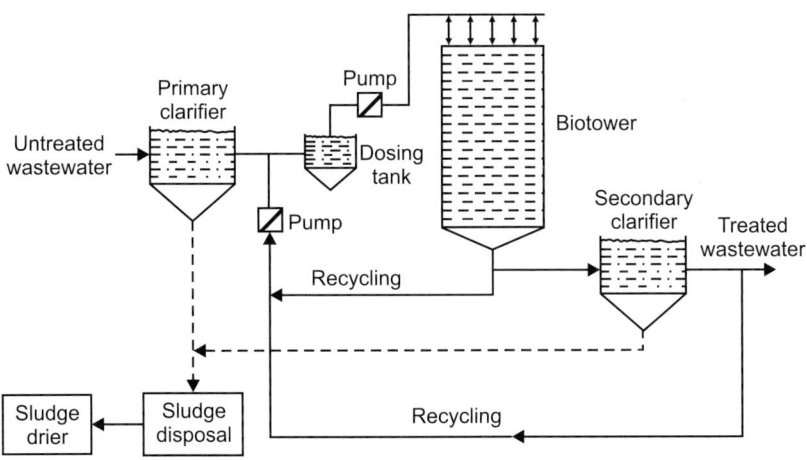

Figure 8.4: Biotower.

Working: Biotowers are operated similar as high rate, trickling filters. The effectiveness of plastic modules is less than random packing. The flow rate should be at high level to ensure that all surfaces are wetted throughout the entire depth. Endogenous respiration of waste throughout most of the depth of the tower. Ammonia will convert in to nitrate if carbon content of the wastewater falls below about 20 mg/l. An efficient biotower should be able to produce a nitrified effluent.

Advantage and disadvantages of biotower

1. Biotower allow greater loading rate.
2. The plugging of medium is not a problem in biotower.
3. There is proper ventilation that minimises odour problems and conditions.
4. Reactor is compact in nature.
5. Reactor operation is very simple.
6. Disadvantages include relatively high pumping cost due to large recycle requirement.

Rotating biological contactors (RBC)

Rotating biological contactors (Fig. 8.5) were first installed in Germany in 1960 and late in the United States. It is a unique adaption of the attached-growth process. An RBC consists of a series of closely spaced circular disks mounted on a common shaft are rotated through series of tanks in which wastewater flows on a continuous basis.

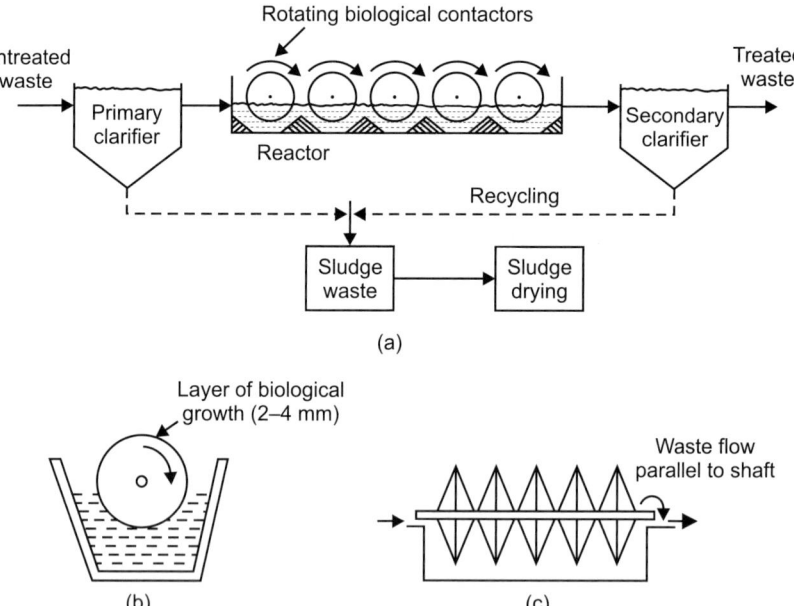

Figure 8.5: (a) Rotating biological contactor system, (b) RBC end view and (c) RBC side view.

The RBC unit is partially submerged (40%) in tank containing the wastewater, and the disks rotate slowly at about 1–1.6 revolution per minute. In the air driven units, an array of cups is fixed to the periphery of the disks. As the RBC disks rotate out of the wastewater, aeration is accomplished by exposure to the atmosphere. RBC systems require pretreatment of primary clarification and secondary clarification for separation.

Process design consideration

The similarity between RBC and trickling filter is design considerations. Both systems develop a large biofilm surface area and rely on mass transfer of oxygen and substrate from the bulk liquid to the biofilm. The organic loading affects BOD removal efficiency and the nitrogen loading after a minimal BOD concentration is reached.

The design of an RBC system must include the following considerations:

1. Staging of the RBC units.
2. Loading criteria.
3. Effluent characteristics.
4. Secondary clarifier design.

Staging of RBC units: Staging is the making compartment of the RBC disks to form a series of independent cells. A low effluent substrate concentration and high specific substrate removal rates are generally the ultimate goal, reduced disk area requirements can be realised only by using staged RBC units. The RBC process (Fig. 8.6) application typically consists of a number of units operated in series. The number of stages depends on the treatment goals, with two to four stages for BOD removal and six or more stages for nitrification.

Loading criteria: BOD loading in the range of 12 to 20 gm BOD/m^2.d for the first stage. Assuming a 50 per cent soluble BOD fraction the total BOD loading ranges from 24 to 30 gm BOD/m^2.d. For some designs that involve higher strength wastewaters, the loading criteria are met by using a step feeding approach.

Component of RBC:

Shaft: The RBC shafts are used to support and rotate the plastic disks. The length of shaft is limited to 8 meter with 7 meter occupied by disks. Steel shafts coated to protect against corrosion and thickness ranges from 13 to 30 mm.

Disk materials: Disk is made up of high density polyethylene. Standard density disks define as disks with a surface area of 9300 m^2 per 8 m shaft. Medium and high density material are used typically in the middle and final stages of an RBC system where thinner biological growths occurs.

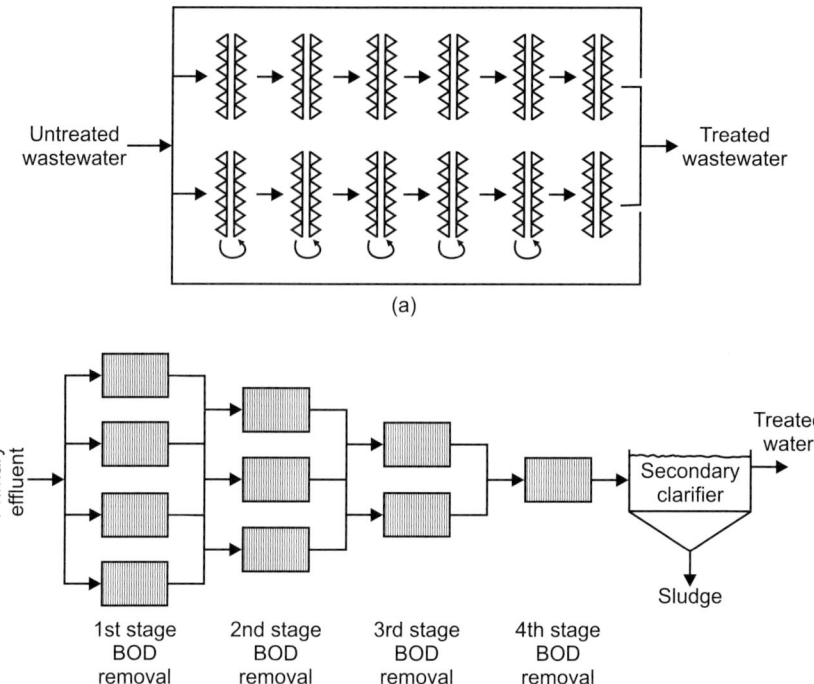

Figure 8.6: Stages of RBC.

Drive system and tankage: RBC units are rotated by mechanical drive units attached directly to the central shaft. Motors are typically used. A typical 1.5 meter depth tankage is used for RBC system to obtain in a stage volume of 45 m³ for a shaft.

Settling tanks: It is similar to trickling filter settling tanks in that all of the sludge from the tanks is removed to the sludge processing facilities.

Advantages of RBC

1. They are simple to operate and have low maintenance.
2. It accommodates shock loading.
3. It does not have the channeling problem.
4. It has reduced power costs, and less operational cost.
5. It requires less space than activated sludge plant.
6. Effluent quality is good as after tertiary treatment.
7. Problems like clogging, ponding filter are eliminated.
8. Lower head loss compared to the trickling filters.

Limitations of RBC

1. Lack of operational control due to over simplicity of the process.
2. Process is still new and people have less experience.
3. Undesirable heavy growth may occur.
4. High total vs. soluble BOD in RBC effluents.
5. Dissolved oxygen may remain limited.
6. Enclosures required for RBC to protect it from Sun, cold and heavy precipitation.

8.2.3   Fluidised bed bioreactor (FBBR)

Fluidised bed bioreactor (Fig. 8.7) were introduced in 1980. In this reactor the wastewater is fed upward to a bed of 0.4 to 0.5 mm sand or activated carbon. The depth of the bed is in the range of 4 to 5 m. The specific surface area is about 1100 m^2/m^3 of reactor volume. It is a combination of attached growth and suspended growth system. Biological film is developed and maintained on solid support medium consisting of particles small enough to be maintained in suspension by the upward flow of liquid being treated. Upflow velocities are 35 to 40 m/h.

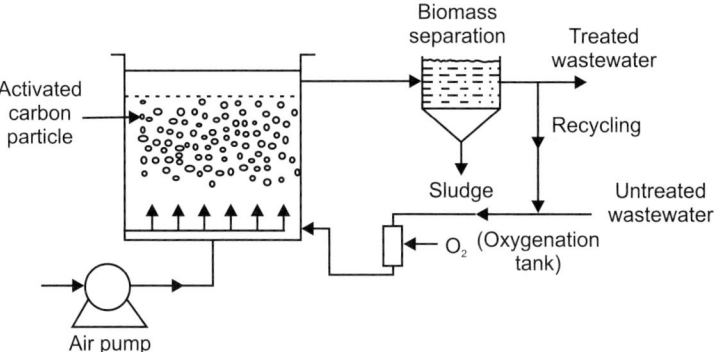

Figure 8.7: Fluidised bed bioreactor.

Packed-bed reactors are one of the most common separation devices and reactor configurations used in the chemical industry. In wastewater treatment applications, micro-organisms immobilised on their internals are used to degrade the contaminants in the wastewater.

Packed-bed reactors consist of a vessel enclosure (which can be open or closed depending on the duty) provided internally with a packing material. The packing is designed so that it has a large surface where the liquid phase, the gas phase (if any) and the immobilised organisms can interact. Typically, the packing for biological wastewater treatment is made of loose materials, such as pebbles, lava rock, or plastic particles.

Packed-bed reactors can be used for both anaerobic and aerobic processes. Anaerobic packed beds (also called anaerobic filter reactors) are closed vessels in which only the liquor to be treated is circulated, typically in the upflow direction, over the bed. The same configuration can also be used for aerobic treatment, even when filamentous organisms are used. However, this approach requires that the stream itself be oxygenated separately so that the micro-organisms can still be supplied with oxygen.

This process can be especially advantageous if the compound to be treated is volatile and can be stripped out by bubbling air directly into the column. Recently, this approach has been used to treat a stream contaminated with methylene chloride by passing the stream through a column containing an immobilised bed of a single aerobic organism.

In the vast majority of cases, however, aerobic packed-bed reactors require the additional presence of a gas phase. In this case the liquid phase is added from the top of the reactor, from which it trickles down by gravity and the air is sparged at the bottom. If the reactor is open, air moves through the bed by natural convection.

Reactors are generally cylindrical with perforated distribution plates and tapered or conical entry sections. Fluidisation of support particles is allowed but clumping is prevented.

For aerobic application recirculated effluent is passed through on oxygenation tank to pre-dissolve oxygen. Adding air to the reactor would discharge packing to the effluent. Aerobic FBBR are frequently used to treat ground water contaminated with hazardous substances.

Designs of FBR

There are two types of design available for industrial scale application.

1. Simon Hartly Captor: Simon Hartly developed this design in Manchester Institute of Science and Technology. The biomass is generating in pads. Pads are retained in reactor. These pads can be periodically removed and layer of biomass is squeezed and empty pads are returned to the reactor. The design is given in Fig. 8.8.

2. Dorr Oliver Oxitron: This design of FBR is developed by Dorr Oliver. In this design, sand particles are used as support medium. Sand particle are cleaned and then recycled. The oxitron design is given in Fig. 8.9.

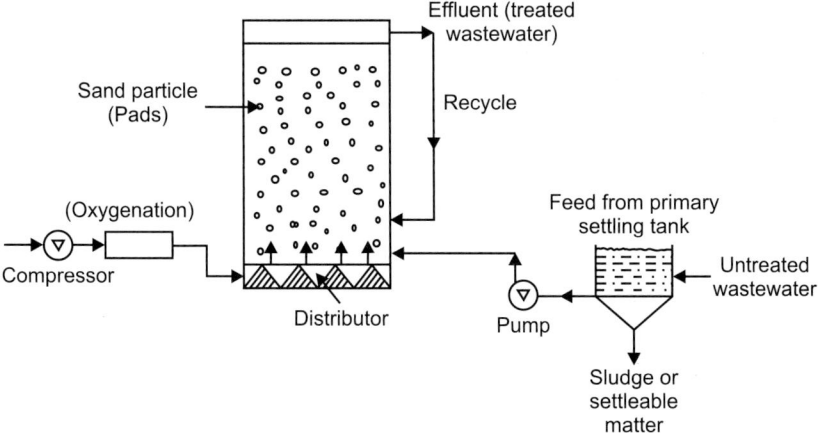

Figure 8.8: Simon Hartely Captor plant.

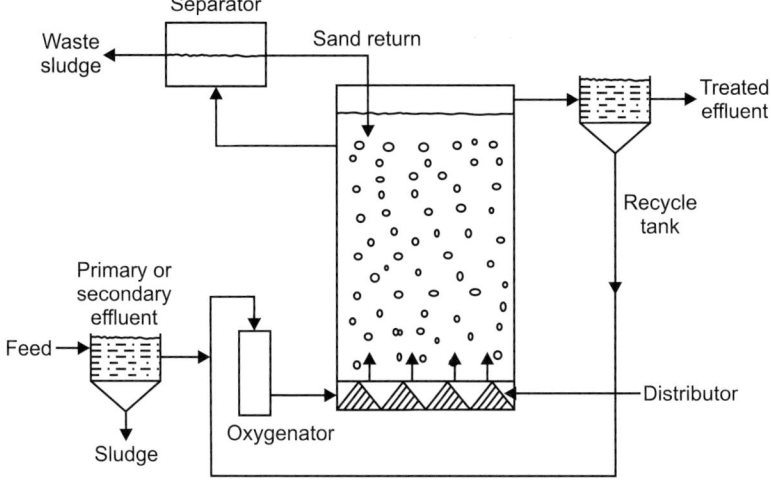

Figure 8.9: Dorr Oliver Oxitron plant.

Advantages of FBRs

1. It is compact structure, only piping to be done on site.
2. It provides an extra space for micro-organism necessary to degrade the xenobiotic and toxic compounds.
3. It is economical and quick for treatment.
4. High quality effluent is produced low in TSS and COD concentration.

5. It is suitable for high strength industrial waste.
6. The oxygenation method prevents stripping and emission of toxic organic compounds to the atmosphere.
7. Capital and operating costs are very low. Secondary clarifiers can be possible eliminated for solid separation and recycling.
8. Biomass sludge production.
9. Sludge transport and disposal costs are lower.

Expanded bed reactor (EBR)

The operation is similar as fluidised bed processes. The expanded bed system uses the operating mode of bed reactor. For biological application, and expanded bed is a different process than fluidised bed in certain aspects.

These are:

1. Velocities to maintain the delicate attached living film.
2. Separation, retardation and bio-coagulation of fine suspended.
3. Achievement of maximum biomass concentrations.

Expanded bed reactor (Fig. 8.10) with above care becomes a better than fluidised bed reactor. Shearing of microbial film is minimum in the expanded bed reactor. Comparison of performance of different treatment systems is shown in Table 8.1.

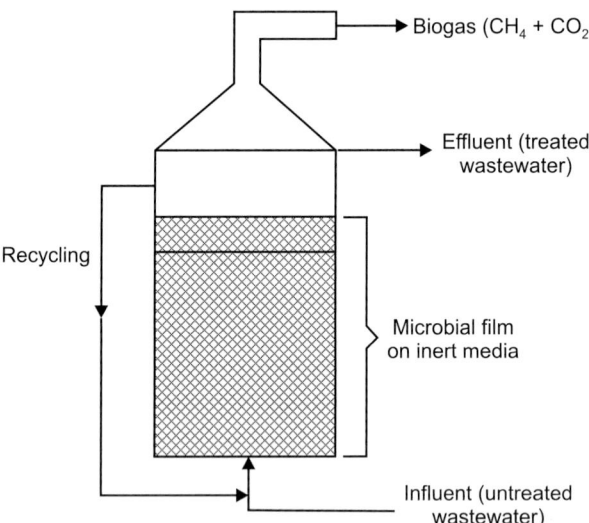

Figure 8.10: Expanded bed reactor.

Table 8.1: Comparison of performance of different treatment systems.

Characteristic	Trickling filter	Activated sludge	Rotating biological contactor	Activated sludge (pure O²)	FBBR
Biomass concentration MLVSS	2000 to 7000 mg/l	700 to 2500 mg/l	10000 to 20000 mg/l	3000 to 5000 mg/l	10000 to 50000 mg/l
Surface area m^2/m^{-3} reactor volume	15–30	28–37	40–50	–	800–1200
Process loading rate at BOD removal per m^3 of reactor volume per day	0.5 to 1.2	0.8 to 1.5	–	1.8 to 2.6	8 to 18

8.3   Suspended growth system

8.3.1   Activated sludge process

Activated sludge process is a process of aerobic fermentation introduced in 1914. In this system high concentration of micro-organisms is maintained by recycling the active sludge. Biosorption and flocculation remove the organic matter rapidly while oxidation and biosynthesis proceed at a lower rate. The activated sludge process is currently one of the most widely used technologies for wastewater purification.

Micro-organism derives energy from the carbonaceous organic matter present in aerated wastewater to produce new cells by a process known as synthesis. The activated-sludge process is one of the oldest wastewater treatment processes and the basic concept is now implemented in a number of different ways. Historically, the practice of blowing air through wastewater to reduce its pollutant concentration has been used since 1890. In so doing, the growth of aerobic organisms which can feed on the pollutant is promoted, thus preventing the growth of anaerobes and the generation of noxious odours. However, it was not until the 1910s that a significant improvement in the process was made by recycling part of the biomass generated during the aeration process (the so-called activated sludge) back to the aeration basin. The introduction of this recycling step led to an increase in the biomass concentration within the aeration tank, thus speeding up the rate at which the degradation process would proceed.

The content of the reaction vessel are referred to as Mixed Liquor Suspended Solid (MLSS) or Mixed Liquor Volatile Suspended Solids (MLVSS) and consist mostly of micro-organisms and inert and non-biodegradable suspended matter. This system consists of different types of micro-organisms which obtain energy by converting ammonia nitrogen in to nitrate nitrogen in a process termed nitrification. The biological components of these processes are collectively known as the activated sludge.

The effluent from the aerated bioreactor, containing a significant amount of biomass, is fed to a settling tank or clarifier (sludge separator), a device capable of separating the clear supernatant from the bulk of the biomass. The supernatant is fed to a polishing treatment process (if necessary) or discharged. The biomass (sludge) is partially recycled to the aeration bioreactor. The excess is disposed of or treated separately to reduce its volume and water content and to improve its stability. Excess sludge constitutes a significant waste product of the activated-sludge process and several alternatives are used for its treatment and final disposal.

Under unfavourable conditions such as toxic loadings, temperature fluctuations, or pH changes, filamentous organisms dominate the microbial populations in the aeration tank. When this happens the process 'bulks' and the resulting microbial flocs tend to remain suspended instead of settling. As a result, the clarifier is not capable of separating and recycling the biomass and the entire process fails. Bulking can also be affected by the reactor design, as will be seen below.

Activated-sludge processes differ not in their basic operating principle (which is always the same) but in the configurations of the two primary components of the process, namely the aerated bioreactor and the sludge/supernatant separator (clarifier).

8.3.2　Design consideration

1. Nutrient requirements: Dosing of inorganic nitrogen and phosphorus done if required and the ratio of BOD: Nitrogen: Phosphorus must be not more than 100: 5: 1.
2. pH: Working pH should be in the range 6–9.
3. Temperature: Ambient temperature range 30–40°C.
4. Loading rate: 0.2–0.4 kg BOD kg^{-1} MLVSS/day.
5. Aerator efficiency: 2.5 kg O_2 kwh^{-1}.
6. Excess biological sludge: 0.35–0.55 kg ss/kg BOD applied.
7. BOD removal: More than 95%.

System components

1. Aeration tank: Air or oxygen is pumped in to the system to create aerobic environment that needs to microbial community and ensure proper mixing of activated sludge.
2. Secondary clarifiers: Activated sludge solids are separated from the surrounding water by process of flocculation and sedimentation. Flocs settle at the bottom of the clarifier. This separation lead to formation of a secondary effluent having a lower level of activated sludge solids.
3. Aeration source: Compressed air is provided through the bottom aeration using nozzle spargers. Waste water is vigorously mixed by the mechanical agitation process.

Completely mixed reactor

The basic configuration of this type of reactor is a completely mixed and aerated tank in which the composition of the liquor is constant everywhere, as shown in Fig. 8.11a. This can be achieved quite easily in a small tank provided with an appropriately designed agitation system. If the tank volume is significant, multiple agitators or internal recycles and jets are used. These reactors typically consist of concrete basins in which aeration is provided by surface aeration or sparging with air diffusers. Well-mixed systems have the advantage of minimising nutrient depletion (including oxygen depletion) in any part of the basin. In addition, they are quite tolerant of shock loadings since any fluctuation in the composition of the feed is dampened by the dilution produced when the feed is mixed with the reactor.

Plug-flow activated-sludge reactors

Plug-flow systems are typically more efficient to treat most wastewaters. In such systems the wastewater flow through long and narrow aeration tanks, as shown in Fig. 8.11b, thus is minimising any back mixing effect. In practice, it is difficult to obtain a true plug flow in any real system. Furthermore, the presence of air bubbles tends to increase the turbulence of the system and promote axial dispersion. Plug-flow typically results in the growth of a good-quality sludge with good settling characteristics. This is especially important in those cases in which the wastewater composition would promote the growth of filamentous organisms, as in the case in which it contains high levels of easily degradable materials that promote bulking. In this situation, the use of plug-flow typically results in a rapid drop in pollutant concentration in the first part of the reactor and minimises the possibility that the concentration in the rest of the reactor will be such as to promote the growth of filamentous organisms. Hence, the sludge leaving the reactor has excellent settling properties and can be effectively separated in the clarifier.

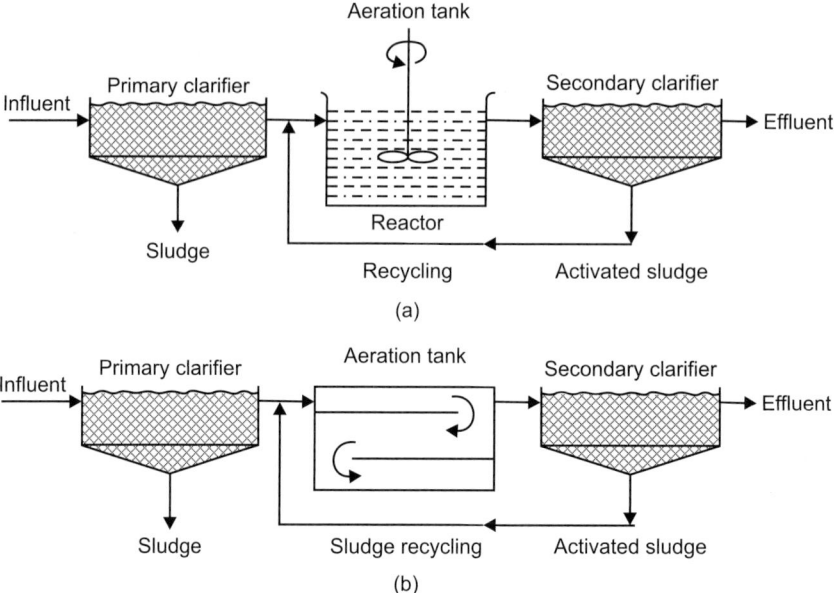

Figure 8.11: Flow diagram of conventional activated sludge treatment process.

One major drawback of plug-flow aeration tanks is their sensitivity to shock loading, since any increase in pollutant concentration in the wastewater is not distributed throughout the entire vessel but is confined to the sludge of wastewater containing it. For this reasons plug-flow reactors are often preceded by a smaller reactor operating as a CSTR, in which concentration fluctuations are partially dampened.

Components of activated sludge process reactor

Screening units: This part of the system remove large objects which can damage the pumps and clog pipes and channels.

Primary clarifier: In this suspended particles are removed from wastewater by gravity sedimentation. Water containing particulate matter is allowed to flow slowly through sedimentation tank and detained long enough to leave the tank are removed manually or by mechanically.

Aeration tanks: Steel or poly fibre glass constructs the aeration tank. This tank retains water up to 24 hours. Content of the tank is know as mixed liquor suspended solid (MLSS). Micro-organisms are kept in suspension for up to 8 hours by diffused air. Treated and settled waste water is discharged through a tank.

Modification of activated sludge process

Tapered aeration: Aeration is more at inlet than outlet that totally depend on the demand of the aeration (Fig. 8.12a).

Step aeration: Aeration and feeding is done at steps in the system throughout length of the tank (Fig. 8.12b).

Contact stabilisation: Recycled sludge is aerated to encourage organisms to utilise any stored nutrients. More wastes are digested. Mixing and aeration is separate in contact stabilisation. Microbes digest the organic matter in the stabilisation tank and are then recycled back to the contact tank-soluble and insoluble food (Fig. 8.12c).

Extended aeration: Long detention time and low feed/mass ratio in aerator to maintain culture in endogenous phase (Fig. 8.12d).

Advantages

1. It can be used for a single household and also for industrial scale.
2. ASP effects oxidation and nitrification in the system.
3. It can remove biological phosphorus.
4. It can separate solids and liquids
5. It can stabilise the sludge.
6. It is capable of removing up to 98% of suspended solids.
7. It is most widely used wastewater treatment process.

Disadvantages

1. It can not remove colour from wastes but may add colour by the formation of coloured intermediates.
2. It does not remove nutrients, so tertiary treatment is necessary.
3. It requires high power supply for agitation.
4. Produced sludge is not well-settled.

8.3.3   Anaerobic biological treatment

Anaerobic treatment methods are recommended when BOD of the effluent is very high. There is no O_2 supply in the anaerobic system. Anaerobic digestion is microbial fermentation of organic matter in to CO_2 and methane. There are very low sludge production and very less energy consumption. The final production is methane which has high calorific value. Micro-organisms can remain dormant for several months and become operational within a week of

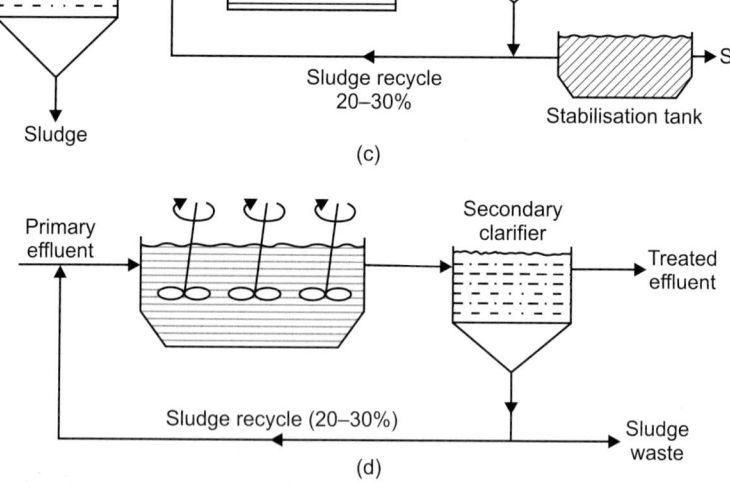

Figure 8.12: Modification in ASP: (a) tapered aeration, (b) step aeration, (c) contact stabilisation and (d) extended aeration.

startup. This treatment system is suitable for seasonally produced wastewaters. Anaerobic organisms have been used to treat wastewater containing large amounts of suspended solids. Because they present many advantages over aerobic processes, such as low sludge production, low power consumption and the generation of methane as a valuable by-product, anaerobic process are now used to treat a variety of highly contaminated wastewaters.

Nevertheless, the use of anaerobic systems has not been as widespread as one might expect, most likely because of the problems commonly associated with their operation, such as sensitivity to toxic pollutants. Indeed, the sequential operation of anaerobic consortia makes them (and especially the methanogens which are the last organisms in the anaerobic chain) more vulnerable to process upsets. However, the poor reputation that some anaerobic processes still have may have also partially resulted from the failure of operators and designers to take advantage of the knowledge accumulated over the last twenty years on the microbiology of anaerobic consortia. There are various reactors that are being used for the treatment of wastewater anaerobically.

8.3.4   Upflow anaerobic sludge blanket reactor (UASB)

UASB is most developed anaerobic treatment process technology. This technology is developed in 1980 by Lettinga and his coworkers in Netherland.

UASB (upflow anaerobic sludge blanket) process, which operates using a column reactor without any packing material, can be described as a system with an internal biomass recycle based on gravity settling.

As shown in Fig. 8.13, the wastewater feed injected at the bottom of the column first meets a thick layer (1.5–2.5 metre) of biomass granules produced by the anaerobic organisms under the appropriate conditions. These granules, forming a 'blanket' of high biomass content (from 60–70 g/l up to 100–150 g/l), are primarily responsible for the removal of the pollutants.

Design considerations

Important design consideration are:

1. Wastewater characteristics: Wastewaters with higher concentration of proteins or fats tend to create problems such as foaming sludge granulation. Particulate versus soluble COD is important in determining the design.

2. Volumetric organic loading: The design of reactor also depend on the loading rate. Removal efficiency of 95 per cent for COD have been achieved at COD loading ranging from 12 to 25 kg COD/m^3.d on a variety of wastes at 28 to 35°C with UASB reactors.

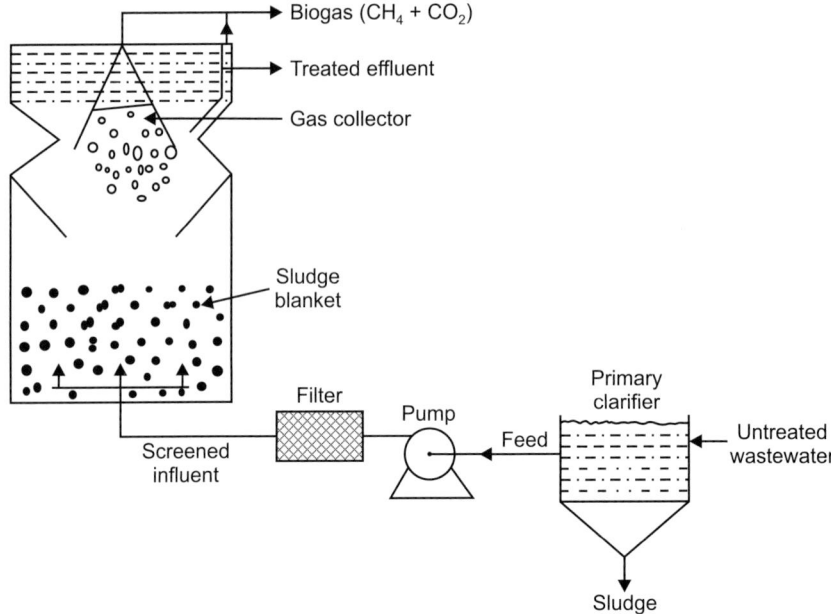

Figure 8.13: Upflow anaerobic sludge blanket reactor.

3. Upflow velocity: Upflow velocity is a critical design parameter velocities of 6 m/h and 2m/h can be allowed for soluble wastewaters. For stronger wastewaters it will be determined by the volumetric COD loading. The upflow velocity is equal to influent flow rate divided by reactor cross-section area.

4. Physical features: Effluent withdrawal, gas collection, gas separation and feed inlet are the physical features that affect the design of the reactor system.

The design of the UASB reactor has the following features. Wastewater enters from the bottom distributed throughout the bottom by liquid distributor. A thick 'sludge blanket' consisting of micro-organisms is formed above the feed distributor at the bottom of the reaction. The upflow velocity plays an important role in stablising sludge blanket. The effluent to be treated is fed by the distributor in to the base of the sludge blanket.

The UASB digester requires the active bacteria in the form of high density granular sludge which is retained in the digester tank despite gassing and upflow velocity of wastewater. The top portion of the reactor is provided with a larger cross section so that the treated wastewater coming from the blanket passes in to narrow zone free of gas bubbles. The gas collection system is also attached at the top.

Limitations: There are certain limitations of UASB reactor system.

1. If the gas production or effluent flow rate is fast then there will be a chance of disturbance in sludge blanket.
2. Wastes with high proportion of insoluble COD can give rise to poor granulation.
3. Digester does not treat particulate waste effectively.

Applications: The UASB reactor have been extensively used to treat food processing wastes, paper mill waste, citric acid wastes, dairy waste, food and softdrink preparation wastes. The UASB has been used in experiments for denitrification in Japan. Several plants are working with high capacity of over 110 m^3 in Japan, Holland and other countries. This process can remove more than 70% of the COD with biogas productivity of 0.85 m^3/kg of the COD destroyed. A full scale version of UASB has successfully treated sugar beet waste at a loading rate of 18 kg COD m^{-3} d^{-1} and hydraulic retention time of 4 hours, achieving 90% COD removal.

The UASB also can be used as a purely methanogenic process with acitogenic phase being carried out in a separate reactor. This type of reactor has been used in industrial applications with removal efficiencies of about 4–10 kg COD/(m^3.day). However, even higher rates (96 kg COD/(m^3.day)] have been reported. Retention times are of the order of 3 to 8 hours.

8.3.5   Anaerobic contact digesters

The anaerobic contact digester is a modified version of Continuous Stirred Tank Reactor (CSTR) and activated sludge process but without oxygen supply. The contact process is the anaerobic equivalent of the aerobic activated-sludge process. The basic reactor configuration consists of a closed vessel, typically provided with agitation, in which the biomass is suspended in flocs and to which the wastewater is continuously fed.

The wastewater retention time is much smaller than the average biomass retention time because the reactor is followed by a settling tank where the biomass is separated from the supernatant and partially recycled to the reactor. A schematic of this process is given in Fig. 8.14. The output of the digester is settled under anaerobic conditions and a part of settled sludge is returned to the digester for the mixing purpose.

This helps in retaining of methanogenic organisms over a wide range of loading. Degassing is necessary before settling of the biomass. This is advantageous as it leads to a higher micro-organisms to BOD/COD ratio, which in turn results in a more rapid and efficient removal of BOD/COD from the effluent stream.

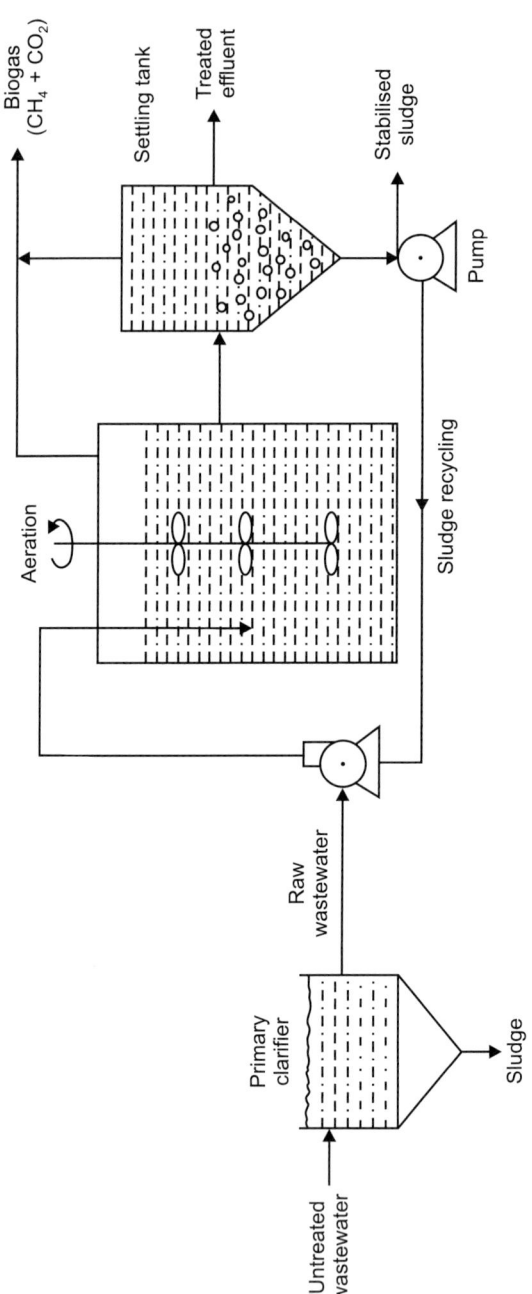

Figure 8.14: Anaerobic contact digester.

A typically reactor has a cylindrical shape with conical or dish bottom and is provided with agitation to homogenise the mixture and suspend the biomass. The gas produced during the process (primarily methane and carbon dioxide) is removed from the top of the reactor. Significantly more complex can be design of the settling tank or biomass separation device. Anaerobic flocs tend to have low density and contain entrapped gas bubbles produced by the anaerobic metabolism. Therefore, they settle very slowly. In addition to traditional settling tanks with conical bottoms other separation devices can be used, such as lamellar separators, in which the slurry from the reactor is passed through slanted channels which promote the coalescence of the suspended solids against the lamellas forming the channels and their sedimentation to the bottom of the reactor. Additional methods to promote solid separation, such as vacuum degassing or centrifugation, have also been attempted.

High biomass content (5 g/l) and significant BOD removal (80 per cent of an initial BOD of 5600 mg/l), with a reactor capacity of 3 to 5 kg COD/(m^3 · day) can be achieved with this type of reactor.

Full-scale contact process reactors are widely used for industrial wastewater treatment. A 300 m^3 reactor with 300 m^3 settler is reportedly being used for treating pectin waste and is design for a loading rate of 5 kg COD per m^3/day at a biomechanics plant. Such units are also in operation in countries like Japan, France and Germany.

8.3.6   Fixed film reactor/packed bed reactor

Packed-bed reactors are one of the most common separation devices and reactor configurations used in the chemical industry. In wastewater treatment applications, micro-organisms immobilised on their internals are used to degrade the contaminants in the wastewater.

Packed-bed reactors consist of a vessel enclosure (which can be open or closed depending on the duty) provided internally with a packing material. The packing is designed so that it has a large surface where the liquid phase, the gas phase (if any) and the immobilised organisms can interact. Typically, the packing for biological wastewater treatment is made of loose materials, such as pebbles, lava rock, or plastic particles.

Packed-bed reactors can be used for both anaerobic and aerobic processes. Anaerobic packed beds (also called anaerobic filter reactors) are closed vessels in which only the liquor to be treated is circulated, typically in the upflow direction, over the bed. The same configuration can also be used for aerobic treatment, even when filamentous organisms are used. However, this approach requires that the stream itself be oxygenated separately so that the micro-organisms can still be supplied with oxygen.

This process can be especially advantageous if the compound to be treated is volatile and can be stripped out by bubbling air directly into the column. Recently, this approach has been used to treat a stream contaminated with methylene chloride by passing the stream through a column containing an immobilised bed of a single aerobic organism. Upflow fixed film reactor is shown in Fig. 8.15.

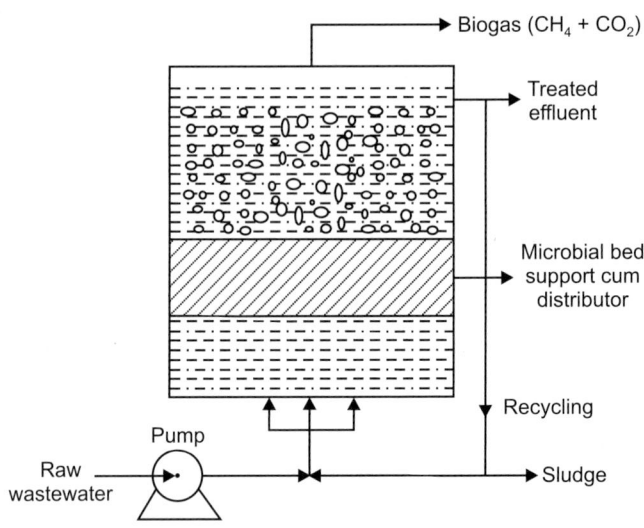

Figure 8.15: Upflow fixed film reactor.

In the vast majority of cases, however, aerobic packed-bed reactors require the additional presence of a gas phase. In this case the liquid phase is added from the top of the reactor, from which it trickles down by gravity and the air is sparged at the bottom. If the reactor is open, air moves through the bed by natural convection. It is actual a type of an immobilised whole cell reactor. They are simple in design, easy to construct and operate. They have advantages over CSTR. Depending upon the entry of wastewater, these reactors may be termed either upflow or down flow reactors.

A solid matrix of inert support material is used to provide the surface for microbial attachment. The high specific biomass concentration achieved due to whole cell immobilisation and flock retention makes it possible to attain a low Hydraulic Retention Time (HRT).

Limitations: The system is not suitable for treating wastewater containing large amounts of calcium salts as these salts may clog the bed and channel the flow. Clogging and channeling may also occur if the effluent has a high concentration of suspended solids.

Application of fixed reactors/packed bed reactor

The application of fixed reactors/packed bed reactor includes the treatment of different types of effluents containing 1–10% dry matter like vegetable processing wastes, animal waste, wheat starch wastes, waste sulphite liquors, molasses wastes and food processing wastes. Down flow FFR is in use to treat confectionary wastes. A 13000 m^3 reactor is also in use to treat wastes from a run production distillery.

8.3.7   Sequential batch reactor/periodic biological reactor

Sequential batch reactor is called as periodic biologic reactor (Fig. 8.16). It is one of the most recent advances in biological treatment processes. Sequential batch reactors will reduce the problems associated with wastewater variations and eliminate sludge recycling.

At starting period of reactor development in 1915 to 1920, the reactors were of fill and draw variety (Periodic operations). But after 1920 continuous mode system come in pictures which were low cost and low maintenance systems. After a lot of research work ultimately in 1970 results in the development of sequential batch reactors. In 1980 SBR were used in the treatment of industrial discharges which contain high level of hazardous wastes in 1990's emphases is on projects for the biological treatment of groundwater. A sequencing batch reactor (SBR) is a reactor in which an activated-sludge process is carried out in a time-oriented, sequential manner using a single vessel for all the phases of the process. The same steps involved in a conventional, continuous activated-sludge process (such as aeration, pollutant oxidation, sludge settling and recycling) are now conducted in batch one after the other.

In an SBR process, each cycle starts with the reactor nearly empty except for a layer of acclimated sludge on the bottom. The reactor is then filled up with the wastewater and the aeration and agitation are started. The biological degradation process begins during the filling steps and proceeds, once the reactor has been filled up, until a satisfactory level of degradation of the pollutant is achieved.

Principle of SBR

SBR works in different stages like fill period, react period, settle period, draw period and idle period. All these stages are being carried out in a single tank.

The wastewater is added to reactor during fill period. Reaction taking place during the fill period are controlled by adjusting mixing and aeration intensity and frequency. After the liquid in the reactor reaches the max level the

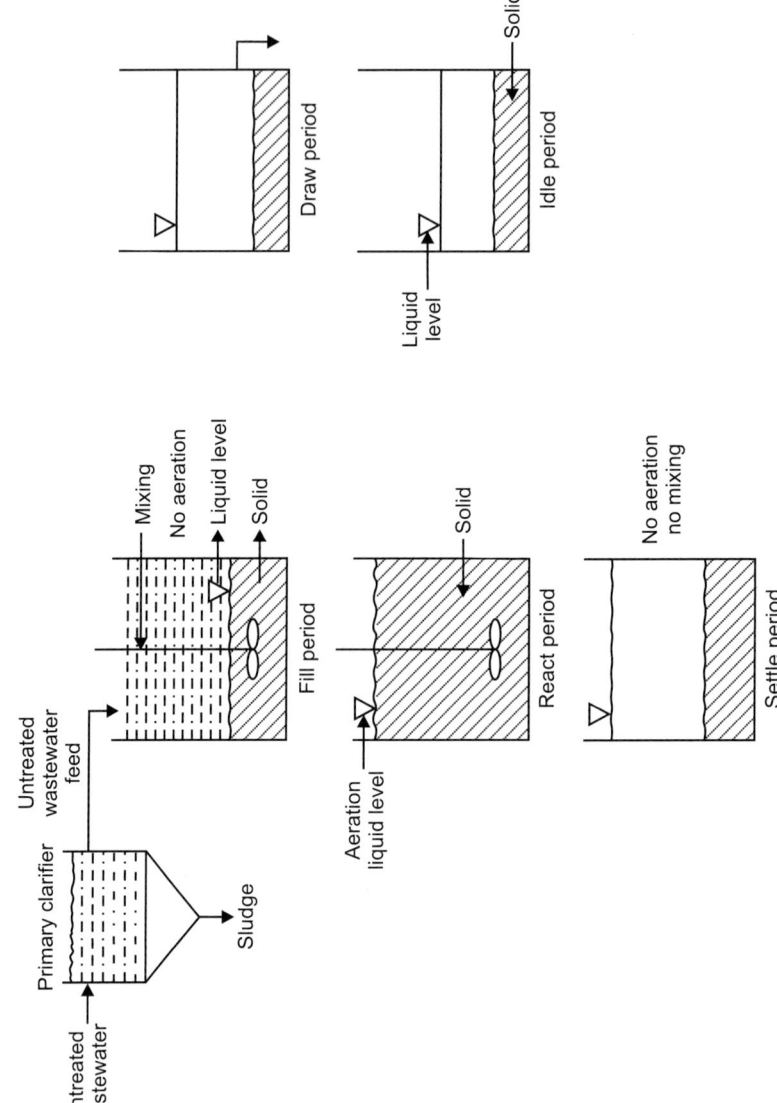

Figure 8.16: Sequential batch reactor (periodic biological reactor).

wastewater is diverted to react periodically. This react period is controlled by adjusting mixing and aeration. Settle period is followed by the draw stage where treated waste water is decanted. Settled organisms remain in the reactor during the ideal waiting period.

The main advantages of SBRs are that they can accommodate large fluctuations in the incoming wastewater flow and composition without failing. The same may not be true in conventional activated-sludge processes, in which an increase in the incoming flow rate results in a lower residence time of the wastewater in the aeration tank and of the sludge in the clarifier, with potential failure of one of them or both. In addition, toxic shocks or significant changes in organic loading may produce alterations in the make-up of microbial populations of conventional activated-sludge processes, with consequent bulking or process failure.

Instead, the wastewater residence time in SBRs can be extended until the microbial population has recovered and completed the degradation process. Similarly, the settling time can be varied to allow complete settling before discharging. In other words, SBR processes, like all batch processes, are more flexible. On the other hand, the use of SBRs to treat a continuous wastewater flow requires the simultaneous use of multiple reactors and/or the presence of holding facilities to store the wastewater until an SBR becomes available. SBRs have been used also in denitrifying applications.

Efficiency of SBRs
Efficiency of SBRs comes from these facts:
1. Frequent alternation of factors such as availability and lack of carbon sources, electron-donors and electron acceptors allow simultaneous enrichment of a variety of microbial strains in multispecies bio-communities.
2. Exploitation of metabolic capabilities of various strains achieved.
3. Bacteria maintain a high metabolic rate even with low substrate concentrations.

Application of SBRs
SBRs are applied for these purposes:
1. Nitrification and denitrification of secondary effluents.
2. Landfill leachates.
3. Fluid from soil remediation sites.
4. SBRs are also used for bioremediation of contaminated soil containing petroleum hydrocarbons.

8.3.8   Anaerobic hybrid reactor

A laboratory scale Anaerobic Hybrid Reactor (AHR) was made of per-spex tube with an internal diameter of 10.4 cm and overall height of 60 cm with a total capacity of 5 litres. The top third of the reactor (10 cm) was filled with polypropylene spherical beads. This packed section performed dual functions of retaining the suspended sludge within the reactor and exerting a polishing effect on the wastewater through the activity of bio-film developed on the packing material. At the lower part of the reactor an inlet was fixed. At the upper part of the reactor, above the packing column, an outlet for the effluent was made. The third outlet fixed on the topmost part of the reactor was meant for the flow of gas, and a gas flow meter was connected to it to measure the biogas collected.

At low temperatures, the low hydrolysis rate and a decrease in the degradable organic matter fraction were found to cause the deterioration of the overall anaerobic reactor performance. UASB COD removals of ~65% at 20°C and of 55–65% at 13–17°C were observed by several authors. A decrease in the effluent quality was also observed, together with a decline in the gas production rate. It has been observed that a 78% decrease in the gas production rate when the temperature was reduced from 27°C to 10°C. The low gas production coincided with a 25% lower COD removal at 10°C than at 27°C, indicating suspended solids accumulation in the reactor.

One possible way to improve the performance of a UASB reactor at low temperatures is to provide surface area for biomass attachment and growth in the reactor volume above the sludge blanket. This can be accomplished by replacing the typical gas/solids separator of the classical UASB reactor with filter media. Elmitwalli and others compared the performances of a hybrid UASB-filter and a classical UASB reactor at 13°C. The hybrid UASB-filter reactor reached 64% COD removal, a 4% better removal than the classical UASB. A better colloidal fraction removal was attributed to the attached biomass on the filter.

AHR is one of High Rate Anaerobic Reactors (HRAR) originally proposed by Maxham and Wakamiya in 1981 and is a conglomeration of the positive features of both the Anaerobic Filter (AF) and Upflow Anaerobic Sludge Blanket (UASB) reactor. UASB reactor with separator and hybrid UASB reactor with plastic filter rings are shown in Fig. 8.17.

The attached growth on the media in the upper portion of the reactor together with the formation of a granular or flocculent sludge bed in the bottom section add up significant biomass inventories leading to increased process stability, improved gas/solid/liquid separation and higher removal efficiency.

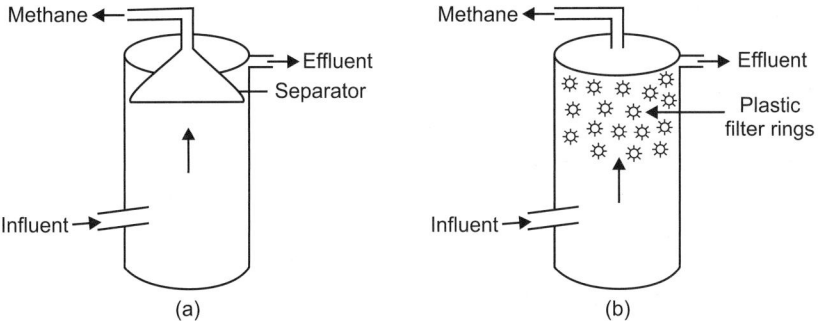

Figure 8.17: (a) UASB reactor with separator, and (b) Hybrid UASB reactor with plastic filter rings.

Another advantage of this kind of design is its ability; even without granular sludge it retains high amounts of biomass inside the reactor.

Although hybrid reactor design is expected to work efficiently without granular sludge, desirable to cultivate granular biomass. Upflow hybrid anaerobic filter is shown in Fig. 8.18.

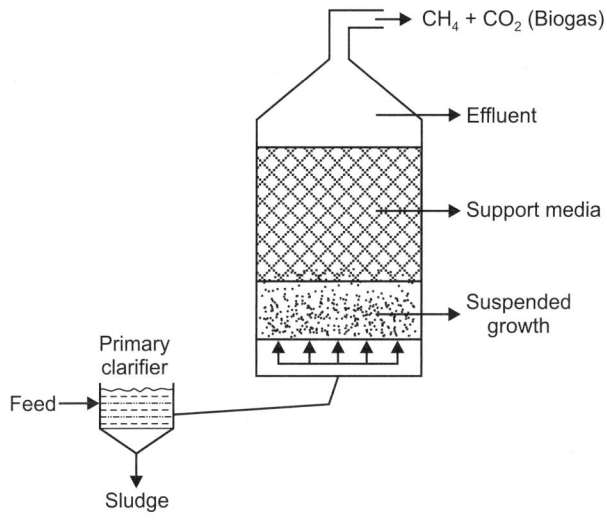

Figure 8.18: Upflow hybrid anaerobic filter.

8.3.9   Reactor operation

The reactor was operated continuously at six hydraulic retention times (HRTs) of 30, 18, 12, 8, 6 and 3h and the corresponding organic loading rates were 3.20, 5.32, 8.04, 11.988, 16.048, and 32.256 kg COD m^{-3} d^{-1} by keeping the initial substrate concentrations constant, closely around 4.0 g COD/L.

Stoichiometry and design kinetics for waste treatment process

Before starting the optimised design procedure five fundamental questions should have been answered:

Basis of design: In the design of waste water treatment plants, often neither quantity nor characteristics of the waste water to be treated are known and have to be estimated, for instance based on the size of the population and its expected growth, the fraction of the population served by a sewer system and the expected future development of organic and hydraulic contributions per capita. For any rational design approach, it will be necessary to attribute values to all of these parameters.

1. Wastewater characteristics: Important parameters wastewater characteristics are given below:
   (a) Influent flow rate.
   (b) Concentration and composition of the organic material in the influent.
   (c) Concentration of the inorganic suspended solids in the influent.
   (d) Temperature profile.
   (e) Value and stability of pH.
   (f) Nutrient concentration.
   (g) Especially in the case of industrial waste waters: the presence of toxic components.

2. Costing of the activated sludge system: To evaluate the attractiveness of different design alternatives, the relevant costing data are required, which will ultimately define the investment and operational costs. To estimate the total investment costs, indicative cost factors are supplied for the main treatment units. Together with the operational costs, the annualised total investment costs will allow a cost evaluation based on total annual costs, costs per people equivalent and costs per cubic meter of treated wastewater.

3. Treatment objectives: Ultimately, the selected wastewater treatment configuration will depend on the treatment objectives and the legal effluent discharge requirements.

4. Available treatment options: The optimised design configurations of the activated sludge system has been discussed already.

5. Limitations and constraints.

Bioreactor design and operation

The goal of an effective bioreactor is to control, contain and positively influence the biological reaction. To accomplish this, the Biochemical engineer must take into consideration two areas. One is the suitable reactor parameters for the desired biological, chemical and physical (macrokinetic) system. The macrokinetic system includes microbial growth and metabolite production. Microbes can include bacteria, yeast, fungi, and animal, plant, fish and insect cells, as well as other biological materials.

The other area of major importance in bioreactor design involves the bioreaction parameters, including:

1. Controlled temperature.
2. Optimum pH.
3. Sufficient substrate (usually a carbon source), such as sugars, proteins and fats.
4. Water availability.
5. Salts for nutrition.
6. Vitamins
7. Oxygen (for aerobic processes).
8. Gas evolution and product and by-product removal.

In addition to controlling these, the bioreactor must be designed to both promote formation of the optimal morphology of the organism and to eliminate or reduce contamination by unwanted organisms or mutation of the organism.

8.3.10 Process parameters of anaerobic bioreactor

Degradation of unwanted components/contaminants in the anaerobic treatment depends on several parameters. The main parameters are related to reactor operating conditions [temperature, pH, Organic Loading Rate (OLR), HRT, SRT, and upflow velocity] and influent characteristics such as particle size distribution. These parameters and their effects are discussed in the following paragraphs.

Temperature

Temperature an important physical characteristic that affects the acceptability of water as well as water chemistry and water treatment. Anaerobic bacteria are classified into 'temperature classes' on the basis of the optimum temperature; the mesophiles survive in mesophilic temperature around 30°C to 40°C, while thermophiles are considered the first micro-organism existing at thermophilic temperature around 50°C to 65°C. Temperature even affects all wastewater treatment processes to some degree, for example: (i) biological waste treatment: cold water reduces the efficiency of high-rate trickling filters by approximately 30%; low temperature inhibits nitrification (by 75% from 30°C to 10°C) more than BOD (biological oxygen demand) removal, (ii) digestion: the minimum solid retention time varies from 2 days at 35°C to 10 days at 20°C; the heat requirement of the digester depends on outside temperature, (iii) microbial growth: temperature affected the richness and diversity of microbial populations.

Temperature affects particle removal through influencing the wastewater viscosity and conversion of organic matter. Because water viscosity is physically coupled to temperature, changes in temperature can influence the activity of microscopic organisms through both physiological and physical means. Increasing the wastewater temperature leads to enhancing mixing by reducing viscosity, more hydraulic turbulence in a reactor, enhanceing the sedimentation, and better entrapment and adsorption due to contact between sludge and solids, and more biogas will be produced. A sudden temperature changes can lead to a change in the physical and chemical properties of the wastewater, which can considerably affect the design and operation of the treatment system.

Low temperatures

Generally temperature has a significant effect on the intracellular and extracellular environment of bacteria, and it also acts as an accelerator of the conversion processes. At low temperatures the startup period may take longer, but it can be successfully accomplished by inoculating the reactor with digested sludge. Anaerobic treatment of raw domestic sewage (COD = 500–700 gm^{-3}) on different UASB reactors can be accomplished at 12–18°C (HRTs of 7–12 h with total COD and BOD removal efficiencies of 40–60% and 50–70%, respectively). And also the possibility of applying anaerobic digestion of dilute dairy waste water at 10°C at OLRs up to 2 kg COD m^{-3}d^{-1} can gain over 84% of OD removal efficiency.

High temperatures

The rates of reaction proceed much faster at higher temperatures, therefore producing more efficient operation and smaller tank sizes. And also treatment proceeds much more rapidly at thermophilic temperatures (around 50°C to 65°C), and the digestion under high temperature conditions offers many advantages such as higher metabolic rates, consequently higher specific growth rates, but frequently also higher death rates as compared to mesophilic bacteria, but also the additional heat required to maintain such temperatures may offset the advantage obtained. Then, most treatment systems are designed to operate in the mesophilic range or lower.

pH

pH is an expression of the intensity of the basic or acid condition of a liquid, a measure of the acidity of a solution. Commonly, methanogens in wastewater treatment systems are most active in the neutral pH range (7.0). The concentration range suitable for most organisms is 6.0–9.0; beyond this range, digestion can proceed, but with less efficiency. The biomass inhibited at pH 9 was able to regain activities after adjusting the pH to neutrality, but that inhibited at pH 5 was not. At acidic conditions produced can become quite toxic to the methane bacteria. For this reason, it is important that the pH is not allowed to drop below 6.2 for a significant period of time. Because this parameter is very important, thus the system needs to control the pH. When the methane gas production stabilises, the pH remains between 7.2 and 8.2.

McCarty reported that an optimum pH range of anaerobic treatment is about 7.0 to 7.2, but it can proceed quite well with a pH varying from about 6.6 to 7.6.

8.3.11 Hydraulic retention time (HRT)

HRT also known as hydraulic residence time is a measure of the average length of time that a soluble compound remains in a constructed bioreactor. Hydraulic retention time is the volume of the aeration tank divided by the influent flow rate: where, HRT is hydraulic retention time (d) and usually expressed in hours (or sometimes days), we is the volume of aeration tank or reactor volume (m^3), and is the influent flow rate (m^3/d).

Generally HRT is a good operational parameter that is easy to control and also a macroconceptual time for the organic material to stay in the reactor. In bioreaction engineering studies, the reverse of HRT is defined as dilution rate, for which if it is bigger than the growth rate of microbial cells in the reactor, the microbe will be washed out, and otherwise the microbe will be accumulated in the reactor. Either of these situations may result in the breakdown of the biological process happening in the reactor.

8.3.12 Organic loading rate (OLR)

At the industrial scale a range of high-rate anaerobic fluidised-bed (AFB) reactors such as upflow anaerobic sludge blanket (UASB), upflow-staged sludge bed (USSB), expanded granular sludge bed (EGSB), internal circulation (IC), and inverse anaerobic fluidised bed (IAFB) reactors can bear very high loading rates, up to 40 kg COD/($m^3 \cdot d$). The organic loading rate (OLR) and volumetric biogas production (VBP) of the spiral automatic circulation (SPAC) reactor in our laboratory could reach up to 306 kg COD/($m^3 \cdot d$). Several authors reported that up to a certain limit, the treatment efficiency of complex wastewaters, for example, potato maise, slaughterhouse, in high rate anaerobic reactors increases with increase in OLR. A further increase in OLR will lead to operational problems like sludge bed flotation and excessive foaming at the gas-liquid interface in the gas-liquid-solid (GLS) separator, as well as accumulation of undigested ingredients.

As a result, the treatment efficiency deteriorates. Also accumulation of biogas in the sludge bed was noticed, forming stable gas pockets that lead to incidental lifting of parts of the bed and a pulse-like eruption of the gas from this zone. The OLR can be varied by changing the influent concentration and by changing the flow rate.

Thus, implies changing the HRT and by changing the flow rate, under these conditions OLR can be expressed in the following form:

$$V = \frac{Q \times C}{OLR}$$

where, V   = Volume of reactor (m^3)

     Q   = Flow rate (m^3/d)

     C   = COD (kg COD/m^3)

   OLR = Organic loading rate (kg COD/m^3/d)

When the solids removal efficiency in upflow reactors is related to the OLR, it becomes crucial to distinguish between these parameters. For this reason, OLR is an inadequate design parameter to assure good performance of anaerobic reactors.

8.3.13   Sludge retention time (SRT)

SRT is known to be the key parameter affecting biochemical and physical properties of sludge. The success of UASB reactors is mainly dependent on the sludge retention time (SRT), which is the key factor determining the ultimate amount of hydrolysis and methanogenesis in a UASB system at certain temperature conditions. The SRT should be long enough to provide sufficient methanogenic activity at the prevailing conditions. The SRT is determined by the loading rate, the fraction of suspended solid (SS) in the influent, the removal of SS in the sludge bed, and the characteristics of the SS (biodegradability, composition, etc.).

Methanogenesis starts at SRT between 5 and 15 days at 25°C and between 30 and 50 days at 15°C, the maximum methanogenesis found at 25°C amounted to 51% and 25% at 15°C. Maximum hydrolysis occurs at 75 days SRT and amounted to 50% at 25°C and 24% at 15°C. The SRT and temperature have a significant influence on the hydrolysis of proteins, carbohydrates, and lipids. The most substantial portion of the digestion of proteins, carbohydrates, and lipids occurs within the first 15 and 10 days at process temperatures of 25°C and 35°C, respectively.

Upflow velocity

The upflow velocity is one of the main factors affecting the efficiency of upflow reactors. An increase in upflow velocity from 1.6 to 3.2 m/h resulted in a relatively small loss in SS removal efficiency, from 55% to nearly 50%, which indicates the role of adsorption and entrapment.

Particle size distribution

The particle-size distribution (PSD) of a powder, granular material, or particles dispersed in fluid is a list of values or a mathematical function that defines the relative amount, typically by mass, of particles present according to size. The effluent quality from classical filters is highly related to the specific size of the filtering media. Most studies indicate that smaller media size gives more efficient removal.

Inner components of anaerobic bioreactor

The inner components play an important role in enhancing OLR of the reactor, help in improving the quality of fluidisation, separate the gas bubble from the sludge granules, and therefore enhance the treatment efficiency and so on. The inner components in a biological fluidised bed reactor can be divided into the transverse inner components, longitudinal inner components, and biofilm-packing material.

Effluent Treatment

9.1 Introduction

The type and nature of any product depends upon medium or substrate used in production process. Based on type of the medium used, the range of waste materials are produced accordingly. Thus, treatment methods to be applied depends upon characteristics of waste and various factors like physical state of the effluent, degree of hazard of pollutant, chemical complexity of the effluent and so on. The level of pollution is increasing day by day due to increased population, increased industrial development, awareness on damages caused by pollution causing industrial units in order to treat them before disposal into environment. Effluents from production units contain many hazardous toxicants that adversily affect the flora and fauna by interacting with the microbes and drastically decreasing the dissolved oxygen levels of that area. Effluent can be treated using biological, physical and chemical methods. Industrial effluent can be treated by oxidative ponds, spray irrigation, well disposal, and incineration, etc.

Filtration and sedimentation are major processes in physical treatment of effluent. Chemical treatment process done by flocculation, coagulation, aggregation methods which are done by addition of various flocculants and coagulants like alum, ferric sulphide, calcium hydroxide, etc. In biological treatment, trickling filters, biologically aerated filters, rotating biological contractors, activated sludge process come with aerobic way and anaerobic digesters, anaerobic filters, up-flow anaerobic sludge blankets come with anaerobic treatment processes.

9.2 Aerobic and anaerobic treatment

Biological treatment consists of aerobic and anaerobic processes. It is an important part of any wastewater treatment plant. This method can be used to treat wastewater from either municipality or industrial waste containing soluble organic impurities or a mix of the two types of wastewater sources. There is economic advantage of biological treatment over other treatment processes like chemical oxidation, thermal oxidation, etc. Biological treatment using aerobic activated sludge process has been in practice for well over a century.

Aerobic treatment process occurs in the presence of air and utilise aerobic micro-organisms which use molecular/free oxygen to assimilate organic impurities, i.e., convert them in to carbon dioxide, water and biomass. The anaerobic treatment process takes place in the absence of air by those micro-organisms, called anaerobes which do not require air (molecular/free oxygen) to assimilate organic impurities. The end products of anaerobic treatment are methane and carbon dioxide gas and biomass.

9.2.1   Steps involved in aerobic treatment process

Aerobic biological treatment is normally used for treatment of industrial effluent for their organic impurities. The major process used worldwide is activated sludge process. It is an aerobic biological process that utilises micro-organisms such as bacteria, and protozoa for the decomposition of organic matter. This process involves the production of biomass of micro-organisms which effectively stabilise the organic content of wastes in presence of oxygen. This biomass is known as activated biomass which convert organic matter to carbon dioxide and water which are safe for disposal in the environment. This is effectively achieved by a series of metabolic reactions carried out by the micro-organisms. Figure 9.1 shows steps of aerobic treatment of effluent.

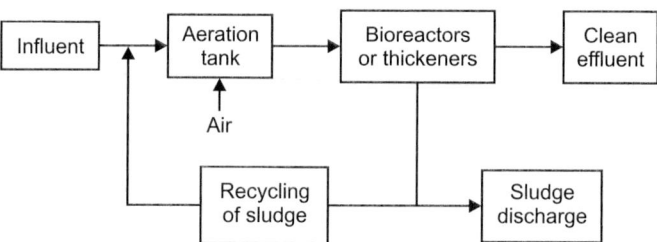

Figure 9.1: Steps of aerobic treatment of effluent.

Aerobic treatment can be used for waste treatment of various industries like sugar, soap, solvent and oil extraction industries, edible oil refineries, food, dairy, soft drink bottling, breweries, starch, pesticides and bulk drug pharmaceutical industries, chemical and mining industries, etc. This can also be used for sewage treatment and common industrial wastewater treatment.

9.2.2   Steps involved in anaerobic treatment process

Anaerobic treatment is a biological wastewater treatment process which is used for treatment and reduction of organic wastes such as organic sludge or concentrated organic industrial waste. Organic solids are major components of industrial waste. The quantity of organic solids are decreased in the sludge after anaerobic treatment process and this lead to easier disposal of waste due to less volume. During this treatment process, consortia of microbes convert organic matter in to biogas (methane) which can be used as a clean energy source. Steps of anaerobic treatment of effluent are shown in Fig. 9.2.

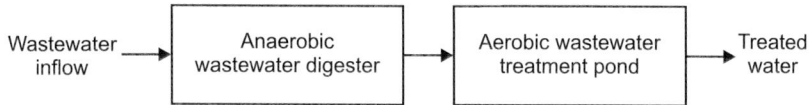

Figure 9.2: Steps of anaerobic treatment of effluent.

Anaerobic digestion process is a natural process that is effectively utilised to treat waste. This digestion occurs in anaerobic bioreactor or digesters, in which the anaerobic bacteria are maintained in high concentrations, thus increasing the effective sludge retention time. This process also results other by-products those are biogas (capable of providing heat) and compost for soil improvement.

Digests are commonly used for sewage, municipal wastewater or industrial wastewater treatment. They significantly help improve the quality of effluent being released into the environment and are a major component in water recycling from high-organic-load wastewater. In comparison to aerobic treatment, anaerobic biological treatment plants is used to treat high-strength wastewater to a level that will permit discharge to a municipal sewer system.

Anaerobic digestion process takes place in three steps or stages. The first stage involves liquification of solid material in the sludge. This process is called hydrolysis. The second stage is rapid and involves digestion of the soluble solids that resulted from the previous stage. This process is carried out by acids producing anaerobic bacteria. The microbes involved in this stage are facultative anerobes, are heterotrophic and found in soil. They belong to diverse genera such as *Escherichia, Flavobacterium, Alcaligenes, Aerobacter, Pseudomonas*, etc., and can function in a large pH range. Final stage is called the gasification stage. In this stage, the organic acid produced in the previous stage is used by certain microbes as substrate and methane and carbon dioxide gases are produced. This stage is slower and is also called methanogenesis as it leads to production of methane. Microbes involved in this process are also anaerobic and belong to the *Methanococcus, Methanobacterium,* and *Methanoscarcina*genera.

9.2.3   Steps involved in sewage treatment process

Sewage is wastewater carrying domestic wastes, agricultural wastes or overland flow. This is carried in sewers or drains. Sewage contains both organic and inorganic wastes, it also contains grit, solids, oil and grease. Sewage is treated in sewage treatment plants (Fig. 9.3) to make it suitable for further disposal. Sewage treatment process involves three sequential treatment steps these include primary, secondary and tertiary treatment. Wastewater treated in sewage treatment plants can be used to recharge ground water and for agricultural purposes. Treatment of sewage can be done by following steps: pre-treatment, primary treatment, secondary treatment and tertiary treatment procedures involved in treating sewage. This treatment is done by analysing the physical, chemical and biological contaminants present in sewage coming from a particular source. Wastewater coming from industry as effluent is passing through screening unit to separate out larger components under primary treatment, then after grit chamber to sediment settalable grits. Wastewater coming from grit chamber is pass through primary settling tank or clarifier, in this step sludge settle down at bottom to reduce the volume. In secondary treatment, wastewater is aerated to increase dissolve oxygen and then treated in biological reactors. After treatment in reactor, water goes to secondary clarifier to settle sludge. Some part of sludge (activated sludge) is recycled to reactor to maintain microbial count. Water from secondary clarifier/tank is chlorinated to polish the treated water. Sludge is thicked/concentrated and digested in anaerobic digester and then disposal of sludge takes place.

9.2.4 Steps involved in treatment process of sugar industry effluent

The sugarcane received from the field contains about 70% moisture on an average. Majority of this water has to be discharged as factory wastewater. The effluent characteristics from a typical sugar plant are presented in Table 9.1

Table 9.1: Characteristics of wastewater from sugar mill.

Parameter	Concentration
BOD	1250 mg/l
COD	2250 mg/l
pH	5–7
Temperature	25 to 35°C
Total suspended solids	620 mg/l
Total dissolved solids	2020 mg/l
Total volatile solids	1320 mg/l
Oil and grease	65 mg/l
Sulphates	500 mg/l
Phosphorus	60 mg/l
Calcium	185 mg/l

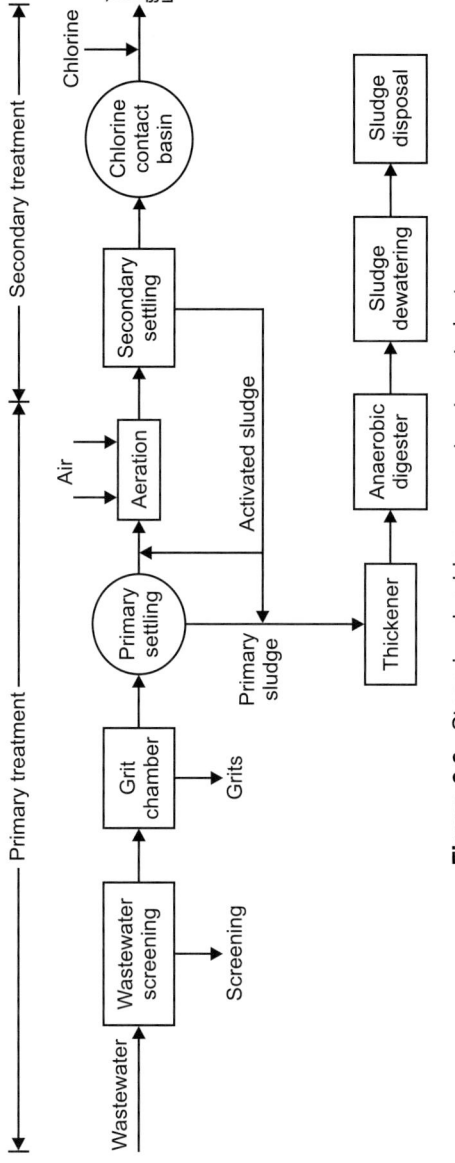

Figure 9.3: Steps involved in sewage treatment plant.

The pollution load of sugar mills can also be reduced if we could use advance technological practices with in the plant. Judicious use of water in various plant practices, and its recycle, wherever practicable, will reduce the volume of waste to a great extent. Volume of mill house waste can be reduced by recycling the water used for splashing. Figure 9.4 shows treatment steps for sugar mill effluent waste.

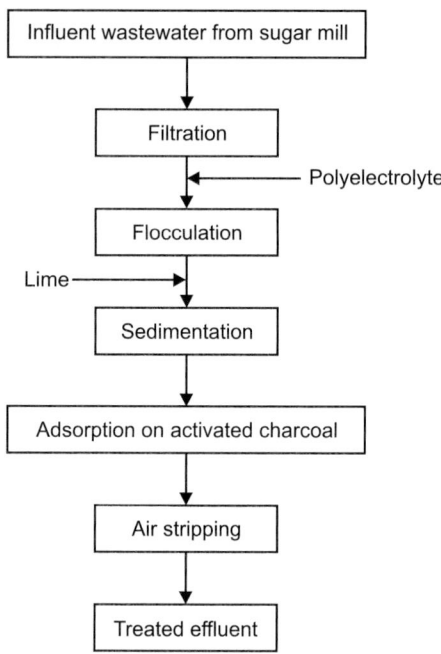

Figure 9.4: Treatment steps for sugar mill effluent waste.

Dry cleaning of floors or floor washings using controlled quantity of water will also reduce the volume of waste to a certain extent. The organic load of the waste can only be reduced by a proper control of the operations. Overloading of the evaporators and the vacuum pans and the extensive boiling of the syrup lead to a loss of sugar through condenser water, this in turn increases both volume and strength of the waste effluent.

Wastewater as influent is passing through filtration unit to separate out separable components as physical treatment. In next step, this wastewater is floculated with treatment of polyelectrolyte. Flocs of waste are treated with lime and settle down in sedimentation step. For adsorption step, activated charcoal can be used as adsorbent, followed by air stripping to increase dissolved oxygen and remove fouling smell from treated water.

9.2.5   Steps involved in treatment process of vegetable oil industry effluent

Vegetable oil or refined oil processing industry is a major source of environmental pollution in developing countries. The waste coming out from oil refinery creates serious environmental problem to aquatic life due to its high organic content. In vegetable oil industry, wastewater mainly comes from the degumming, deacidification, deodourisation and neutralisation steps. In the neutralisation step sodium salts of free fatty acids and sulphuric acid generates highly acidic and oily wastewaters. Effluent characteristics generated by oil processing industry, depends largely on the type of oil processed. Effluent is high in COD, oil and grease, sulphate and phosphate content, resulting in both high inorganic as well as organic loading of the relevant wastewater treatment. Treatment steps for vegetable oil industry effluent are shown in Fig. 9.5.

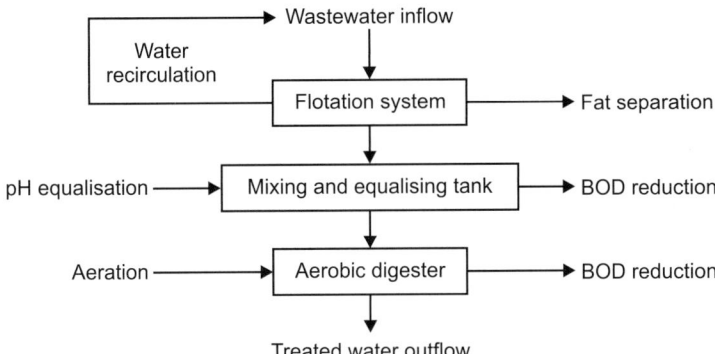

Figure 9.5: Treatment steps for vegetable oil industry effluent.

Vegetable oil industry effluent contains oil and fat coming from different parts of processing unit. It is important to remove fat for easy digestion by microbes. For this purpose, a flotation system is used to separate fat present in effluent followed by recirculation of water. After separation of fat, pH of wastewater is maintained using equalisation tank. In this step BOD reduction is happening. This treated water is pumped in to aerobic digester for further BOD reduction and treatment to get treated water, which can be used for different purposes.

9.2.6   Steps involved in treatment process of potato processing industry effluent

The potato processing industry generates large quantities of organic wastes. Treatment of this industrial effluent is targeted to remove organic materials from discharge. Proper treatment of potato processing wastewaters is necessary to minimise their undesirable impact on the environment.

The type of processing unit depends upon the product selection, for example, potato chips, frozen French fries and other frozen food, dehydrated mashed potatoes, dehydrated diced potatoes, potato flake, potato starch, potato flour, canned white potatoes, prepeeled potatoes, and so on. The major processes in all products are storage, washing, peeling, trimming, slicing, blanching, cooking, drying, etc. There is increasing demand for quality improvement of water resources in parallel with the demand for better finished products. These requirements have obliged the potato industry to develop methods for providing effective removal of settlable and dissolved solids from potato processing wastewater, in order to meet national water quality limits. In addition, improvement and research have been devoted to the reduction of wastes and utilisation of recovered wastes as by-products.

Because potato processing wastewater contains high concentrations of biodegradable components such as starch and proteins, in addition to high concentrations of Chemical Oxygen Demand (COD), Total Suspended Solids (TSS) and Total Kjeldahl Nitrogen (TKN), the potato processing industry presents potentially serious water pollution problems. An average-sized potato processing plant producing French fries and dehydrated potatoes can create a waste load equivalent to that of a city of 200,000 people. About 230 million litres of water are required to process 13,600 T of potatoes. This equals about 17 L of waste for every kilogram of potatoes produced. Raw potato processing wastewaters can contain up to 10,000 mg/l COD. Total suspended solids and volatile suspended solids can also reach 9700 and 9500 mg/l, respectively. Wastewater composition from potato processing plant depends on the processing method, to a large extent.

In general, the following steps are applied in potato processing: washing the raw potatoes; peeling, which includes washing to remove softened tissue; trimming to remove defective portions; shaping, washing, and separation; final processing or preservation; and packaging. Amount of different components of potato waste is given in Table 9.2.

Table 9.2: Percentage of components in potato waste.

Component	Amount (%)
Carbon as C	42.00
Total phosphorus as P	0.040
Total organic nitrogen as N	1.000
Volatile solid	95.2
Total sulphur as S	0.080

Following are the steps involved in the treatment of waste generated during above mentioned potato processing steps in potato processing industry are shown in Fig. 9.6.

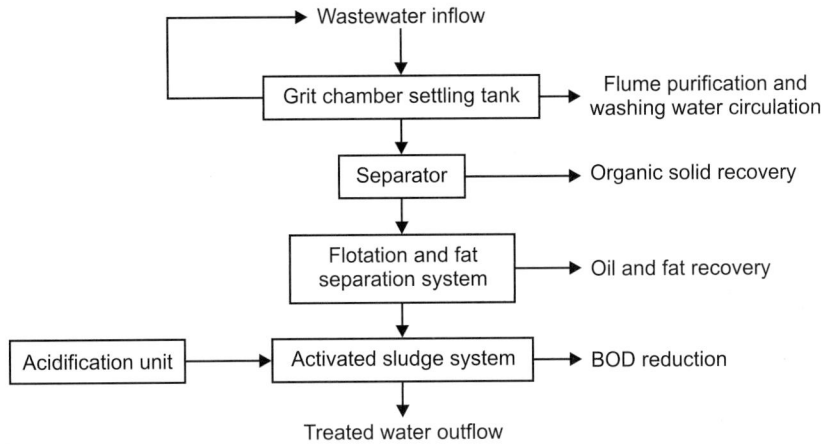

Figure 9.6: Steps involved in waste treatment process in potato processing unit.

First step of treatment process is physical treatment in which solid components settled down in grit chamber settling tank. After this organic solids are recovered using separator. Oil and fat content present in effluent is separated by flotation and fat separation system as presence of oil and fat will reduce the growth of micro-organisms. This waste is now pumped in to activated sludge reactor for further treatment and BOD reduction.

9.2.7   Steps involved in treatment process of dairy industry effluent

The dairy industry effluent is the largest source of food processing wastewater. Various steps in the milk processing plant generate vast amount of waste, including production, processing, packaging, transportation, storage, distribution, and marketing, impact the environment.

This is highly diversified nature of industry, in which various product processing, handling, and packaging operations create wastes of different quality and quantity. If produced waste is not treated properly, it could lead to increased disposal and severe pollution problems. Steps involved in dairy waste treatment process are shown in Fig. 9.7.

Wastes generated from the dairy industry contain high concentrations of organic material such as proteins, carbohydrates, and lipids, high concentrations of suspended solids, high biological oxygen demand (BOD) and chemical

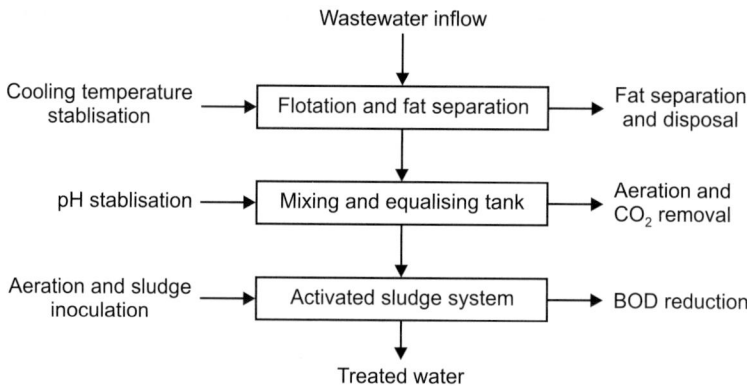

Figure 9.7: Steps involved in dairy waste treatment process.

oxygen demand (COD), high nitrogen concentrations, high suspended oil and/ or grease contents. BOD and COD values of different type of milk processing waste is given in Table 9.3.

Table 9.3: BOD and COD values for typical dairy products and domestic sewage.

Product	BOD₅ (mg/l)	COD(mg/l)
Skim milk	90,000	145,000
Whole milk	114,000	182,000
Cream	400,000	747,000
Butter milk	60,000	135,000
Whey	44,000	65,000
Domestic sewage	350	510

Effluent coming from dairy industry may be divided into three major categories:

1. Processing wastewater: This type of effluent include water used in the cooling and heating processes.

2. Cleaning wastewater: This effluent is mainly coming from the cleaning of equipment that has been in contact with milk or milk products, spillage of milk and milk products, whey, pressings and brines.

3. Sanitary wastewater: This is normally piped directly to a sewage works.

Following are the steps involved in the treatment of waste generated during milk processing in milk processing unit.

Wastewater coming from different part of processing units of plant, contains fat. This fat containing effluent is treated in fat separator to separate it out followed by mixing and pH stabilisation to maintain pH required for micro-organisms in next step. In further step wastewater coming from equalisation tank is treated in activated sludge process, in which complex organic matter is digested by micro-organism to reduce BOD.

9.2.8   Steps involved in distillery waste treatment

In India bulk of the alcohol is being produced from sugar cane molasses. Molasses is a thick viscous by-product of the sugar industry which is acidic in nature, rich in salts, dark brown in colour and it also contains sugar which could not be crystallised. Distillery waste treatment steps are shown in Fig. 9.8.

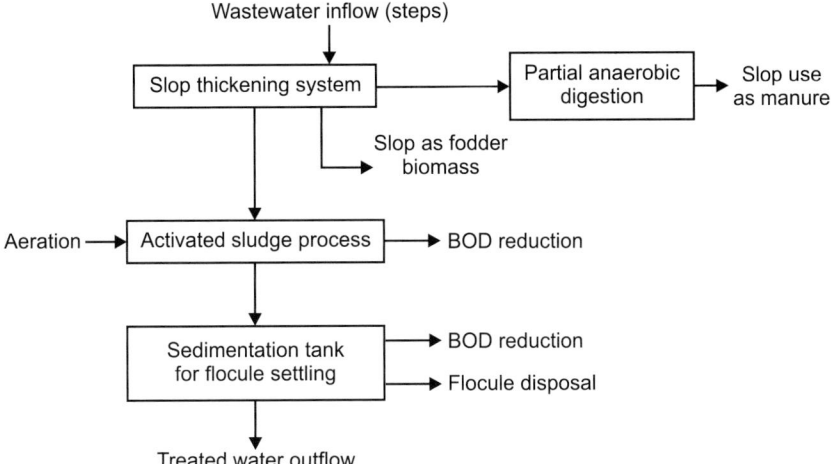

Figure 9.8: Distillery waste treatment steps.

The liquid wastes from distillery can mainly be divided into three category.

1. Spent wash: It is generated from the separation (centrifuge) and distillation process.

2. Cleaning water: It is generated from the different plant components, i.e., fermenters, distillation columns, floors.

3. Refrigeration water: It is generated from cooling after distillation.

Characteristics of distillery wastewater is given in Table 9.4. wastewater from distillery unit is dark brown and containing high BOD and COD values. This wastewater is known as slop. Thickening of wastewater is required for anaerobic digestion. Influent is pass through slop thickening system and slop produced can be used as fodder biomass to animals. In next step water is treated in activated sludge reactor in which micro-organisms will digest organic components of waste and thus BOD is reduced.

Table 9.4: Characteristics of distillery wastewater.

Parameter	Range
Colour	Brown to dark brown
pH	4.5 to 5.5
Temperature	72°C to 80°C
Total suspended solids (mg/l)	12500 to 15000
Total dissolved solids (mg/l)	46000 to 74000
BOD (mg/l)	32000 to 48000
COD (mg/l)	85000 to 10000

After activated sludge process, water transfer to sedimentation tank where flocules is settled and BOD is reduced further and we get treated water.

Bioremediation

10.1 Introduction

Bioremediation is the process of removal of complex material by degrading environmental pollutants using living micro-organisms. It is a method to remove out pollutants from the environment, restoring contaminated sites and preventing future pollution. Bioremediation activity depends on natural capacity of micro-organisms to degrade organic compounds. This capacity could be improved by providing optimum growth conditions to micro-organism or by applying the genetically modified micro-organisms (GMMs). This technology has been used to eradicate environmentally hazardous chemicals and detoxify them into nontoxic forms. Micro-organisms play important role in this toxic removal technology, several members of microbial group like algae, fungi and bacteria are known to solubilise, transport and deposit the metals, and detoxify dyes and complex chemicals. The toxic waste materials are present in vapour, liquid or solid phases; therefore, bioremediation technology varies depending upon nature of toxic material.

10.2 Principles of bioremediation and biodegradation

10.2.1 Biodegradation

Biodegradation is the process in which micro-organisms reduce complex organic pollutants into smaller chemical compounds. Most of the biodegradable matters are usually organic, and are generally derivatives of plant and animal matter. The micro-organisms take this matter as food material and convert them to smaller compounds by enzymatic or metabolic processes.

10.2.2 Type of biodegradation

Biomineralisation

Biodegradation is basically categories in to two type. The first category is called as biomineralisation. Mineralisation is the process in which micro-organisms feed on organic compounds and by a chemical process, reduce them to inorganic material such as water, carbon dioxide, and other such inorganic compounds. In mineralisation process total degradation of the organic matter occurs.

Biotransformation

The second category of bioremediation is called biotransformation. Biotransformation essentially differs from mineralisation. In biotransformation process, organic matter is not degraded totally. Some part of it is degraded and another part is converted into other smaller chain organic compounds.

The converted smaller chain organic compounds may be either toxic or non toxic. In the case of the pesticide dichloro diphenyl trichloroethane (DDT), the biotransformation yields more toxic compound. Another example of biotransformation is the fermentation process, in which sugar, a long chain organic compound, is transformed into ethanol.

Relative biodegradability of different compounds: Order of biodegradation is as follows from simple to complex compounds.

Simple hydrocarbons and petroleum fuels $\rightarrow$ Aeromatic hydrocarbon $\rightarrow$ Alcohol and esters $\rightarrow$ Nitrobenzenes $\rightarrow$ Clorinated hydrocarbons $\rightarrow$ Pesticides

Bioremediation utilise abilities of micro-organisms for degradation of toxic polluants. These include natural attenuation, bioaugmentation or biostimulation. Bioremediation may be enhanced by engineered techniques, either by addition of selected micro-organisms or by stimulation, where nutrients are added for this purpose. Genetic engineering is also used to improve the biodegradation capabilities of micro-organisms. There are several factors affecting the efficiency of bioremediation process and risks associated to the use of genetically modified micro-organisms. Biodegradation abilities and different factors responsible for microbial action are presented in Fig. 10.1.

Role of micro-organisms in biodegradation of pollutants

Biodegradation is the natural way of recycling wastes, or breaking down organic matter into simple nutrients that can be used and reused by other organisms. In the microbiological sense, 'biodegradation' means degradation of all organic materials by bacteria, yeast and fungi, and possibly other organisms.

Bioremediation and biotransformation methods are naturally occurring, microbial catabolic diversity to degrade, transform or accumulate a huge range of compounds including hydrocarbons, polychlorinated biphenyls, polyaromatic hydrocarbons, radionuclides and metals.

Some biodegradable pollutants

Due to industrial development to produce a range of products, highly toxic organic compounds have been synthesised and released into the environment for direct or indirect application over a long period of time. These products are different fuels, polychlorinated biphenyls, polycyclic aromatic hydrocarbons,

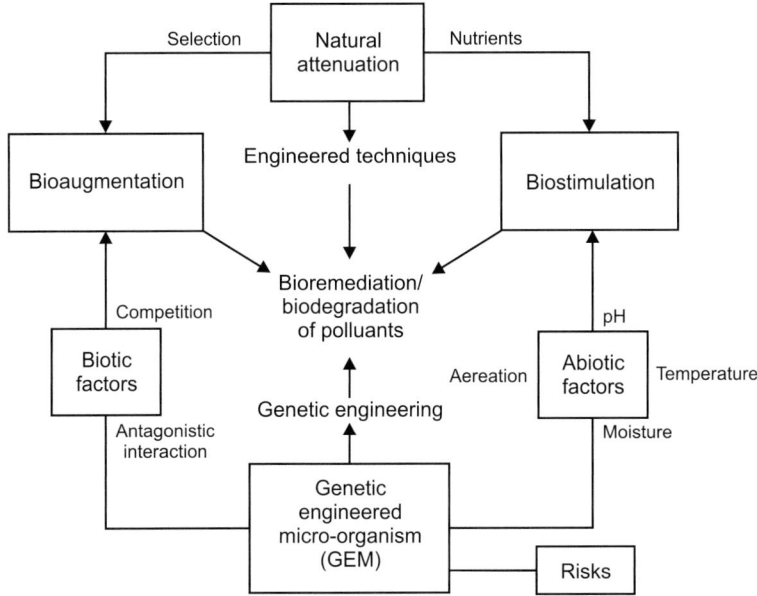

Figure 10.1: Biodegradation ability of micro-organism and affecting factors.

pesticides and dyes. There are some other synthetic chemicals like radionuclides and metals those are not biodegradable using native flora compared with the naturally occurring organic compounds that are easily degraded in the natural environment. Hydrocarbons, polycyclic aromatic hydrocarbons, polychlorinated biphenyls, pesticides, dyes, radionuclides, heavy metals are categorise as biodegradable pollutants.

10.3   Concept and requirement of bioremediation

10.3.1   Type of bioremediation

On the basis of removal and transportation of wastes for treatment, basically there are two methods of bioremediation:

1. *In situ* bioremediation.
2. *Ex situ* bioremediation.

In situ bioremediation

In situ bioremediation is the cleaning up approach where micro-organisms feed on contaminants and dissolve contaminants for biotransformation. Biotransformation is a very complex process. Minimal site disruption, simultaneous treatment of contaminated soil and ground water, minimal exposure of public, site personnel, and low costs are potential advantages of *in situ* bioremediation method.

Limitations of in situ bioremediation: Following are limitations of *in situ* bioremediation.

1. Time consuming method as compared to other remedial methods.
2. Seasonal variation of microbial activity resulting from direct exposure to prevailing environmental factors, and lack of control of these factors.
3. Problematic utilisation of treatment additives as nutrients, surfactants and oxygen. The micro-organisms act well only when the waste materials help them to generate more cells. When the native micro-organisms lack biodegradation capacity, genetically engineered micro-organisms may be added to the site during *in situ* bioremediation.

There are two types of *in situ* bioremediation, intrinsic and engineered *in situ* bioremediation.

Intrinsic in situ bioremediation

Intrinsic bioremediation is conversion of environmental pollutants into the harmless forms through the natural capabilities of naturally occurring microbial population. There is increasing interest on intrinsic bioremediation for control of all or some of the contamination at waste sites. The inherent capacity of micro-organisms to degrade the contaminants should be analysed and tested at laboratory and in field trails before use for intrinsic bioremediation. There are several conditions of site that favour intrinsic bioremediation. These conditions are ground water flow throughout the year, carbonate minerals to buffer acidity produced during biodegradation, supply of electron acceptors and nutrients for microbial growth and absence of toxic compounds. The other environmental factors such as pH, concentration, temperature and nutrient availability determine whether or not biotransformation takes place. Presence of metals such as Hg, Pb, As and cyanide at toxic concentration can create problem for microbial growth during bioremediation of that waste. Degradation of pollutants using bacteria in ground water is dependent on the type and concentration of compounds, electron acceptor and duration of bacteria exposed to contamination. Therefore, ability of bacteria used to degrade contaminants must be determined in laboratory by microbial studies before use.

Engineered/accelerated in situ bioremediation

Intrinsic bioremediation is giving good results at some places, but it is slow process due to poor availability and growth of micro-organisms, limited ability of electron acceptor and nutrients, cold temperature and high concentration of contaminants. When site conditions are not matching with microbial growth requirement, in this case bioremediation requires engineered systems to supply materials that stimulate micro-organisms growth.

Engineered *in situ* bioremediation accelerates the desired biodegradation reactions by encouraging growth of more micro-organisms under optimum physico-chemical growth conditions. Oxygen and electron acceptors (e.g., NO_3^{1-} and SO_4^{2-}) and nutrients (e.g., nitrogen and phosphorus) promote microbial growth in surface shown in Fig. 10.2.

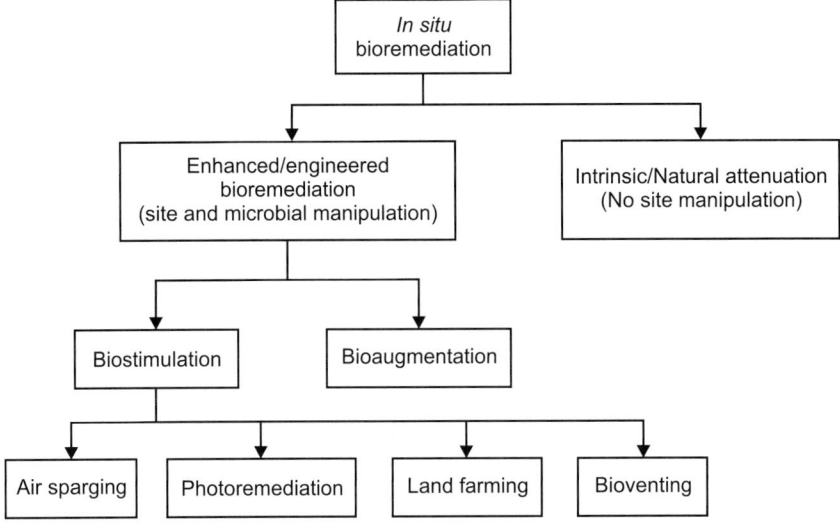

Figure 10.2: *In situ* bioremediation.

Ex situ bioremediation

Ex situ bioremediation involves removal of waste materials and their collection from the contaminated site or place to facilitate microbial degradation. *Ex situ* bioremediation technology includes most of disadvantages and limitations as it is costly process due to costs associated with solid handling process, e.g., excavation, screening and fractionation, mixing, homogenising and final disposal. Contaminated material may be in liquid or solid form.

On the basis of phases of contaminated materials under treatment *ex situ* bioremediation is classified into two part as per following :

1. Solid-phase system (including land treatment and soil piles), i.e., composting.
2. Slurry-phase systems (involving treatment of solid-liquid suspensions in bioreactors).

Solid-phase treatment: Solid-phase system includes organic wastes which is in solid form (e.g., leaves, animal manures and agricultural wastes), and problematic wastes (e.g., domestic and industrial wastes, sewage sludge and municipal solid wastes). The traditional clean-up practice involves the processing of the organic materials and production of composts which may be used as soil conditioning.

Composting: Composting is a self-heating, substrate-dense, managed microbial degradation system used to digest organic matter. This is solid-phase biological treatment technology which is suitable to the treatment of large amount of contaminated solid materials.

It has been seen that many hazardous compounds are nondegradable using micro-organisms due to complex chemical structure, toxicity and compound concentration that do not support to microbial growth. Microbial growth is also affected by other factors such as moisture, pH, inorganic nutrients and particle size. During composting of hazardous wastes, micro-organisms requires proper amount of supplements for support of microbial self-heating. Arrangement in open composting is presented in Fig. 10.3.

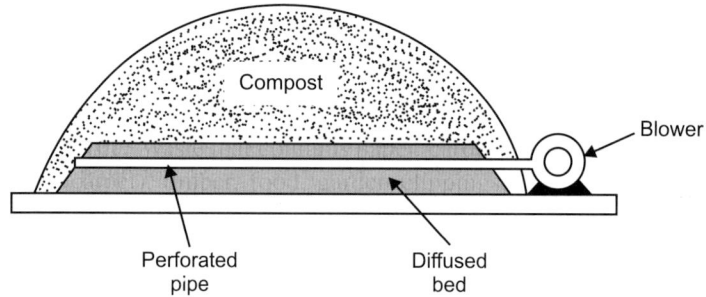

Figure 10.3: Open composting

The aliphatic, aromatic hydrocarbons and certain halogenated compounds considered as hazardous compounds disappear through composting process. Volatilisation, assimilation, adsorption, polymerisation and leaching are the possible steps leading to disappearance of hazardous compounds present as contaminants.

Composting can be done in open system, i.e., land treatment, and in closed system also. The *open land system* can be inexpensive treatment method, but limitation is the control of temperature fluctuation from summer to winter. Therefore, rate of biodegradation of waste materials decreases. Another limitation is land treatment system which becomes oxygen limited, depending on amount of substrate, depth of waste, application, etc. The efficiency of open treatment system can be increased by passing air through blower. This approach is referred to as *engineered soil piles* and *forced aeration treatment*. The *closed treatment system* is preferred over the open land treatment system because controlled air is supplied to maintain the microbial activity. As a result of microbial growth and volatilisation of hazardous compounds, internal temperature gradually rises. Therefore, use of blowers for air circulation and exhaust for removal of toxic volatiles are set up in closed treatment system (Fig. 10.4). Ventilators supply oxygen and remove heat through evaporation of water.

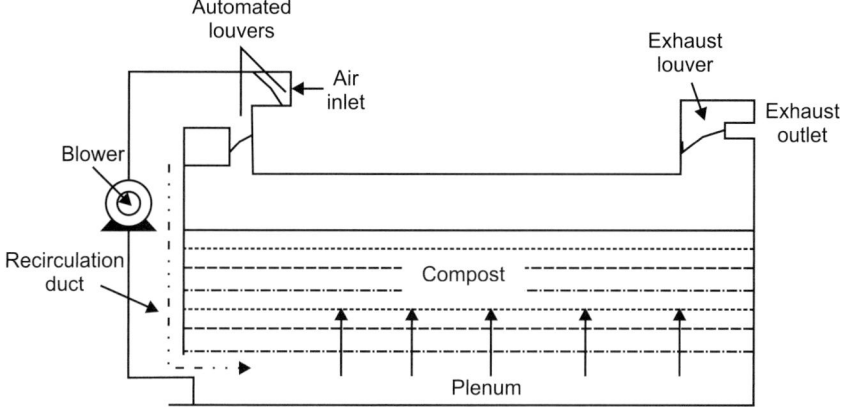

Figure 10.4: Closed composting.

Composting process

Composting is a solid-phase biological treatment therefore target compounds must be either solid or a liquid associated with a solid matrix. The hazardous compounds should be biologically transformed. To do this, the waste material should be pretreated or prepared so that biological treatment potential should maximise. This is done by adjustment of several physical, chemical and biological factors (Fig. 10.5). The hazardous wastes must be solubilised so that they may be available to micro-organisms very easily. The hazardous compounds and soil organic matters act as source of carbon and energy for micro-organisms. Enzymes secreted by micro-organisms during growth phase are used to degrade toxic compounds. Availaility of water, O_2, inorganic nutrients and pH, increase the rate of decomposition of hazardous compounds.

If there is low substrate-density or site-specific conditions, analogue or non-analogue, non-hazardous carbon sources that can stimulate microbial growth and enzyme production can be added to compost. Presence of sufficient amount of water enhances microbial growth. Addition of inorganic nutrients influences microbial growth and rate of decomposition of hazardous wastes.

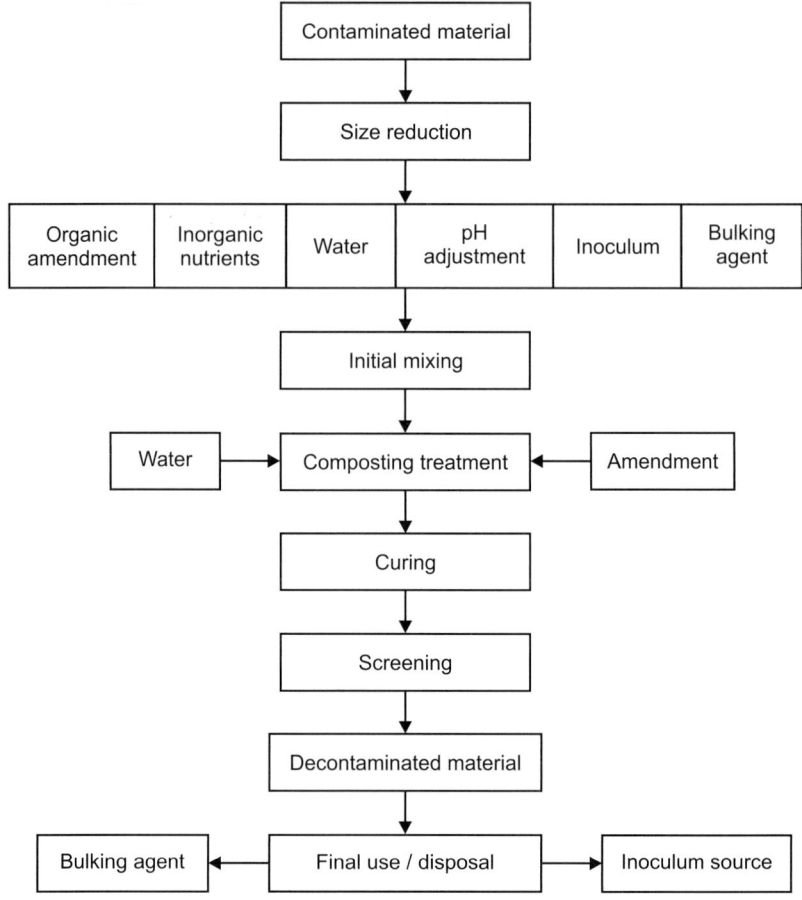

Figure 10.5: Steps of composting treatment.

It has also been noted that a pH range of 5.0–7.8 promoted the highest rates of degradation of hazardous wastes. But lignin degradation has been found the most rapid at pH of 3.0–6.5. This shows that optimal pH levels can be species, site and waste specific.

10.3.2 Soil treatment by *in situ* bioremediation

Bioventing

Bioventing (Fig. 10.6) is a advance technology that stimulates the natural *in situ* biodegradation of any biodegradable compound in soil by supplying oxygen to existing soil micro-organisms. In comparison to soil vapour vacuum extraction, bioventing uses low air flow rates to provide only enough oxygen

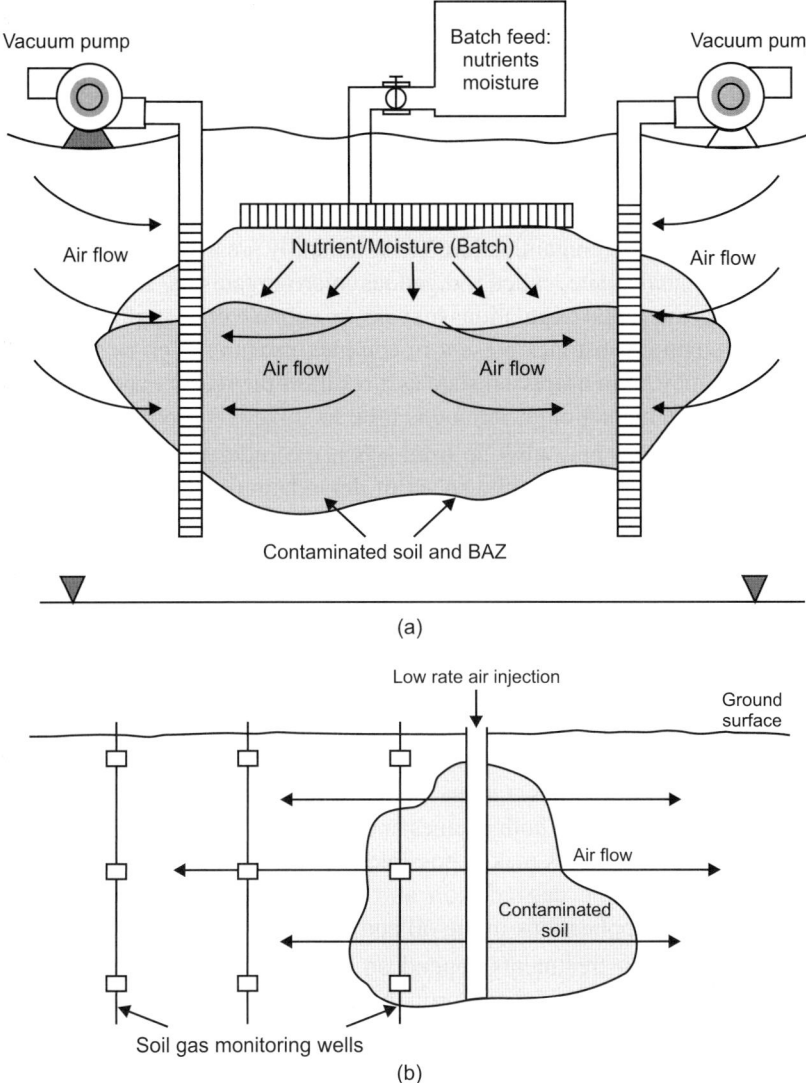

Figure 10.6: (a) Bioventing system and (b) air injection bioventing system.

to accelerate microbial activity. Oxygen is supplied through direct air injection into contaminated soil site. Degradation of adsorbed fuel residuals as well as volatile compounds are degraded as vapours and move slowly through biologically active soil. Bioventing technique has been successfully used to remediate soils contaminated by petroleum hydrocarbons, non-chlorinated solvents, some pesticides, wood preservatives, and other organic chemicals.

On other hand bioremediation cannot degrade inorganic contaminants, bioremediation can be used to change the valence state of inorganics and cause adsorption, uptake, accumulation, and concentration of inorganics in micro or macro-organisms.

Bioaugmentation

Biodegradation of contaminants occurs in presence of micro-organisms naturally at the site of contamination. These naturally present micro-organisms on the contaminated site, called indigenous micro-organisms. In some cases, if indigenous microbial populations may not be capable of degrading the wide range of potential substrates present in complex mixtures such as petroleum or that they may be in a stressed state as a result of the recent exposure to the site, then bioaugmentation technique is used to solve this problem.

Bioaugmentation may also be used when the indigenous hydrocarbon-degrading population is low, the speed of degradation is the primary factor, and when seeding may reduce the lag period to start the bioremediation process. For successful application of bioaugmentation, the seed micro-organisms must be able to degrade most contaminants, maintain genetic stability and viability during storage, survive in foreign and hostile environments. This method effectively compete with indigenous micro-organisms, and move through the pores of the sediment to the contaminants.

Different microbial species have different enzymatic abilities and preferences for the degradation of contaminants. Some micro-organisms degrade linear, branched, or cyclic alkanes. Others prefer mono or polynuclear aromatics, and others jointly degrade both alkanes and aromatics. The study of microbes in bioremediation systems makes possible the selection of micro-organisms with potential for the degradation and production of compounds with biotechnological applications in the oil and petrochemical industry.

Bioaugmentation treatments depend on the use of inocula consisting of microbial strains or microbial consortia that have been well adapted to the site to be remediated. Foreign micro-organisms have been applied successfully but their efficiency depends on ability to compete with indigenous micro-organisms, predators and various abiotic factors. Factors affecting proliferation of micro-organisms used for bioaugmentation including the chemical structure and concentration of pollutants, the availability of the contaminant to the micro-organisms, the size and nature of the microbial population and the physical environment should be taken into consideration when screening for micro-organisms to be applied.

Bioaugmentation involves the introduction of micro-organisms isolated from the contaminated site or genetically modified to support the remediation of contaminated sites based on the confirmation that indigenous organisms within the contaminated site cannot biodegrade contaminants.

Biosparging

Biosparging (Fig. 10.7) is the method in which the atmospheric air is injected into the aquifer. Biosparging is used in both saturated and unsaturated soil zones. The technique was developed to reduce the consumption of energy. The injection of air into the aquifer results the formation of small channels for the air to move to the unsaturated soil zone. In order to form the several branches in these channels to supply the air in to soil biosparging results the transportation of volatile contaminants to the unsaturated zone. Soil vapour extraction is used to extract the developed volatile vapours and then treat them at the surface. For effective biosparging, the sparge points must be installed below the contamination zone because air always flows in upward direction. The upflow of air will form a cone. The degree of branching and the angle of the cone are determined by the amount of air pressure during the injection. Monitoring wells are installed around the point and then the groundwater level and dissolved oxygen content are measured to determine the zone of influence for the sparge point. In order to effectively remove contaminants from the soil using biosparging, the soil should be relatively homogeneous throughout the contamination zone.

10.3.3   Reactors for bioremediation

Aerated lagoons

Slurry-phase lagoon system which is very similar to aerated lagoon used for treatment of small common municipal wastewater is shown in Fig. 10.8. For maximising growth of micro-organisms, nutrients and aeration are supplied to the reactor. Mixers are fitted to mix different components and form slurry, whereas surface aerators provide air required for microbial growth.

The process may be used as single-stage or multistage operation depending upon requirement. This reactor is not appropriate for treatment of waste containing volatile materials or components. This is the limitation of slurry phase lagoon system.

Low-shear airlift reactors (LSARs)

To solve the limitation of slurry phase lagoon in case of volatiles containing waste, low shear airlift reactor has been developed. The LSARs are useful when waste contains volatile components; tight process control and increased efficiency of bioreactors are required.

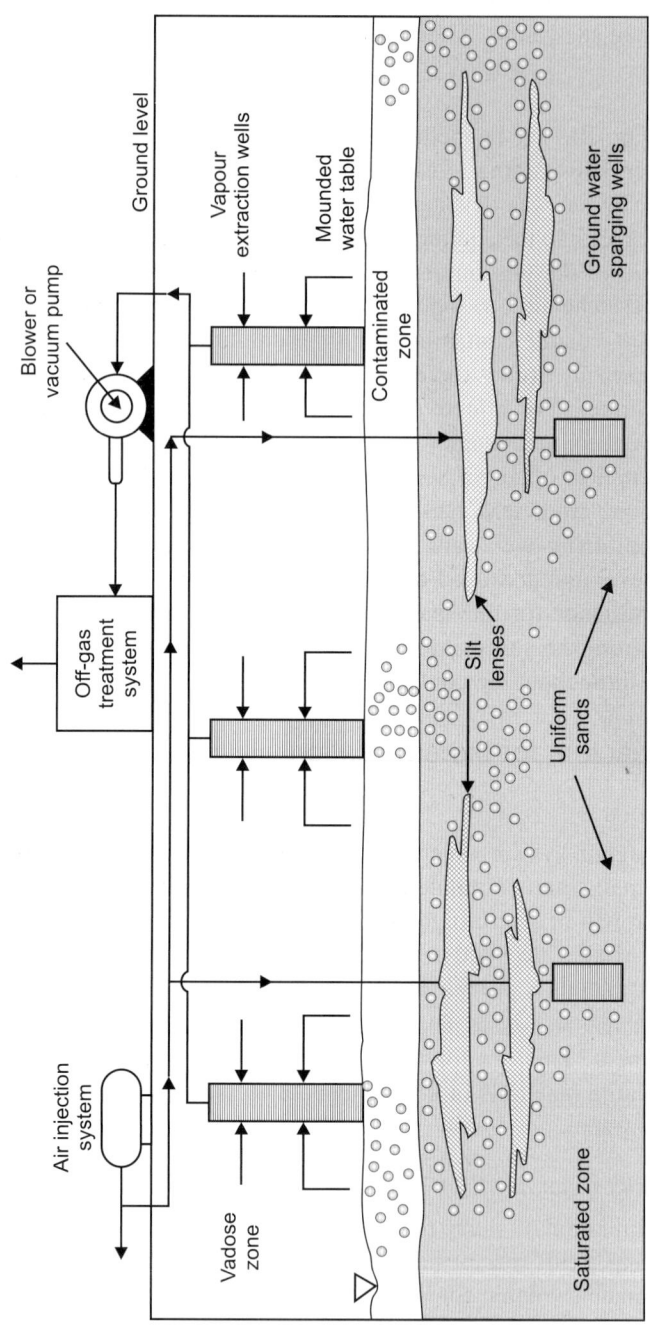

Figure 10.7: Biosparging system.

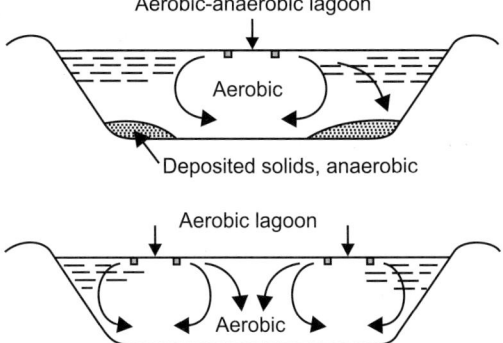

Figure 10.8: Aerated lagoons.

Figure 10.9 shows a low-shear airlift slurry-phase bioreactor. LSARs are like cylindrical tank which is made up of stainless steel. In this bioreactor pH, temperature, nutrient addition, mixing and oxygen can be controlled as per requirement. Impellers are mounted on shaft to fulfill the need and driven by motor set up at the top. The rake arms are connected with blades which is used for resuspension of coarse materials that tend to settle on the bottom of the bioreactor. Air diffusers are also arranged along the rake arm. Airlift provides to bottom circulation of contents in reactor.

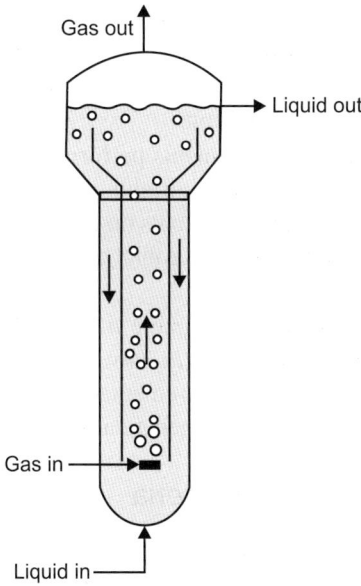

Figure 10.9: Low-shear airlift reactor.

Baffles maintains the hydrodynamic behaviour of slurry-phase bioreactors. Contaminated material should be pre-treated using size fractionation of solids, soil washing, milling to reduce particle size and slurry preparation. To enhance the rate of biodegradation, some surfactants such as anthracene, pyrene, perylene, etc., are added to waste. These act as co-substrate and utilise as carbon and energy source. Co-substrates also induce the production of beneficial enzymes.

Factors affecting slurry-phase biodegradation: Following factors play important role in slurry phase biodegradation.

1. pH (optimum 5.5–8.5)
2. Moisture content
3. Temperature (20–30°C)
4. Ageing
5. Mixing
6. Nutrients (N, P, micronutrients)
7. Microbial population (naturally occurring micro-organisms are satisfactory, genetically engineered micro-organisms for layer compound may be added).
8. Reactor operation (batch and continuous cultures).

10.4 Bioremediation of hydrocarbons

Petroleum and its products are best examples of hydrocarbons and have much economic importance. Oil is made up of a variety of hydrocarbons, viz., xylanes, naphthalenes, octanes, camphor, etc. If these are present in more amount in the environment, these cause pollution.

In toxic environment micro-organisms perform, if the growth conditions, e.g., temperature, pH and inorganic nutrients are as per requirement. Oil is insoluble in water and is less dense. It floats on water surface and forms slicks. It has been seen that in storage tank microbial growth is not possible although water and air are supplied.

The micro-organisms which are capable of degrading petroleum include *pseudomonas*, various *corynebacteria, mycobacteria* and some yeasts. However, there are two methods for bioremediation of hydrocarbons/oil spills, by using mixture of bacteria, and using genetically engineered microbial stains.

10.4.1 Use of mixture of bacteria

A large number of bacteria live in interfaces of water and oil droplets. Each strain of bacteria consumes a selective type of hydrocarbons, so, methods have been developed to introduce mixture of bacteria not a single strain.

Mixture of bacteria have been used successfully to control oil pollution in water or oil spills from ships. Bacteria living in interface degrade oil at a very slow rate. The rate of degradation could be accelerated with human efforts. Artificially well developed mixture of bacterial strain along with inorganic nutrients such as phosphorus and nitrogen are pumped into the ground or applied to oil spill areas as required for treatment. This increases the rate of bioremediation at target site.

10.4.2   Use of genetically engineered bacterial strains

Anand Mohan Chakrabarty, an India borne American scientist in 1979, obtained a strain of *Pseudomonas putida* that contained the XYL and NAH plasmid as well as a hybrid plasmid derived by recombinating parts of CAM and OCT (these are incompatible and cannot co-exist as separate plasmids in the same bacterium). This strain could grow rapidly on crude oil because it had capability of metabolising hydrocarbons more efficiently than any other single plasmid.

10.5   Bioremediation of industrial waste

Different type of pollutants are discharged in the environment from a large number of industrial units. For example, textile industry alone contributes a significant amount of pollutants to water resources such as enzymes, acids, alkali, alcohols, phenols, dyes, heavy metals, radionucliods, etc. Traces of zinc, cadmium, mercury, copper, chromium, lead are found in dyes. Bioremediation of toxic textile effluents can be done by use of either free living microbial system or immobilised microbial system and enzymes. Actinomycetes have more capacity to bind metal ions as compared to fungi and bacteria. Uptake mechanism of living and dead cells differ from bacteria to fungi. Due to these differences they have potential application in industries to treat industrial effluents. The living microbial cells accumulate metals intracellularly at a higher concentration, whereas dead cells precipitate metals in and around cell walls by several metabolic processes. *Aspergillus niger* biomass contains up to 30 per cent of chitin and glucan. Chitin phosphate and chitosan phosphate of fungi absorb greater amount of U than Cu, Cd, Mn, Co, Mg and Ca.

10.5.1   Bioremediation of dyes

Bioremediation of heavy metals

Micro-organisms like bacteria, algae, fungi, actinomycetes and higher plants accumulate high amount of heavy metals in their cells. Species of different microbial groups are discussed below.

Algae: Algal species have capability to grow even in presence of heavy metals. The species of *Chlorella, Anabaena inaequalis, Westiellopsis prolifica, Stigeoclonium tenue, Synechococcus* sp. can grow in presence of heavy metals. This capacity of these several species of *Chlorella, Anabaena,* marine algae have been used for the removal of heavy metals from contaminated sites. Although operational conditions limit the practical application of these organisms. The naturally occurring cells showed higher efficiency for Cd^{++} and Ni^{++} as compared to laboratory cells.

Fungi: Fungi also having capability to accumulate heavy metals in their cells and follow different mechanisms for removal of heavy metals from the solution. These mechanisms are discussed below:

1. Metabolism-independent accumulation: The positively charged ions in the solution are attracted to negatively charged ligands in cell materials. Biosorption of metal ion occurs on microbial cell surface. Some factors like composition of biomass and other factors affect biosorption. In case of *Rhizopus arrhizus,* adsorption depends on ionic radius of Li^{3+}, Mn^{2+}, Cu^{2+}, Zn^{2+}, Cd^{2+}, Ba^{2+}, Hg^{2+} and Pb^{2+}. However, binding of Hg^{2+}, Ag^{2+}, Cd^{2+}, Al^{3+}, Ni^{2+}, Cu^{2+} and Pb^{2+} strongly depends on concentration of yeast cells.

2. Metabolism-dependent accumulation: In this mechanism, heavy metal ions are transported into the fungal and yeast cells through cell membrane. In this metabolic processes ions are precipitated around the cells, and synthesised intracellularly as metal-binding proteins. Uptake of Cu^{2+}, Cd^{2+}, Co^{2+}, Ni^{2+}, Zn^{2+} by fungi is energy-dependent. Similarly, intracellular uptake is affected by certain external factors such as pH, anions, cations and organic materials, growth phase, etc. Metal uptake by growing batch culture shows maximum during lag phase and early log phase in *Aspergillus niger, Penicillium spinulosum* and *Trichoderma viride.*

3. Extracellular precipitation and complexation: In this mechanism, fungi produce numerous extracellular products which can precipitate heavy metals. For example, many fungi and yeast sythesise and release high affinity Fe-binding compounds that chelate iron known as siderophores. The Fe^{3+} chelates which are formed outside the cell wall are taken up into the cell. In *Saccharomyces cerevisiae* removal of metals is done by their precipitation as sulphides, e.g., Cu^{2+} is precipitated as CuS.

10.5.2 Bioremediation of xenobiotics

In modern agriculture system, huge amount of pesticides are being used by modem society to improve the quantity and quality of the food production world wide. It is applicable as common practice to use pesticide and it has become an integral part of modern agriculture system. These compounds used as pesticids are complex in structure and artificially made, i.e., xenobiotics persist in environment and do not undergo biological transformation. Micro-organisms can play an important role in degradation of xenobiotics as they have capability to degrade, and maintain steady state concentrations of chemicals in the environment. The complete degradation of a pesticide molecule to its inorganic components require an oxidative cycle to removes its potential toxicity from the environment.

Objectives for biodegradation of xenobiotics

Objective for biodegradation of xenobiotic compounds is to understand the mechanism of micro-organisms by which they show their activity in presence of such complex compounds and also to develop bioremediation methods for removing or detoxifying high concentration of dangerous pesticide residues. The characters of pesticide degradation using micro-organisms are located on plasmids and transposons, and are grouped in clusters on chromosome. Understanding of the characters provides significant information to the development of degradative pathways and makes the task of gene manipulation easier to construct the genetically engineered microbes capable of degrading such complex compounds as pollutants.

Microbial degradation of xenobiotics

Biodegradation of pesticides occurs by aerobic micro-organisms under aerobic conditions. Pesticides are considered as of wide varieties of chemicals, e.g., chlorophenoxyalkyl caboxylic acid, substituted ureas, nitrophenols, triazines, phenyl carbamates, organochlorines, organophosphates and many more. Duration of persistence of herbicides and insecticides in soil is given in Table 10.1.

Organophosphates (e.g., diazion, methyl parathion and parathion) are the most frequently used insecticides in agriculture practices. Biodegradation through hydrolysis by *Pseudomonas diminuta* and *Flavobacterium* are considered as the most significant steps in the detoxification of organophosphorus compounds. Organomercurials (e.g., Semesan, Panodrench, Panogen) have been practiced in agriculture since the birth of fungicides. Numerous species of *Aspergillus, Penicillium* and *Trichoderma* have been isolated from Semesan treated soil. They have shown ability to grow over 100 ppm of fungicide *in vitro*. The major fungicides used in agriculture are water soluble derivatives such as Ziram, Ferbam, Thiram and can be degraded by micro-organisms.

Pentachlorophenol (PCP) is a broad spectrum multipurpose biocide which can be used as fungicide, insecticide, herbicide, algicide, disinfectant and antifouling agent. Bioreactors using alginate immobilised and polyurethane

Table 10.1: Different pesticides and their duration of persistence in nature.

S.No.	Name of pesticides	Time taken for disappearance
1	Chlorinated insecticides	
	Aldrin	3 years
	DDT	4 years
	Chlordane	5 years
	Heptachlor	2 years
2	Organophosphate insecticides	
	Diazinan	12 years
	Malathion	1 week
	Parathion	1 week
3	Herbicides	
	2,4,5-T	30 weeks
	Atrazine	1.5 years
	Propazine	40 weeks
	2,4-D	4 weeks

foam immobilised PCP degrading *Flavobacterium* cells can be used to remove PCP from contaminated water. Absorption of PCP by polyurethane immobilised matrix plays crucial role in reducing the toxicity of PCP. Steps of PCP degradation has been shown in Fig. 10.10.

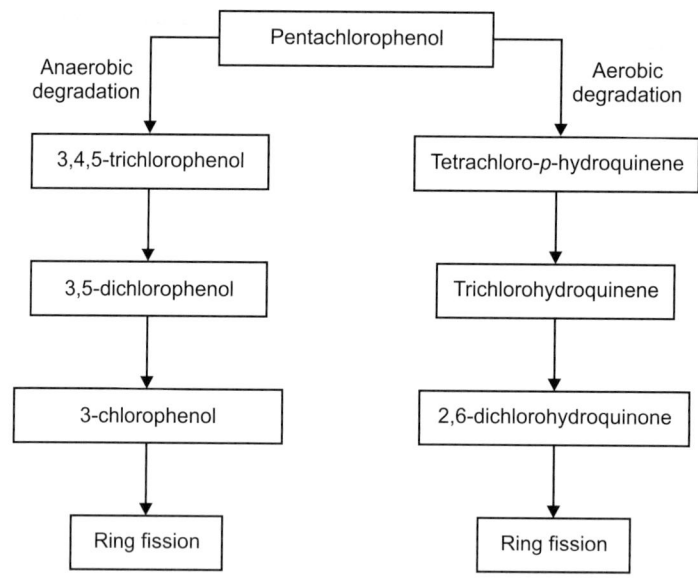

Figure 10.10: Steps of PCP degradation.

10.6   Phytoremediation

Phytoremediation is a bioremediation process that uses various types of plants to remove, transfer, stabilise, extract or destroy contaminants in the soil and groundwater.

10.6.1   Concept of phytoremediation

There are different types of phytoremediation mechanisms used to remove or detoxify contaminants from soil and water is discussed as follows.

Rhizosphere biodegradation

In this process, the plant secreats natural substances through its roots and these are nutrients required for growth of micro-organisms in the soil. The micro-organisms grow rapidly and accelerate biological degradation of contaminants present in soil.

Phytostabilisation

In this process, chemical compounds produced by the plant immobilise contaminants, rather than degrade them.

Phytoaccumulation (phytoextraction)

In phytoaccumulation process, rhizosphere part of the plant roots absorb the contaminants along with other nutrients and water. The contaminant is not degraded but stored in the part of plant such as shoots and leaves. This method is mostly used for wastes containing metals. It has been seen that water-soluble metals are taken up by plant species selected for their ability to take up large quantities of lead (Pb). The metals are stored in the plants aerial shoots, which are harvested and either smelted for potential metal recovery or are disposed of as a hazardous waste. Generly bioavailable metals for plant uptake include cadmium, nickel, zinc, arsenic, selenium, and copper.

Moderately bioavailable metals are cobalt, manganese, and iron. Lead, chromium, and uranium are not very bioavailable. Chelating agent can play a major role to get metal bioavailable, for example, lead can be made much more bioavailable by the addition of chelating agents to soils. Similarly, the availability of uranium and radio-cesium 137 can be enhanced using citric acid and ammonium nitrate, as chelating agents.

Hydroponic systems for treating water streams (Rhizofiltration)

Rhizofiltration is similar to phyto-accumulation, but the plants used for this purpose are grown in greenhouses with their roots in water not in soil. This system can be used for *ex situ* groundwater treatment. Groundwater is pumped to the surface to irrigate these plants and at that duration these plants capture contaminants in different part of plants. Typically hydroponic systems utilise an artificial soil medium, such as sand mixed with perlite or vermiculite. As the roots become saturated with contaminants, they are harvested and disposed of.

Phytovolatilisation

This is the process in which plants take up water containing organic contaminants and release the contaminants into the air through their leaves as volatile components.

Phytodegradation

This process is based on the degradation capability of specific plant species for a particular contaminant. In this process, plants actually metabolise and degrade contaminants within plant tissues.

Hydraulic control

In hydraulic control process, we can use trees as they have capability to carry water from very deep compare to plants. They indirectly remediate by controlling groundwater movement. Trees act as natural pumps when their roots reach down towards the water table and establish a dense root mass that takes up large quantities of water. For example, A poplar tree, pulls out of the ground 30 to 35 gallons of water per day, and a cottonwood can absorb up to 340 gallons per day.

10.6.2 Limitations and concerns

The toxicity and bioavailability of products after biodegradation, is not always known. This degradation by-products may be mobilised in groundwater or bio-accumulated in animals or other aqatic life. It is needed to determine the fate of various compounds produced during degradation of contaminants in the plant metabolic cycle to ensure that plant parts/droppings and products do not contribute toxicity or harmful chemicals into the food chain. It is also needed to understand whether contaminants that collect in the leaves and wood of trees are released when the leaves fall in the autumn or when firewood or mulch from the trees is used. Disposal of harvested plants containing contaminants can be a problem if they contain high concentration of heavy metals as contaminants.

The location of contaminants inside soil in a limiting factor for it remediation. The treatment zone is determined by plant capacity to reach root up to which depth. it is limited to shallow soils, streams, and groundwater. If the plant root is not capable to reach up to that depth where contaminants are present in water then pumping the water out of the ground and using it to irrigate plantations of trees may be the option to treat contaminated groundwater in such case. Generally, the use of phytoremediation is limited to sites with lower contaminant concentrations and contamination in shallow soils, streams, and groundwater.

However, researchers are finding that the use of trees (rather than smaller plants) allows them to treat deeper contamination because tree roots have capability to reach up to more depth into the ground.

The success of phytoremediation may be seasonal, depending on location and climatic conditions of the area where the plant are to be grown. These climatic factors will also influence its effectiveness. The success of remediation also depends upon the selection of plant species from plant community. Bioremediation using plants is time taking process as the establishment of the plants may require several seasons of irrigation.

It is important to consider extra mobilisation of contaminants in the soil and groundwater during bioremediation if possible. High concentration of contaminant also limits this process as contaminant concentration is too high, plants may die. Phytoremediation is not effective for strongly absorbed contaminants such as polychlorinated biphenyls (PCBs). Phytoremediation also requires a large surface area of land for remediation.

Application of phytoremediation

Phytoremediation is used for the removal/treatment of metals, radionuclides, pesticides, explosives, fuels, Volatile Organic Compounds (VOCs) and Semi Volatile Organic Compounds (SVOCs). Researchers are also trying to find out the role of phytoremediation to remediate perchlorate, a contaminant that has been shown to be persistent in surface and groundwater systems. It may be used to cleanup contaminants found in soil and groundwater. For radioactive substances, chelating agents are sometimes used to make the contaminants available to plant uptake.

10.6.3   Mechanisms of heavy metal uptake by plant

Contaminant uptake by plants and its mechanisms have been being explored in different ways. Understanding of this mechanism could be used to optimise the factors to improve the performance of plant uptake. During the remediation process, plants act both as 'accumulators' and 'excluders'. Accumulators survive despite concentrating contaminants in their aerial tissues. They biodegrade or biotransform the contaminants into inert forms in their tissues. The excluders restrict contaminant uptake into their biomass.

Plants have developed highly specific and very efficient mechanisms to obtain essential micronutrients from the environment, even when present at low concentration. Plant roots, aided by plant based chelating agents, plant induced pH changes and redox reactions are able to solubilise and take up micronutrients from very low levels in the soil. Plants have also developed highly specific mechanisms to translocate and store micronutrients. These mechanisms are also used in the uptake, translocation, and storage of toxic elements, whose chemical properties simulate those of essential elements. Therefore, mechanisms of micronutrient uptake having great interest to phytoremediation.

10.6.4   Classification of phytoremediation

Phytoextraction

Phytoextraction is the uptake/absorption and translocation of contaminants by plant roots into the the plants shoots, that can be harvested and burned to obtain energy and recycling the metal from the ash (Fig. 10.11).

Phytostabilisation

Phytostabilisation is the process of remediation in which certain plant species are used to immobilise the contaminants in the soil and groundwater. This occurs through absorption and accumulation in plant tissues, adsorption onto roots, or precipitation within the root zone preventing their migration in soil, as well as their movement by erosion and deforestation.

Rhizofiltration

Rhizofiltration is the process in which adsorption or precipitation of contaminants takes place onto plant roots or absorption and sequesterisation in the roots. Contaminants that are present in solution form surrounds the root zone by constructing wetland for cleaning up contaminated wastewater.

Phytovolatilisation

Phytovolatilisation is the uptake and removal of a contaminant by a plant, with release of the contaminant or a modified form of the contaminant to the atmosphere from the plant as transpiration occurs. Phytovolatilisation occurs when growing trees and other plants take up water along with the contaminants present in water. These contaminants pass through the plants to the leaves and volatilise into the atmosphere at comparatively low concentrations. Plants also play an important role in physically stabilising the soil with their root system. This is also helpful for preventing erosion, protecting the soil surface, and

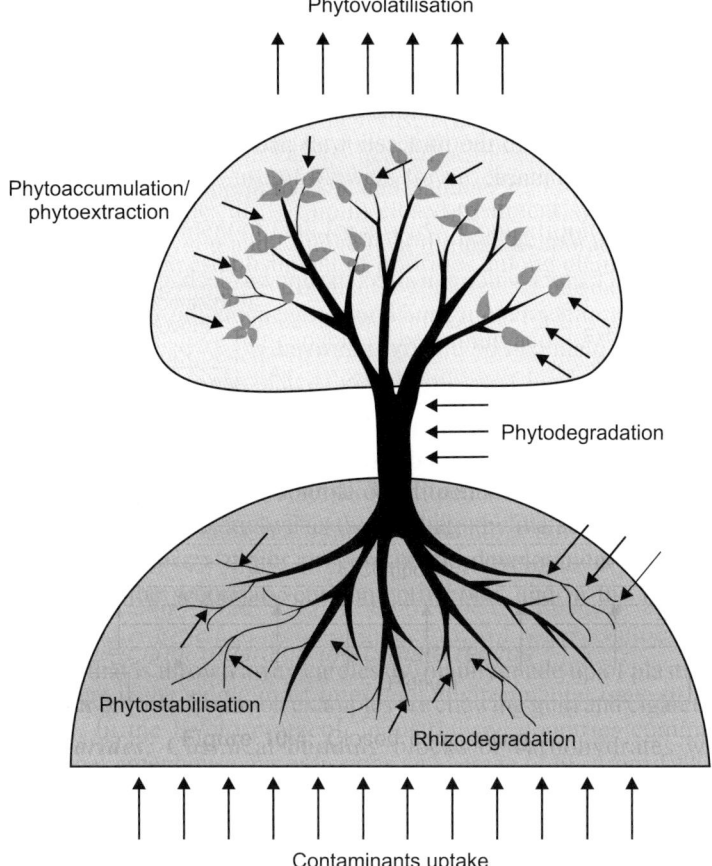

Figure 10.11: The mechanisms of heavy metals uptake by plant through phyto-remediation.

reducing the impact of rain. At the same time, plant roots release nutrients that help to improve the growth of microbes to convert in to a rich microbial community in the rhizosphere. Presence of bacterial community and its composition in the rhizosphere region is affected by complex interactions between soil type, plant species, and root zone location. Population of micro-organisms is generally higher in the rhizosphere compare to the root-free soil. This is due to availability of nutrients near by this rhizosphere part of soil and also due to a symbiotic relationship between soil micro-organisms and plants. Due to this symbiotic relationship, bioremediation processes can be enhanced. Plant roots also acts as surfaces provider for absorption or precipitation of metal contaminants. In this remediation process the root zone acts as focus of interest. The contaminants can be absorbed by the root to be subsequently stored or metabolised by the plant. Degradation of contaminants in the soil by plant enzymes released from the roots is also an important phytoremediation mechanism. Many contaminants follow route in which passive uptake takes place, via., micropores in the root cell wall and finally into the root, where degradation can take place.

Factors affecting the uptake mechanisms

There are several factors which can affect the uptake mechanism of heavy metals. By having better understanding and knowledge about these factors, the uptake performance by plant can be greatly improved.

Plant species: Selection of potential plants species or varieties is very important as plant species having better remediation power remediate contaminant very fast. The uptake of a compound is affected by natural characteristics of plant species. The effectiveness of the phytoextraction technique depends upon the identification and selections of suitable plant species that hyper accumulate heavy metals.

Properties of medium: Soil conditioning is most important agricultural practice in which pH adjustment, addition of chelators and use of appropriate fertilisers takes place. This practice also help to improve the growth and to enhance remediation. For example, the amount of lead absorbed by plants is affected by the pH, organic matter, and the phosphorus content of the soil.

Root zone: The root zone is major area of action in phytoremediation. Through this part of plant contaminants can be absorbed, stored and metabolise in to the plant tissue. Degradation of contaminants in the soil by plant enzymes secreted from the roots is another phytoremediation mechanism. A morphological adaptation due to drought stress condition enhance root diameter and reduced root elongation as a response to less permeability of the dried soil.

Vegetative uptake: Vegetative uptake by plant is affected by the environmental conditions like temperature which affects growth and root length. Morphology of root structure vary in natural soil conditions and that under greenhouse condition. The success of phytoremediation, depends on a contaminant specific hyper accumulator. Metal uptake by plants also depends on the bioavailability of the metal in the liquid phase. Bioavailability depends on the retention time of the metal, as well as the interaction with other elements and substances in the water. Factors such as pH, redox potential, and organic matter content affect the tendency of the metal to exist in different ionic and plant-available form. Plants will affect the soil by lowering the pH and oxidise the sediment. This affects the availability of the metals in bioavailable form of heavy metals by the addition of physicochemical factors, such as chelating agents and micronutrients.

Addition of chelating agent: The remediation process can be improved by increasing the uptake of heavy metals by the plants can be influenced by increasing the bioavailability of heavy metals. This availability can be increased by addition of biodegradable physicochemical factors such as chelating agents, and micronutrients. This can also be improved by stimulating the heavy metal uptake capacity of the microbial community around rhizosphere part of the plant. The application of chelating agents in heavy metal contaminated soils may promote leaching of the contaminants into the soil. Bioavailability of heavy metals in soils decreases above pH 5.5–6. Therefore, use of a chelating agent is benificial in alkaline soils. It has been observed that plant exposure to chemicals such as EDTA for a longer period up to 15 days, could improve metal translocation in plant tissue as well as the overall phytoextraction activity. Selection of appropriate concentration of chelating agents plays crucial role. For example, application of a synthetic chelating agent (EDTA) at 5mmol/kg yielded positive results. Plant roots release citric and oxalic acids, which affect the bioavailability of metals. In chelate assisted phytoremediation, synthetic chelating agents such as NTA and EDTA are added to enhance the phytoextraction of soil polluting heavy metals. The leaching of metals can be improved for bioavailability of metal to plant by presence of a ligand. This ligand accelerate the uptake of heavy metals through the formation of metal-ligand complexes to leach metals below the root zone.

10.7   Advantages and limitations of bioremediation

10.7.1   Advantages of bioremediation

Natural process

Bioremediation is a natural process and accepted by the public as waste treatment process for contaminated material such as soil. Microbes able to degrade the contaminant, increase in numbers and release harmless products. The residues for the treatment are usually harmless products such as carbon dioxide, water, and cell biomass.

Complete destruction

Bioremediation is useful for the complete destruction of a wide variety of contaminants. Many hazardous compounds can be transformed to harmless products. This reduces the chance of future liability associated with treatment and disposal of contaminated material.

On site treatment

Bioremediation can be carried out on site treatment, without causing a major disruption of normal activities. This removes the need to transport huge quantities of waste off site and thus reduce potential harm to human health and the environment that can arise during transportation.

Cost effective process

Bioremediation is less expensive compare to other methods that are used for removal of hazardous waste.

10.7.2 Limitations of bioremediation

Limited up to biodegradable compounds: Bioremediation is limited to those compounds that are biodegradable. This method is susceptible to rapid and complete degradation. Products of biodegradation may be more persistent or toxic than the parent compound.

Specificity

Biological processes are highly specific. Important site factors required for success include the presence of metabolically capable microbial populations, suitable environmental growth conditions, and appropriate levels of nutrients and contaminants.

Scale up limitation

It is difficult to scale up from bench and pilot scale studies to full scale field operations.

Technological advancement

Research is needed to develop and engineer bioremediation technologies that are suitable for sites with complex mixtures of contaminants that are not evenly distributed in the environment. It may be present as solids, liquids, and gases.

Time taking process

Bioremediation takes longer time compare to other treatment options, such as excavation and removal of soil from contaminated site.

Regulatory uncertainty

We are not certain to say that remediation is 100% completed, as there is no accepted definition of clean. Due to that performance evaluation of bioremediation is difficult, and there is no acceptable endpoint for bioremediation treatments.

Bioenergy from Waste

11.1   Introduction

The continuous growth of plants on our planet exceeds men's primary energy requirements many times over. Of course, only part of the biomass that grows can actually be supplied for energy use, due to ecological, technical and economic reasons. However, there remains a huge amount of biomass that is very suitable for exploitation. Biomass resources comprise those which are received from agriculture and forestry as well as from agro industry and wood industry. It also includes waste sources from construction and demolition as well as municipal wastes.

The potential biomass available in India seems to be sufficient to support the ambitious renewable energy targets in an environmentally responsible way. Agricultural waste generated after harvesting the crops, waste of forestry and organic waste generated from various sources, such type of waste can be utilised for production of various biofuels like methane, biohydrogen, ethanol, etc. Biomass can be used for generation of heat, power and transport fuels in an environmentally friendly way. Consequently, it is useful for both, i.e., reduction in emission of green house gases and achieve the Indian renewable energy targets.

Recent concerns arise that biofuel production competes with food production. However, in India the production of many agricultural products is more than saturated. In order to guarantee profitable market prices, production limits were introduced and high premiums are paid for some agricultural products and set-aside land. Therefore the production of biofuels does not compete with food production at the moment. But once the demand for biomass increases, the production of biofuels will not only compete with the food sector, but also with chemical industries and regenerative raw materials.

Useful features of biofuels:

1. Most of biofuels are derived from biomass, which is renewable low cost and locally available and no commitment of foreign exchange.
2. They lead to relatively low CO_2 emission then fossil fuels.
3. The substrate is often a waste, including municipal waste use of such materials for biofuel production not only generates more valuable products from low cost substrate but also help in cleaning up the environment.

11.2   Biofuel versus fossil fuel

Biofuels are not new. In fact, Henry Ford had originally designed his Model T to run on ethanol. There are several factors that decide the balance between biofuel and fossil fuel use around the world. Those factors are cost, availability, and food supply.

All three factors are actually interrelated. Availability of fossil fuels has been of concern almost from day one of their discovery. The cost of fossil fuel is very high due to processing cost as pumping fuel from the ground is a difficult and expensive process, which adds more cost of these fuels. Availability of fossil fuel depends upon our ability to recover fossil fuels from the ground. If availability decreases, the supply will decrease, which will lead to an increase in price.

It was originally thought that biofuels could be produced in almost limitless quantity because they are renewable. Unfortunately, our energy needs far outpace our ability to grown biomass to make biofuels for one simple reason, land area. There is very limited covered area of land, farming for biofuels will decrease covered area for food product farming. As the population grows, our demands for both energy and food grow. Today, we do not have sufficient land to grow both biofuel and enough food to meet out our needs. The result of this limit has an impact on both the cost of biofuel and the cost of food. For wealthier countries, the cost of food is less of an issue.

However, for poorer nations, the use of land for biofuels, which drives up the cost of food, can have a tremendous impact. The balance between food and biofuel production can be achieved by using advanced technologies. When this factor is combined with an increased ability to extract oil from the ground using advance technology, the price of fossil fuel is actually lower than that of biofuel for the most part.

11.3   Type of energy resources, renewable, non-renewable resources and availability

11.3.1   Hydrothermal energy

Hydrothermal energy is the process of producing heat energy from water. Produced heat is not associated with high temperature rather a relative heat content or relative temperature difference. Hans Krock first time mentioned the abundance of this renewable energy source. According to Krock, the energy coming through the surface layer of the tropical ocean is about 10,000 times greater than the energy used by human societies. It is the only energy resource on Earth that can replace fossil fuel. Fluid, heat, and permeability are resources to generate electricity. Conventional hydrothermal resources contain all three components naturally. Conventional hydrothermal resources naturally contain the permeability, fluid, and heat needed to generate electricity. This constitutes the majority of current global geothermal resource developments.

11.3.2   Wind energy

The sun's heat also drives the winds, whose energy is captured with wind turbines. The Earth's rotation also contributes to the winds, particularly through the Coriolis effect. Wind power is the energy converted to electricity using the air flows that occur naturally in the earth's atmosphere. This natural air flow provide kinetic energy to move turbine. Wind turbine blades capture kinetic energy from the wind and convert it into mechanical energy that is used to spin a generator that produces electricity. Wind is a type of renewable energy. There are three major types of wind power mentioned below.

1. Utility-scale wind: Utility scale wind turbines consist of more than 100 kilowatts with electricity delivered to the power grid and distributed to the end user by electric utilities or power system operators.
2. Distributed or 'small' wind: Capacity of this type of turbines is up to 100 kilowatts or smaller to directly supply power to home, farm or small business.
3. Offshore wind: This type of wind turbines operates in large bodies of water, usually on the continental shelf.

Working of turbine

Working of turbine is very simple. When wind passes through a turbine, the blades of turbine capture the kinetic energy and start rotating. This kinetic energy converts into mechanical energy. This rotation turns an internal shaft connected to a gearbox. This gearbox increases the speed of rotation by a factor of 100. That spins a generator to produce the electricity. Turbine stands at 80 meters tall, tubular steel towers support a hub with three attached blades and a 'nacelle,' which hold the shaft, gearbox, generator, and controls. Wind automatically rotates the turbine to face the strongest wind and angle or 'pitch' its blades to optimise the energy captured. A modern turbine generates power over 90% of the time. It will start to generate electricity when wind speeds reach 3–4 meters per second, and cut off at about 20 meters per second to prevent equipment damage.

Wind energy technologies use the energy in wind for practical purposes, such as generating electricity, charging batteries, pumping water, and grinding grain. Mechanical or electrical power is created through the kinetic energy of the wind. Wind power is proportional to the cube of its speed, if double the wind speed, power available to a wind generator increases by a factor of eight. Wind energy is now the second fastest-growing source of electricity in the world, with a global installed capacity of 462,895 megawatts MW at the end of 2017. There are over 75,000 MW of wind capacity operational in the US only, as of September 2016.

11.3.4   Nuclear energy

Our surroundings and even smallest thing is made up of atoms. The mass of each atom is concentrated in the centre which is called the nucleus, and the rest of the mass is in the form cloud of electrons surrounding the nucleus. The other components are protons and neutrons, that are known as subatomic particles. In case of certain circumstances, the nucleus of a very large atom can divided in two parts. In this process the nucleus is break down in to two parts, This process is known as nuclear fission.

A certain amount of the large atom's mass is converted to pure energy following Einstein's famous formula:

$$E = MC^2$$

where, M is the small amount of mass and C is the speed of light.

Nuclear energy was recognised as a potential source of energy during 1930s to 1940s. The negative aspect of atomic energy is atomic weapons that can be cause of destruction. During second world America tested the nuclear weapons for destruction of Japanese cities. India is developing country having great demand of energy which can be fulfilled by established new nuclear reactors across the country. Technology developed in the Manhattan Project successfully used this energy in a chain reaction to create nuclear bombs. The atomic energy very helpful in the propulsion of the nuclear navy, providing submarines with engines that could run for over a year without refuelling. This technique of energy production was quickly transferred to the public sector, where commercial power plants were developed and deployed to produce electricity.

More over 400 power reactors in the world (about 100 of these are in the USA) have been successfully established. They produce base-load electricity 24×7 without emitting pollutants (including CO_2) into the atmosphere. The radioactive nuclear waste is produced in very little amount which must be stored carefully. The nuclear energy is produced by two fundamental nuclear processes: fission and fusion.

Fission: Nuclear fission is the process of splitting to large atoms like Uranium, Thorium, Plutonium, etc., into two smaller atoms, called nuclear fission. It is necessary to split an atom, we have to hit it with a neutron. Several neutrons are also released which again hit the other nearby atoms, resulting a nuclear chain reaction is started which produces a huge amount of energy. All commercial nuclear power plants in operation use this reaction to generate heat which they turn into electricity.

Fusion: Nuclear fusion is the process in which two small atoms such as Hydrogen or Helium are combined to produce heavier atoms and energy is released. These reactions can release more energy than fission without producing radioactive by-products and nuclear waste. Sun is the major source of energy on the earth. The fusion reactions occur in the sun, generally using Hydrogen as fuel and producing Helium as waste. This reaction has not been commercially developed yet and is a serious challenge to researchers worldwide, due to its promise of nearly limitless, no or low-pollution, and non-proliferative energy.

Energy densities of various energy sources: Energy densities of various energy sources in MJ/kg and in length of time that 1 kg of each material could run a 100 W load. Natural uranium has undergone no enrichment, reactor-grade uranium has 5% U-235. Although one kilogram of weapons grade uranium can provide power to entire USA for three minutes. All numbers assumed 100% thermal-to-electrical conversion.

Table 11.1 shows how long a 100 Watt light bulb could run from using 1 kg of various fuels. The natural uranium undergoes nuclear fission and thus attains very high energy density (energy stored in a unit of mass).

Table 11.1: Energy density of various energy sources.

Material	Energy density (MJ/kg)	100 W light bulb time (1 kg)
Wood	11	1.3 days
Ethanol	27.3	3.2 days
Coal	32.8	3.9 days
Crude oil	42	4.9 days
Diesel	45.9	5.4 days
Natural uranium	5.7×10^5	183 years
Thorium	7.95×10^7	25310 years

11.3.5 Fossil fuels

The other major types of fuels are fossil fuel. The main resources of fossil fuels include petroleum oils, coal and natural gas. These are non-renewable resources that formed after the prehistoric plants and animals died and were gradually buried by layers of rocks and soil. Millions of years have been passed to form different types of fossil fuels formed. The formation of fossil fuels are depending on what combination of organic matter was present, how long duration it was buried, what was temperature of reaction and pressure conditions existed as time passed.

Fossil fuel industries are responsible for the mining of these energy sources. These substances are burned to produce electricity, after refining these can be used as fuel for heating or transportation. Over the last two decades, nearly three-fourths of human-caused emissions came from the burning of fossil fuels.

Fossil fuels, including coal, oil and natural gas, are currently the world's primary energy source. Formation of fossil fuels takes place millions of years from organic materials, fossil fuels plays an important role in global economic development over the past century. Although the sources of fossil fuels are finite or limited and they are also highly harmful to the environment.

Oil or petroleum fuels

Fossil fuels or petroleum is the world's primary fuel source for transportation. Most fossil fuels are pumped out of underground reservoirs, but it can be found embedded in shale and tar sands also. After extraction, crude oil is proceed in oil refineries to purify fossil fuels, gasoline, liquefied petroleum gas, lubricants and other nonfuel products such as pesticides, fertilisers, pharmaceuticals, grease and plastics. Top exporters of oil are United States include Canada, Mexico, Saudi Arabia, Venezuela, and Nigeria. Fossil oil poses major environmental problems due to highly consumption for the use of transportation makes it difficult to reduce consumption. Although the environmental degradation caused by oil spills and extraction, combustion of oil releases fine particulates which can lead to serious respiratory problems due to increase in concentration of suspended particulate matter in the environment, and is a major source of greenhouse gas emissions.

Coal

The combustion of coal releases air pollutants such as acid rain-inducing sulphur dioxide, nitrogen oxides (NO_x), and mercury. The process of coal mining can also be very damaging to the environment, it may result to increase in the destruction of vegetation and top-soil. Rivers and streams can also be destroyed or contaminated by mine wastes. Burning coal in electric power plants is a major source of carbon dioxide (CO_2) emissions, and its use has other repercussions as well. Mining coal disturbs the land and modifies the chemistry of rainwater runoff, which in turn affects stream and river water quality. It also releases substantial amounts of methane, a potent greenhouse gas. Of all the fossil-fuel sources, coal is the least expensive for its energy content and is a major factor in the cost of electricity.

Natural gas

The major composition of natural gas is methane (CH_4) that can also be generated by the decomposition of municipal waste in landfills and manure from livestock production. Methane is a greenhouse gas that contributes more potentially (20 times) than carbon dioxide. Collecting and burning the biogas to produce usable heat and power, prevents the methane from being released from the landfill or feedlot into the atmosphere directly. The combustion of natural gas is eco friendly and cleaner than coal and fossil oil, with no emission of sulphur dioxide and far very less nitrogen oxide and particulate emissions. Natural gas releases almost one third carbon dioxide than fossil oil and approximately half than coal.

Although the current dependence on fossil fuels, some options exist to minimise and control the harmful fossil fuel economy. Improving the energy efficiency of vehicles, buildings, industrial processes, appliances and equipment is the most immediate and cost effective way to reduce energy use. By planning for communities where people can safely and conveniently use public transport, walk, or bike, instead of using private vehicles, also reduces energy demand. At present there are several alternative resources that can supply clean, renewable energy to replace fossil fuels, including solar energy, hydrolic energy, biofuels, biomass, wind energy, geothermal, and tidal energy.

11.4   Classification of biofuels – first, second, third and fourth generation

The classification of biofuels can be applied to first generation and second generation biofuels. PPO, biodiesel, bioethanol and ETBE are first generation biofuels since the conversion and engine technologies are widely developed and approved in practice. They offer the greatest short-term potentials of biofuels today. Although they differ in properties, technical requirements, economical aspects and potential, they can contribute to guarantee long-term mobility.

The second generation biofuels are not yet commercial available since the conversion technologies require great improvement. This group of biofuels includes, e.g., BTL fuels and ethanol from starch. BTL fuels are a promising option for the future, but will not achieve relevance to the market before 2018. However, the boundaries first and second generation fuels are fluently and not exactly defined. Currently biogas is shifting from first to second generation biofuel. First biogas stations are built at the moment. Biomethane from biogas can be used in natural gas vehicles without any adjustments.

The third generation biofuel refers to biofuel derived from algal biomass. The diversity of fuel that algae can produce results from two characteristics of the microorganism. First, algae produce an oil that can easily be refined into diesel or even certain components of gasoline. More importantly, however, is a second property in it can be genetically manipulated to produce everything from ethanol and butanol to even gasoline and diesel fuel directly.

Fourth generation biofuels are derived from specially engineered plants or biomass that may have higher energy yields or lower barriers to cellulosic breakdown or are able to be grown on non-agricultural land or bodies of water. In fourth generation production systems, biomass crops are seen as efficient carbon capturing machines that take CO_2 out of the atmosphere and store it in their branches, trunks and leaves.

11.4.1 Conversion of organic waste in to biofuels

Biogas

At present time automobile industries are also manufacturing pure or hybrid natural gas vehicles as standard models. One of the promising future options for sustainable transport fuels is the subsidisation of natural gas by biomethane. Biogas or biomethane is the most efficient and clean burning biofuel which is available easily today. It can be produced from nearly all types of biomass including wet biomass which is not usable for most other biofuels. Another motivational use of gaseous biofuels for transportation.

11.4.2 Raw material for biogas production

The raw material for the production of biomethane is biogas, which can be processed from various feedstock sources. For biogas production much more different feedstock sources can be used than for common liquid biofuels. For instance biodiesel can be only made from plant materials containing certain amounts of oil. In contrast, biogas is produced from nearly all types of organic materials including vegetable and animal feedstocks. The origin of the feedstock can vary, ranging from livestock waste, manure, harvest surplus, to vegetable oil residues. Dedicated energy crops are becoming more and more practice as feedstock source for biogas production. Recently, wastewater sludge, municipal solid wastes and organic wastes from households have been introduced as feedstock. Another feedstock source is the collection of biogas from landfill sites. Pathways for different biofuels is shown in Fig. 11.1.

The main advantage of biogas production is the ability to use so-called 'wet biomass' as feedstock source. Wet biomass is not used for the production of other biofuels such as biohydrogen, biodiesel. The examples of wet biomass

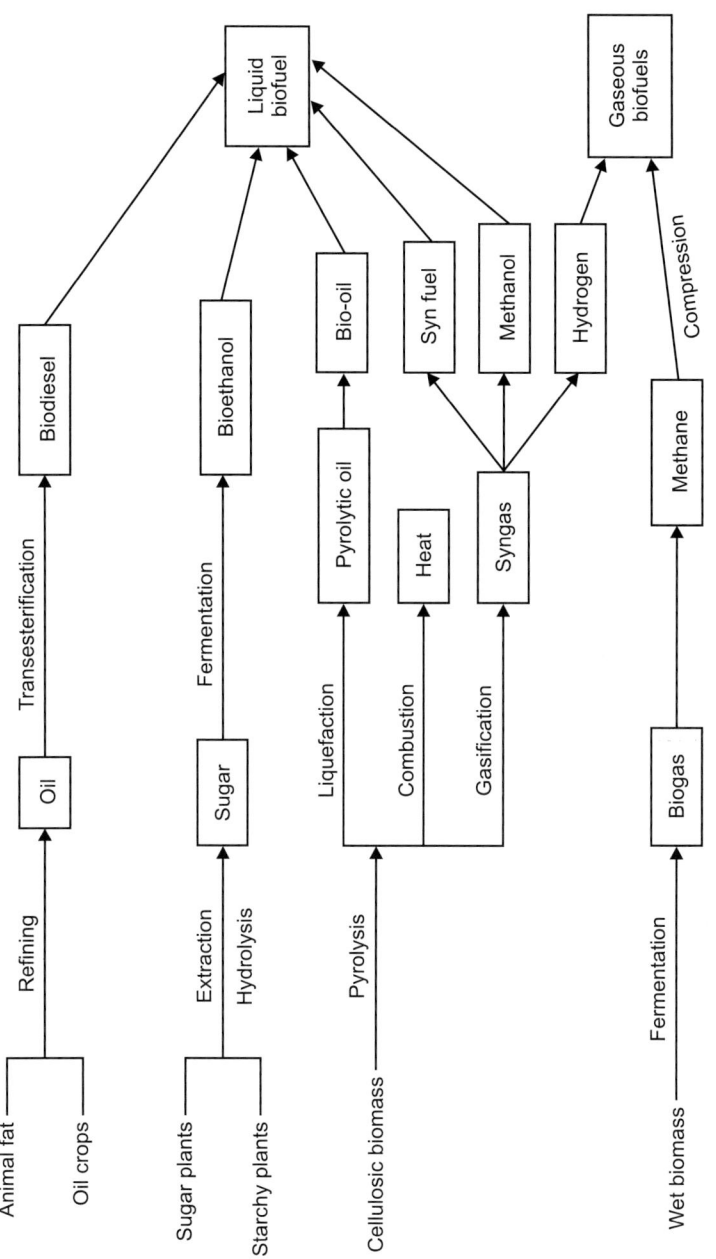

Figure 11.1: Pathways for different biofuels.

are sewage sludge, manure from dairy and poultry farms as well as residues from food processing industries. All of these are characterised by moisture contents of more than 60–70%.

The waste materials is not only utilised for biogas production, it also creates some additional benefits. Thus, it contributes to reduce animal wastes, odours and green house effects. The digestion or hydrolysis process effectively eliminates environmental hazards, such as over production of liquid manure. Thus biogas production is an excellent way for livestock farmers to comply with increasing governmental regulations of animal waste.

Sources of biomass

1. Land crops.
2. Aquatic plants.
3. Wastes – manure, domestic, rubbish, municipal waste sewage.
4. Agro industry waste – wood and crop residue like straw, bagasse, molasses, press mud, paper sludge.

Wastes which can be used for biogas production at various level

1. Village, farm level: Agricultural waste/vegetable wastes.
2. House hold level: Animal waste/domestic garbage.
3. City level: Municipal garbage/sewage.
4. Industry level: Industrial effluents/solid wastes of dairy/distillery, brewery, food processing units, chemical industries.

11.4.3 Biomethane production

The production of biomethane includes two steps. Firstly, biogas has to be produced from feedstock sources. Secondly, the biogas has to be further processed and cleaned in order to receive biomethane which is suitable for transport applications.

Digestion process

Biogas is produced by means of anaerobic digestion. Organic matter is broken down by microbiological activity and in the absence of air. Symbiotic micro-organisms plays different roles at different stages of the digestion process during the break down complex organic materials. These micro-organisms are categorised in to four basic types. Hydrolytic bacteria break down complex organic wastes into sugars and amino acids. Fermentative bacteria then convert those products into organic acids. Acidogenic micro-organisms convert the produced organic acids into hydrogen, carbon dioxide and acetate. At last, the methanogenic bacteria produce biogas (CH_4) from acetic acid, hydrogen and carbon dioxide.

Since these bacteria are sensitive to temperature, this has to be considered in the digestion process. In order to promote bacterial activity, temperatures of at least 20°C are required. It has been observed that higher temperatures reduces processing time and reduce the required volume of the reactor tank by 25% to 40%. Regarding the temperature, bacteria of anaerobic digestion can be divided into psychrophile (25°C), mesophile (32–38°C) and termophile (42–55°C) bacteria. The process temperature depends on the type feedstock used and type of bioreactor/digester used. Thus, digesters have to be heated in colder climates in order to encourage the bacteria to carry out their function.

Digestion time duration ranges from a couple of weeks to a couple of months depending on feedstock, type of bioreactor used in the process and on the reactor temperature also.

Micro-organism used for anaerobic digestion to produce biogas

Anaerobic digestion to biogas production involves three groups of organism.

1. Hydrolysis of organic materials: Fermentative bacteria convert complex organic material into organic acids, alcohols, esters, sugars, CO_2.
2. Acetogenesis: This group is dependent on first and contains hydrogen and acid producing bacteria.
3. Methanogenesis: Methanogenesis bacteria convert acetate and H_2 into biogas which is mixture of CH_4 and CO_2, e.g., *Methanosarcina barkeri, Methanobacterium omelionskii.*

Biogas (CH_4) production from wastes is given more and more importance because it couples degradation of waste to energy production and not energy consumption. Reactions of various designs and size ranging from 2000–20000 m^3 capacity are in use world wide. Metabolism in biogas generation digester is shown in Fig. 11.2.

Soluble organic matter here is suitable and loads of 25–30 kg COD $m^{-3}d^{-1}$ are handled. Each 1 kg COD yield 350 litre of methane.

Effluents rich in carbohydrates are rich in methane production but those with high fat and protein contents are still rich. That is the reason why wastes from the food processing units find more potential in biogas production.

Type of digester

Biogas production is the digestion of feedstock by common technology in specially designed digesters. These must be strong enough to withstand the buildup of pressure and must provide anaerobic conditions for the bacteria

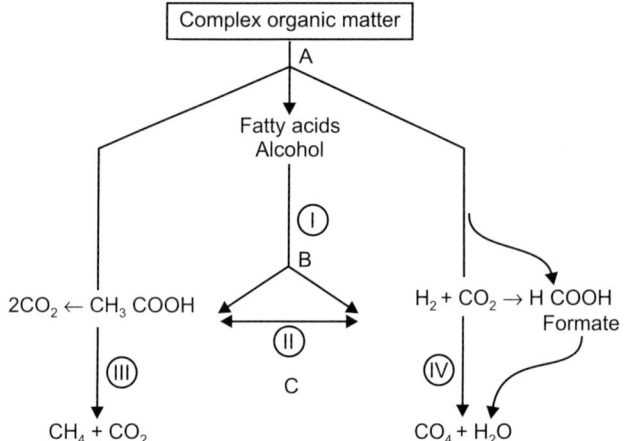

Figure 11.2: Metabolism in biogas generation digester.

inside. In this process anaerobic digester systems can reduce fecal coliform bacteria in manure by more than 99%. Further, the ability of the digester to produce and capture methane from the manure reduces the amount of methane that otherwise would enter the atmosphere. Methane gas in the atmosphere is a contributor to global climate change. Biogas plant and gas collection from landfill site are shown in Fig. 11.3.

Today, there are many different technologies and digester types available. Generally, the size of biogas plants can vary from a small household system to large commercial plants of several thousand cubic meters. Digester size also influences logistics and vice versa. For instance, for larger scale digesters feedstock has to be collected from individual farms and transported to central digester facilities. However, independent from the type of digester, they are often built near the source of the feedstock, and several are often used together to provide a continuous gas supply.

Batch type: The digester used for biogas production is filled at once and after completion of production process the whole system is emptied.

Continuously expanding type: Firstly, the digester is filled up to 1/3, then it is continuously filled until it is full and finally the digester is emptied.

Continuously flow type: The digester is initially filled completely, then the feedstock is continuously added and digested material is continuously removed.

Pug flow type: The feedstock is added regularly at one end and overflows the other end.

Contact type: This is a continuous type, but a support medium is provided for the bacteria.

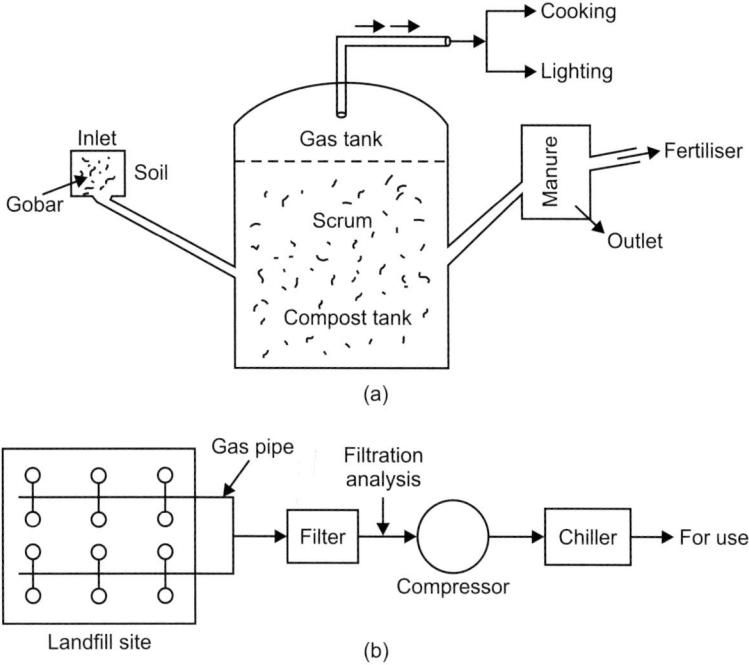

Figure 11.3: (a) Biogas plant and (b) gas collection from landfill site.

Reactors used:

1. Upflow anaerobic sludge blanket reactor (UASB).
2. Upflow fixed film anaerobic filter.
3. Down flow film anaerobic filter.
4. Expanded bed reactor.
5. Fluidised bed reactor.
6. CSTR.

11.4.4   Biogas purification

The digestion of organic matter results the production of biogas, a combination of methane and carbon dioxide, typically in the ratio of 6:4 (55– 80% methane). In addition, there are small quantities of hydrogen sulphide and other trace gases. Since only the methane is usable as transport fuel, methane has to be separated from CO_2 and the remaining components of biogas.

The final product is biomethane, which has methane content between 95 and 100%. Therefore it is very similar to natural gas and suitable for all natural gas applications.

Biomethane can be also produced by gasification. Nevertheless, it has to be recognised that the process of biomass gasification is distinctly different form that of biogas production. Gasification is the process by which solid biomass materials are broken down using heat to produce a combustible gas, commonly known as producer gas.

Factors affecting methane formation:

1. Slurry: Proper solubilisation of organic material. (The ratio between solid and water should be 1:1 when it is house hold type).
2. Seeding: In the beginning, seeding of slurry with small amount of sludge of another digester is taken to activates the digester as active micro-organisms are present in that sludge.
3. pH: For the production of sufficient amount of methane, optimum pH of digester should be maintained between pH 6–8 as the acetic medium lowers down methane formation.

Properties and use of biomethane

The simplest hydrocarbon, methane, is a gas at Standard Temperature and Pressure (STP). Its chemical formula is CH_4. Further, methane is a combustible and odourless gas. It is also a greenhouse gas with a global warming potential of 23 in 100 years. That means that each kg of methane warms the earth 23 times as much as the same mass of CO_2 when averaged over 100 years.

After the digestion and purification process of biomass, biomethane is obtained. In contrast to neat NH_4, biomethane also has small amounts of other compounds than NH_4. Nevertheless, the methane content of biomethane is 95–100%. For fuel purposes it can be concluded, that the higher the methane content the higher is the fuel quality. Biomethane from biogas is chemically identical with natural gas and therefore does not differ in parameters.

11.4.5 Bioethanol

Ethanol can be produced from any biological feedstock that contains appreciable amounts of sugar or materials that can be converted into sugar such as starch or cellulose. Different feedstock sources can be used for ethanol production. They can be divided into sugary, starchy and cellulosic feedstock.

Two examples of feedstock for ethanol production are sugar beets and sugar cane which contain high percentages of sugar. Sugars can be easily fermented. For example, Brazil developed a successful fuel ethanol programme from sugarcane. In Europe, sugar beets are used for ethanol production. Currently, ethanol imports from Brazil are entering the European fuel market. Corn, wheat, barley, rye and other cereals are typical feedstocks containing starch in their kernels. Starch can relatively easily be converted into sugar and then into ethanol. In the USA and Europe, ethanol is manufactured mainly from maize and grain. At the moment substantial capacities for the manufacture of ethanol are being created in Germany. Other starchy crops that can also be used for bioethanol production are sorghum grains, cassava and potatoes. Recent research includes bioethanol production from potatoes and waste potatoes from food processing industry.

Since ethanol from sugar and starch bearing plants is readily available today, these feedstock types are also called first-generation feedstocks. First generation feedstocks are characterised by the fact that only parts of the plants (starch, sugar, oil) are used for biofuel production. Different feed stock for ethanol production is shown in Fig. 11.4.

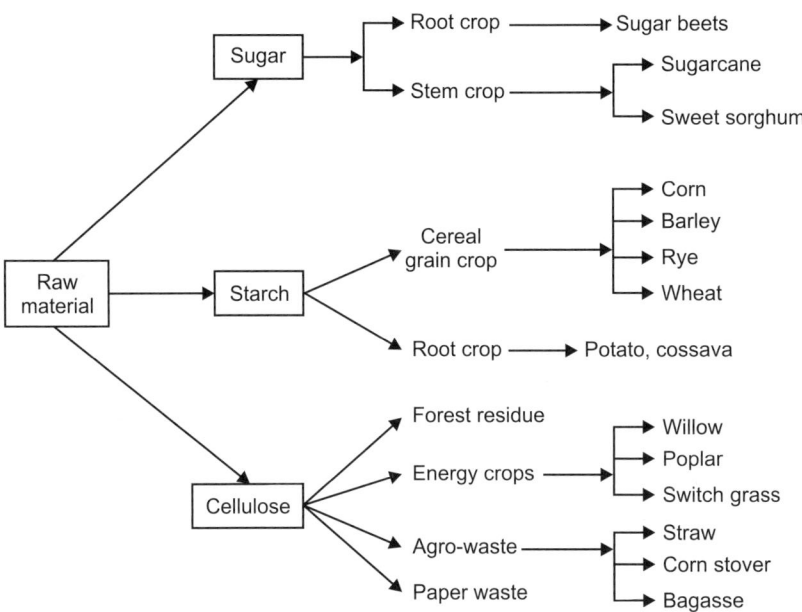

Figure 11.4: Different feed stock for ethanol production.

Contrary to this, next-generation feedstock types provide the opportunity to use nearly the whole plant for biofuel production and not only parts of the plants (grains, tubes, stalks). The advanced technologies are necessary for the use of second generation fuels. Various types of feedstock is available for producing ethanol from biomass that having large amounts of cellulose and hemicellulose. Cellulose and hemicellulose can be converted to sugar by the hydrolysis process, but conversion of starch is more difficult. Considered cellulosic biomass are agricultural wastes (including those resulting from conventional ethanol production), forest residues, municipal solid wastes (MSW), wastes from pulp/paper processes and energy crops. Cellulosic agricultural wastes for ethanol production include crop residues such as wheat straw, corn stover (leaves, stalks and cobs), rice straw and bagasse (sugar cane waste). Forestry wastes include logging residues as well as wood which is not used and thus left in the forest. MSW contains high percentages of cellulosic materials, such as paper and cardboard.

In contrast to cellulosic waste materials, dedicated energy crops, which are grown specifically for ethanol production, include fast-growing trees (poplars), shrubs (willow), and grasses (switch grass). The cellulosic components of these materials range between 30% and 70%.

This new concept of utilising cellulosic feedstock for bioethanol production is not yet applicable on the large scale, but is currently subject to intensive research. The large-scale production of agricultural ethanol requires substantial amounts of cultivable land with fertile soils and water (except for wastes).

Sugar crops

Sugar beet: Sugar beet (*Beta vulgaris* L.) belongs to the subfamily of the *Chenopodiaceae* and to the Family of the *Amaranthaceae*. Its roots contain a high concentration of sucrose and therefore it is grown commercially for sugar production. The three largest sugar beet producers worldwide are the European Union, the United States, and Russia. Only Europe and Ukraine are significant exporters of sugar from beet. Ukraine and Russia have the largest cultivated area, but the largest producers by volume are France and Germany. Despite from the food industry, sugar beet molasses is a valuable feedstock for bioethanol.

Sugar beet is a hardy biennial plant that can be grown commercially in a wide variety of temperate climates. During growth it produces a large (1–2 kg) storage root whose dry mass is 15–20% sucrose by weight. This sucrose and the other nutrients in the root are consumed to produce the plant's flowers and seeds if it is not harvested in the first year. In commercial beet production, the root is harvested in the first growing season, when the root is at its maximum size. Beets are planted from small seeds. In most temperate climates, beets are planted in spring and harvested in autumn. A minimum growing season of 100 days can produce commercially viable sugar beet crops. In warmer climates, sugar beets can be cultivated as winter crop, being planted in the autumn and harvested in the spring.

Sugar cane: Sugar cane (*Saccharum* sp.) is a genus of 37 species of tall grasses and belongs to the family of the *Poaceae* and is native to warm temperate to tropical regions. The species of sugarcane are interbreed, and the esteemed commercial cultivars are complex hybrids. Sugarcane is a grass originally found in tropical region of Southeast Asia. The plants have stout, jointed fibrous stalks which are 2 to 6 meters tall and rich in a sugar bearing sap. Today about 107 countries grow sugar cane whereas Brazil is the world leading producer. Sugar cane is the most significant crop for biofuel production today, supplying more than 40 % of all fuel ethanol. Besides the production of bioethanol, sugar cane is also used for the production of alimentary sugar, molasses, and rum. In a sugar mill the harvested sugarcane is washed, chopped, and shredded by revolving knives. The shredded cane is repeatedly mixed with water and crushed between rollers. The collected juice contains 10–15 % sucrose. The remaining fibrous solids, also called bagasse, can be used as co-product to generate process heat. It makes a sugar mill more than self-sufficient in energy. The surplus bagasse can be used for animal feed, in paper manufacture, or burned to generate electricity for the local power grid.

The juice from sugar cane is further processed, refined, fermented and distilled for bioethanol production.

Starch crops

Cereals: Cereal crops are grasses which are cultivated originally for their edible grains or seeds (actually a fruit called a caryopsis). Worldwide cereal grains are grown in greater quantities and provide more food energy to the human race than any other type of crop. The most planted cereal crops are corn (maize), wheat and rice, which account for more than 80 % of all grain production worldwide.

Although each species has its specific characteristics, the cultivation of cereal crops is similar. In general, they are annual plants and consequently one planting yields one harvest. Nevertheless, in Europe, all cereals can be divided into cool-season and warm-season types.

Recently bioethanol is produced by using waste potatoes which are a co-product of the food industry.

Cellulosic feedstock

Primary cellulosic wastes are produced during production and harvesting of food crops such as, e.g., straw, corn stalks and leaves. Also residues from forestry such as, e.g., wood thinning from commercial forestry belong to primary cellulosic wastes. These types of biomass are typically available in the field or forest and must be collected to be available for further use. Thereby attention has to be paid as there are long-term economic and environmental concerns associated with the removal of large quantities of residues from cropland. Removing residues can reduce soil quality, promote erosion, and reduce soil carbon, which in turn lowers crop productivity and profitability. But, depending on the soil type, some level of removal can be also beneficial. Establishment and communication of research-based guidelines is necessary to ensure that removal of residue biomass is done in a sustainable manner.

Secondary cellulosic wastes are generated during the production of food products and biomass materials. This biomass include nut shells, sugar cane bagasse, and saw dust, and are typically available at, e.g., industries for food and beverage production as well as at saw and paper mills. Tertiary cellulosic wastes become available after a biomass-derived commodity has been used. A large variety of different waste fractions is part of this category: Organic part of Municipal Solid Waste (MSW), waste and demolition wood, sludge, paper, etc.

Bioethanol production

Ethanol, also known as 'ethyl alcohol' or 'grade alcohol', is a flammable, colourless chemical compound, one of the alcohols that is most often found in alcoholic beverages. In common parlance, it is often referred to simply as alcohol. Its molecular formula is C_2H_6O, variously represented as EtOH, C_2H_5OH or as its empirical formula C_2H_6O.

Generally, ethanol can be produced either synthetically from petrochemical feedstock (petroleum) or by microbial fermentation which is applicable to bioethanol production. The process for production of fuel bioethanol from biomass can be broken down as follows:

Feedstock production: Harvesting, reception, storage.

Physical pretreatment: Milling.

Saccarification: Conversion of starch and cellulose into sugar.

Chemical treatment: Dilution of the sugars with water and addition of yeast or other organisms.

Fermentation: Production of ethanol in solution with water along with waste and by-products.

Distillation: Separation of ethanol.

Dehydration: Removal of the remaining water by molecular sieves (anhrour ethanol).

Co-product preparation: Drying of the alcohol free stillage (mash) for high-value animal feed.

These steps in the feedstock-to-ethanol conversion process largely depend on the type of feedstock.

Sugar-to-ethanol process

The simplest way to produce ethanol is the sugar-to-ethanol production. Yeast biomass is used the hexose sugars which can be fermented directly to ethanol. Examples for typical sugary feedstock types are sugar cane and sugar beets which contain substantial amounts of sugar. Although fungi, bacteria, and yeast micro-organisms can be used for fermentation, the specific yeast *Saccharomyces cerevisiae* (Bakers' yeast) is frequently used to ferment glucose to ethanol. Traditional fermentation processes rely on yeasts that convert six-carbon sugars (mainly glucose) to ethanol.

$$C_6H_{12}O_6 + \text{Zymase } (\textit{S. cerevisiae}) \rightarrow 2C_2H_5OH + 2CO_2$$

51.4 g of ethanol and 48.8 g of carbon dioxide will be produced theoretically by 100 g of sugar. In Brazil and in most tropical countries which produce ethanol, sugar cane is the most common feedstock for ethanol production. In these warm countries costs of ethanol production from sugar cane are among the lowest for any biofuels.

Starch-to-ethanol process

Another potential ethanol feedstock is starch. In Europe and in the United states a large portion of bioethanol is produced from the starch component of grain crops, primarily corn and wheat in the US and wheat and barley in Europe.

Starch molecules are made up of long chains of glucose molecules which have to be broken into simple glucose molecules (saccharification). Therefore starchy materials require a reaction of starch with water (hydrolysis). The hydrolysis is performed by diluting the starch with water to form slurry which is then agitated and heated to break the bound between the molecules. During the heating cycle, specific enzymes are added, which break the chemical bonds. Organisms and enzymes for starch conversion and glucose fermentation on a commercial scale are readily available.

The starchy part of the crop plant is only used in conventional starch-to-ethanol processes. Other part of the kernels of corn, barley or wheat, represent a fairly small percentage of the total plant mass. The fibrous portion of these plants like seed husks and stalks remain. Current research on cellulosic ethanol production is focused on utilising these waste cellulosic materials to create fermentable sugars. This leads to more efficient production of ethanol than from using just the sugars and starches directly available.

Cellulose-to-ethanol process

Besides sugar and starch, also cellulose can be converted into ethanol, but the cellulosic biomass-to-ethanol production process is more complicated than the sugar or starch to-ethanol process.

Cellulosic materials are composed of lignin, hemicellulose, cellulose and so these are also called lignocellulosic materials. They have to be converted to five- and six-carbon sugars, before they can be fermented and converted into ethanol. The primary functions of lignin is to provide structural support for the plant. So generally, trees have higher lignin contents then grasses. Unfortunately, lignin which contains no sugars encloses the cellulose and hemicellulose molecules, making them difficult to reach. Cellulose molecules polymer of glucose molecules same as the starch molecules, cellulose has a different structural configuration. These structural characteristics plus the encapsulation by lignin makes cellulosic materials more difficult to hydrolyse than starchy materials. Also hemicellulose is comprised of long chains of sugar molecules. The exact sugar composition of hemicellulose can vary depending on the type of plant. For complete fermentation of cellulosic materials special organisms are required. Bacteria have drawn special attention from researchers because of their speed of fermentation. In general, bacteria can ferment in minutes as compared to hours for yeasts.

There are three basic process types for conversion of cellulose to ethanol: acid hydrolysis, enzymatic hydrolysis, and thermochemical process. The most common type is acid hydrolysis. Virtually any acid can be used. However, sulphuric acid is most commonly used since it is usually the least expensive.

Distillation and dehydration process

Ethanol produced by fermentation results in a solution of ethanol in water. For ethanol to be used as fuel, water must be removed. The oldest method therefore is distillation, but the purity is limited to 95–96% due to the formation of a low-boiling water-ethanol azeotrope. The azeotrope is a solution of two or more liquids substances that retains the same composition in the vapour state as in the liquid state when distilled or partially evaporated under a certain pressure. It means that the composition of this liquid at its azeotropic composition can not be changed by simple boiling.

The purification of ethanol higher than 96% is very difficult by simple distillation. But after blending with gasoline, ethanol purities of 99.5 to 99.9% can be achieved. Currently, the most widely used purification method is a physical absorption process using molecular sieves.

Properties of bioethanol

Ethanol has many favourable properties. For example, the octane number of ethanol is higher than the octane number of conventional petrol. The octane number influences the antiknocking property of the fuel. A high octane number stands for an antiknocking fuel. Knocking describes uncontrolled combustion which puts heavy mechanical and thermal loads on the engine.

On the other hand, the energy yield of ethanol is about one third lower than petrol. One litre of ethanol substitutes only about 0.65 litres of petrol. This is due to the different caloric values of petrol and ethanol. The energy content of petrol is 32.5 MJ/l and 21.2 MJ/l of ethanol.

Another property of ethanol is its low vapour pressure. When stored as a pure fuel (or even as an E-85 blend), it has a lower vapour pressure than gasoline, and thus will have fewer evaporative emissions. In colder climates, the low vapour pressure of pure ethanol can cause cold start problems. Therefore in cold climates ethanol is blended with gasoline (E85). In contrast, lower-level blends of ethanol in gasoline, tend to raise the vapour pressure of the base gasoline to which ethanol is added. When ethanol is blended up to about 40 percent with gasoline, the two fuels combined have higher evaporative emissions than either does on its own.

This example shows that different blends of ethanol and petrol have different properties. Depending on the situation and the desired fuel, ethanol is therefore blended with gasoline at any ratio. Common ethanol blends are E5, E10, E20, E25, E70, E85, E95, and E100, which contain 5%, 10%, 20%, 25%, 70%, 85%, 95%, and 100% ethanol, respectively. Also other varying quantities are possible. In the European Union, so-called flexible-fuel vehicles (FFV) are currently entering the market. They can run with an ethanol proportion of any mixture up to 85 %.

Ethanol is also increasingly used as an oxygenate additive for standard petrol, as a replacement for methyl tertiary butyl ether (MTBE). MTBE is usually mixed with petrol as an additive to improve the octane number. Table 11.2 show the difference in bioethanol and petrol.

Table 11.2: Difference in bioethanol and petrol.

Parameter	Bioethanol	Petrol
Density (kg/l)	0.79	0.76
Viscosity (mm^2/g)	1.5	0.6
Flash point (°C)	< 21	<21
Calorific value (at 20°C MJ/Kg)	26.8	42.7
Octane number	>100	92
Fuel equivalence	0.65	1

11.4.6   Lipid derived biofuel

Biodiesel

Properties of biodiesel: The properties of biodiesel like viscosity and ignition properties are similar to the properties of fossil diesel.

Although the energy content per litre of biodiesel is about 5 to 12 % lower than that of diesel fuel, biodiesel has several advantages. For example the cetane number and lubricating effect of biodiesel, important in avoiding wear to the engine, are significantly higher. Therefore the fuel economy of biodiesel approaches that of diesel. Additionally, the alcohol component of biodiesel contains oxygen, which helps to complete the combustion of the fuel. The effects are reduced air pollutants such as particulates, carbon monoxide, and hydrocarbons. Since biodiesel contains practically no sulphur in it and can be helpful for reducing the emissions of sulphur oxides.

Biodiesel is sensitive to cold weather and may require special anti-freezing precautions, similar to those taken with standard diesel. Therefore winter compatibility is achieved by mixing additives, allowing the use down to minus 20°C. Another problem is that biodiesel readily oxidises. Thus long-term storage may cause problems, but additives can enhance stability.

Biodiesel also has some properties similar to solvents. Therefore it can attack plastic and rubber components such as seals and fuel lines. This causes problems in vehicles which have not been approved or which are filled with biodiesel for the first time after a long mileage with fossil diesel. In this case biodiesel acts like a detergent additive, loosening and dissolving sediments in storage tanks. Residues of the fossil fuel are released, causing the filter to become blocked. It is therefore advisable to change the fuel filter after several tank fillings with biodiesel.

Conventional diesel engines operate readily with up to 100 % biodiesel fuel, but using blends above 20 % may require modest costs in order to replace some rubber hoses that are sensitive to the solvent character of biodiesel.

11.4.7   Raw material for biodiesel production

The choice for a dedicated feedstock is predetermined by agricultural, geographical and climatic conditions. But it also has to be considered, that different feedstock types are characterised by different properties. For instance, the oil saturation and the fatty acid content of different oilseed species vary considerably. Biodiesel from highly saturated oils is characterised by superior oxidative stability and high cetane number, but performs poorly at low temperatures. The major seeds are from sunflower, peanut, sorghum, rapeseed, ricinus, sorghum, jatropha, etc. Different feedstock for biodiesel is shown in Fig. 11.5.

Rapeseed

Rape (*Brassica napus* L. ssp. *oleifera*), also known as canola or colza, belongs to the family of the *Brassicacea* and is closely related to other oil seed crops

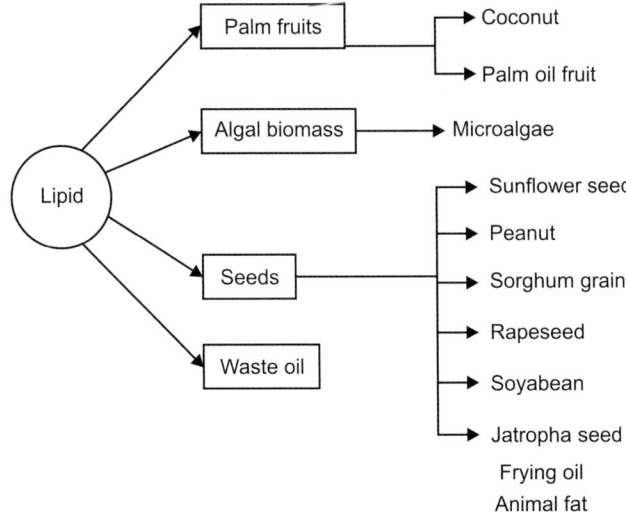

Figure 11.5: Different feedstock for biodiesel.

such as mustard species (*Brassica nigra*, *Sinapis alba*) and Gold-of-pleasure (*Camelia sativa*).

Rape is cultivated and sowed either in autumn (biennial) or in spring (annual). The plant has a long taproot and the stem can grow up to 1.5 m. The seeds are enclosed in pointed pots. Winter rape in Europe is harvested at the end of July with yields of 3 T/ha. Summer rape ripens in September and yields 2.1 T/ha.

Palm oil

The oil palm (*Elaeis guineensis*) is one of the two palm trees (besides coconut palm) that are used for oil production, mainly in South Asian countries. The two largest producers are Malaysia and Indonesia, where palm oil production has grown rapidly over the last decade. Nigeria has the second largest planted area and high potentials are expected in Brazil. While most palm oil is used for food purposes, the demand for palm biodiesel is expected to increase rapidly, particularly in Asia.

Fuel production

Today, mainly oil from plant sources which are exclusively harvested for biofuel production (oil crops) is used for biodiesel processing. So, in this chapter our concentration is firstly on biofuel production from seed oil crops. The amount of fuel production from microalgae, animal fats and waste oils is only small, although the potential is expected to be very high. The harvest of oil crops depends on the plant species and the technique available. Taking rape as an example, the harvest is conducted by using a combine harvester. The seeds are either transported directly to the oil mill or stored first. The first process step of biofuel production then is the oil extraction which can be done by several means.

Oil extraction

The oil extraction of the feedstock is the first process step of biodiesel processing. Regarding the scale of production and the infrastructure, there are two fundamental production process types for vegetable oils:

Industrial: Centralised production by refining in large industrial plants.

Small scale pressing: Decentralised cold pressing directly on farms or in co-operatives.

In small scale cold pressing facilities, the cleaned oil seeds are exclusively mechanically pressed at maximum temperatures of 40°C. Suspended solids are removed by filtration or sedimentation. As a co-product, the press cake is left with a remaining oil content of usually over 10%, which is used as a protein-rich fodder. Due to higher production costs, the decentralised oil production by farmers is not widely applied today, although the chance of additional income for farmers is given. Furthermore, the co-product could be directly used for feeding the animals.

The common way in oil extraction is the treatment of feedstock in centralised industrial large scale plants. First, the feedstock has to be pre-treated. For better illustration purposes, the processing of rape oil is used here as an example for oil extraction. The process flow diagram is shown in Fig. 11.6.

Within the pre-treatment the rape seeds have to be dried first, but only if it will be stored more for than ten days. In this case, the typical water content of rape seeds, which is about 15%, has to be reduced to 9%. Subsequently, the rape seeds are cleaned. Additionally, other seeds that are larger in size, such as sunflower seeds, have to be peeled.

When pressing rape seeds, the press cake is left as co-product. It still contains the remaining 25% of the total rape seed oil content and therefore is further treated. First, the press cake has to be crushed so that the added solvent, which is usually hexane, can extract the oil at temperatures of up to 80°C . The results of this process step are a mixture of oil with hexane, also called miscella, and the so called extraction grist. The solvent is separated from both compounds and recycled to the process.

After these process steps, the oil has more undesired components as in cold pressing. They are removed by refining. The end product is oil designated as fully refined in edible oil quality.

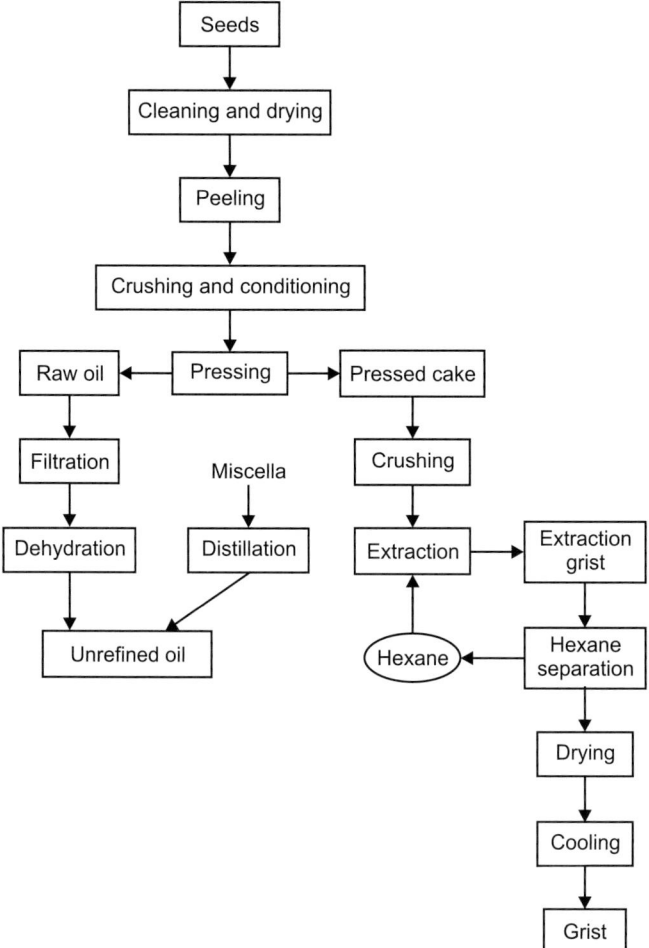

Figure 11.6: Oil extraction process.

Transesterification

The molecular structure of lipid molecules are changed in the chemical process of transesterification during biodiesel production. Thereby the physical properties change. Although even refined pure plant oil (PPO) can be used in refitted diesel engines, biodiesel, which is created by a transesterification step, has several advantages. One advantage is the lower viscosity of biodiesel when compared to PPO. Increased viscosity adversely affects fuel injection duration, pressure, and atomisation of diesel engines. Biodiesel is very similar to fossil diesel and thus can be consumed in common diesel engines which are refitted with only small efforts.

Transesterification, also known as alcoholysis, it is the process in which the refined oil molecule is 'breakdown'. The glycerin is removed for manufacturing of glycerin soap and methyl-or ethyl esters for biodiesel. Organic fats and oils are triglycerides which are three hydrocarbon chains connected by glycerol. The bonds are broken by hydrolysing them to form free fatty acids. These fatty acids are then mixed or reacted with methanol or ethanol forming methyl or ethyl fatty acid esters (monocarbon acid esters). The mixture separates and settles out leaving the glycerin on the bottom and the biodiesel (methyl, ethyl ester) on the top. Now the separation of these two substances has to be conducted completely and quickly to avoid a reversed reaction. These transesterification reactions are often catalysed by the addition of an acid or base. The chemical transesterification reaction is shown in Fig. 11.7.

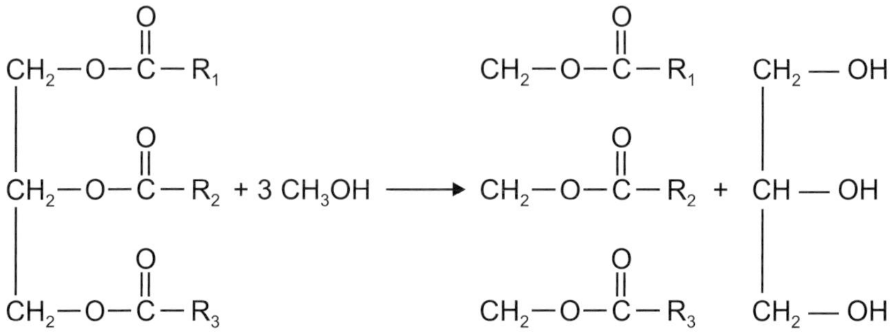

Figure 11.7: Transesterification process.

For the transesterification process, mainly the alcohols methanol and ethanol are used. Theoretically transesterification can be also processed with higher or secondary alcohols. Transesterification with methanol, also called methanolysis, is the most commonly method for biodiesel production. Methanol is characterised by its lower prices and its higher reactivity as compared to other alcohols. This reaction can happen by heating a mixture of 80–90 per cent oil, 10–20 per cent methanol, and small amounts of a catalyst. For the reaction it is necessary to mix all ingredients well, as the solubility of methanol in vegetable oil is relatively low. The received biodiesel after methanolysis is Fatty Acid Methyl Ester (FAME).

Biohydrogen

Biohydrogen gas is a perfect renewable fuel hydrogen when burnt does not cause any pollution but regenerates water. Hydrogen production process operates at a normal temperature. No toxic materials are produced in the process. Biohydrogen can be made directly from biomass in presence of sunlight, or it can be produced by splitting of water molecule into its constituent components of hydrogen and oxygen. Some microbial strains like *Rhodopseudomonas* bacterial produces biohydrogen. Algae is also another source of production. Through recent technologies biohydrogen is produced from a variety of energy sources, stored for later use, piped to where it is used and then converted cleanly into heat and electricity. Hydrogen is the most efficient source of energy. Now a days hydrogen production is being done by steam reforming natural gas, but the natural gas is already a good energy source or fuel. Natural gas is rapidly becoming dangerous and more expensive. As natural gas is a fossil fuel, so it will generate green house gases whenever biohydrogen does not cause any type of pollution. Very high energy is liberated during the combustion of biohydrogen. The major challenge is to increase the production efficiency of biohydrogen, so new technology is needed to increase production, store and transport it. The fuel cell technology is still in early development, it is needing improvements in efficiency and durability.

Micro-organisms:

1. Anaerobic bacteria.
2. Photosynthetic algae, e.g., *clostridium butyricum, enterobacter aerogenes, Rhodopseudomonas palustirs, Rhodopseudomonas rubrum, Rhodobacter sphyroid.*

Substrate (Raw material):

Wastewater, food waste, vegetable waste, other organic wastes.

Bio-hydrogen production mechanisms:

It can be possible by two routes:

1. Anaerobic fermentation.
2. Photolysis of water.

Anaerobic bacterial mechanism of bio-hydrogen production.

An anaerobic bacteria oxidise the substrate by reducing NAD$^+$ to NADH. But for continued substrate oxidation, it is essential to remove NADH which is transferred to H$^+$ ions to produce gas; there by regenerating NAD$^+$, the reaction is catalysed by enzyme 'Hydrogenase' as shown below:

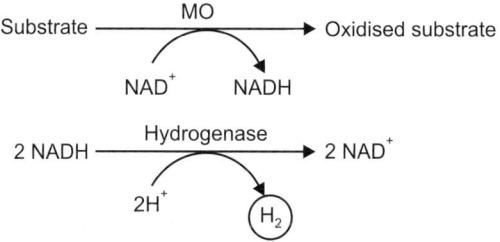

'Hydrogenase' enzyme that has been extracted from 15 species of bacterial and algae. Japanese biotechnologists have immobilised clostridium butyricum and these cells produce H_2 gas for a month when feel with wastewater containing sugar from a alcohol industry. Anaerobic packed bed reactor and agar entrapment used for the purpose.

R. palustris has been grown in anaerobic bioreactor. Plants of agar immobilised organism are used. The system is easy to operate and build 0.78 L/L of H_2 production from sugar refinery and 2.2 L/L H_2 from straw paper mill effluent is reported. *R. gelatinosa* produced more H_2 from organic acid than from sugars like glucose, sucrose, lactose, 50 ml of H_2 is produced per gram of total organic carbon used.

Japans fermentation Research Institute and agency of industrial science and technology have jointly developed a system to efficiently produce the H_2 gas. Bacteria used for the system is *Rhodobactor sphyroid* (photosynthetic bacteria). H_2 gas has 3 times more calorific value per unit weight of petroleum and it does not generate CO_2 or other air pollutants. Energy conversion can be increased up to 20%.

Photosynthetic pathway (Algae)

Some algae also produce H_2. Photosynthetic apparatus splits water molecule into H_2 and O_2. The photosystem-I produces then reduced ferredoxin. Ferredoxin then oxidised and protein (H^+) act as electron acceptors to produced H_2. The efficiency of H_2 production is reasonable at low light intensities.

Upon a dark anaerobic incubation of the algae and the ensuing induction of the hydrogenase, electrons for the photosynthetic apparatus are derived upon a catabolism of endogenous substrate and the attendant oxidative carbon metabolism in the green algae.

Electrons substrate catabolism feed into the photosynthetic electron transport chain between the two photosystems, PS-I and PS-II. Light absorption by Photosystem-I and the ensuing electron transport elevates the redox potential of these electrons to the redox equivalent of ferredoxin and the hydrogenase, thus permitting the generation of molecular H_2.

11.4.8 Advantages and limitation of biofuels

Advantages of biofuels

The advantages of biofuels are given below:

Cost: As well as new technologies are being developed the prices of biofuels are falling which have the potential to be significantly much less expensive than fossil fuels. In fact, bioethanol is already less costly than diesel and gasoline. Although it is absolutely true that the worldwide demand for fuels is increasing exponentially. So the alternative source of biofuels/bioenergy have to be developed and searched because we have a limited stock of fossil fuel as it is decreasing very rapidly.

Raw materials: Biofuels can be produced from a wide range of raw materials including agricultural waste, domestic waste, food industry waste, meat industry waste and other by-products of different industries. This will be helpful for managing the waste material, utilisation and recycling of waste for biofuel production.

Renewable: Biofuels can be produced from waste or very cheap raw materials. The production time and cost is much lower. The process of fossil fuels formation takes a very long time.

Feature security: Biofuels can be produced easily world wide. The dependency on foreign nations can be reduced for fossil fuels by producing biofuels locally. Country like India imports approximately 80% fossils fuels from other countries. It has been observed the cost of fossil fuels are increasing very high rate. So biofuels not only make a nation independent for energy requirement but it is also very helpful to build a nation prosperous by saving currency spent for fossil fuels purchasing.

Economic boostup: As we have discussed that biofuels can be produced locally at very low cost. The production of biofuels will definitely reduce the dependency of a country on other country for fossil fuels. It will save currency which is spending for fossil fuels purchasing, that currency now, will be utilise for other developmental work and will be helpful for boostup the economy of any nation.

Lower carbon emissions: Environmental pollution is another big challenge to all of us. On of the major causes of air pollution is highly consumption of fossil fuels which can not be reduced. Biofuels are eco-friendly fuels it produce significantly less carbon output and fewer toxins, making them a safer option to preserve atmospheric quality and lower air pollution.

Disadvantages of biofuels

There are some following disadvantages of biofuels production and utilisation:

Energy yield: Although biofuels have a lower energy output than traditional fossil fuels, so biofuels are required in greater quantities for producing the same energy level. This has been noticed by energy analysts that biofuels are not worth the work to convert them to ethanol rather than bioenergy or electricity.

Carbon emissions: Some of researchers have been studied to analyse the carbon footprint of biofuels, while they are being cleaner to burn, during the process to producing the biofuels. The production processes of biofuels production, cultivation of crops have hefty carbon emissions. In addition, pretreatment of raw materials and during the production of biofuels (e.g., CH_4) also promotes large amount of carbon emissions.

High cost: In some cases biofuels production and purification cost may be higher (e.g., biodiesel).

Food prices: As some biofuels like ethanol can be produced by grains as a raw materials, this may cause for increase of demand for food crops such as corn, due to higher demand the rates may increase of staple food crops.

Food shortages: The area of agricultural land is shrinking day by day, in such case our first priority should be to make available food to our peoples. In such case the production of biofuels from food grains may lead to shortage of food materials.

Water use: Huge amount of water is consumed during irrigation of biofuel crops as well as in manufacturing process of biofuels.

11.5   Future prospects

11.5.1   Economy of biofuels

In the whole life cycle of biofuels, the relatively high production costs still remain a critical barrier to commercial development, although continuing improvements are achieved. The technologies for pure plant oil (non-edible oil) extraction, purification and conversion to biodiesel have been developed.

The competitiveness of biofuels will increase as prices for crude oil and other fossil sources increase and overstep a critical threshold. Subsidies can be both agricultural aids and market incentives for the biofuel itself. Also tax exemptions have considerable impacts on end-user costs for biofuels.

For first generation biofuels, the feedstock is a major component of overall costs. As crop prices are highly volatile, the overall production costs of biofuels vary. The production scale of biofuels has significant impact on cost. It is more important for ethanol processing than for production of pure plant oil and biodiesel. This advantage for lipid derived fuels is especially important for small scale agricultural producers and SME's. Some country like Brazil, Germany, etc., have established industrial plants for biofuels or bioenergy production. Generally biofuels are expected to have large socio-economic impacts, especially for local actors. Biofuel production opens new market opportunities for agricultural products and thus new income options for farmers. In the future agriculture will not only play a role in food production, but also in energy provision. The increased feedstock production is expected to strongly contribute to the multi-functionality of the agricultural sector. Nevertheless it is difficult to assess the real dimension of additional employment and impact on local economy in the biomass sector.

Second generation fuels are not yet produced on commercial scale. Due to high production costs, they are not competitive at the moment, but as technology improves, they may become an important role in biofuel provision. The great advantage of these fuels is the vast range of feedstock that can be used for biofuel production, as well as the reduced feedstock (e.g., cellulose crops) costs.

After overall process and technologies used for biofuels production we are able to conclude that there are a lot of advantage of biofuels over fossil fuels, but direct cost comparisons may be difficult. Negative externalities associated with fossil fuels tend to be poorly quantified, such as military expenditures and costs for health and environment. Biofuels have the potential to help environment clean and green due not emission of green house gases and decrease the air pollution, production and management of biofuels will create millions of jobs worldwide.

Additionally biofuels decrease dependency from crude oil imports. Consequently biofuels are a more socially and environmentally desirable liquid fuel, a fact that is often neglected in direct-cost calculations. So biofuels are the potential fuels which have no competitiveness with fossil fuels. Biofuels are sustainable energy source so it may actually provide long-term economic benefits to market, eco-friendly environment.

11.5.2   Economical and social aspect of waste treatment

The economic feasibility of using anaerobic treatment process for production of biogas from wastes are:

1. It is dependent on various factors such as availability of a domestic source of energy.
2. Cost of imported fuel.
3. Uses and actual benefits from biogas production, the public and private costs associated with the development and utilisation of biogas production, the public and private costs associated with the development and utilisation of biogas.
4. Technology used to generate biogas.

All these parameters have to be taken into account while a analysing the cost effectiveness of such as project.

An interesting cost benefit analysis and comparison has been reported on the production of 230000 T of nitrogen fertiliser annually using chemical technology and alternate biogas technology are shown in Table 11.3. This analysis has been done for biogas produced using cattle dung as raw material.

Table 11.3: Comparison of chemical technology with biogas technology (cost estimation year 2008).

Item	Chemical technology	Biogas technology
No. of plants	1 (coal based)	26450 (7.8 T/plant/year)
Capital cost	Rs 1150 million	Rs 100 million (Rs 3800/plant)
Foreign exchange	80 million dollars	Nil
Capital – Sole ratio (at 510 dollars/T N_2)	1.2	1.07
Employment	1100	120750 (5 person/plant)
Energy	0.1 million MWh/year consumed	6.35 million MWh/year generated
Effect on rural development	Centralised	Highly decentralised
Potable water	Required	Not required

Thus, this quantity of dung can produce more than 100 million m^3 biogas per day, having an energy equivalent of 560 million kwh or kerosene equivalent of 30000 T.

The potentiality of cattle dung as one the best feedstocks for the production of biogas and biofertiliser in India. Further the large scale utilisation of dung in biogas plant would simultaneously produce gaseous fuel and organic manure, which in turn, will reduce the countrys dependence on fossil fuels as the main source of energy and on naphtha as a fertiliser.

Community biogas plant

People in the rural sector depend mostly on wood, straw, leaves, dung cakes, etc., as their main source of energy. These fuel materials are mostly burnt in primitive ovens, with minimum fuel efficiency. That means, per unit of useful energy, fuel consumption is very large. Others disadvantages are the trees are cut to be used as fuel and thereby cause deforestation.

These problems and effects are being directed at seeking alternative source of energy for the rural population. The alternative energy sources for the rural, sector can be categorised as directly solar and indirectly solar.

Although biomass can be burnt directly as fuel, it is not advisable to do so for two reason. First, all types of biomass have food fertiliser value, which the village people can directly use for their land. Therefore, these materials should not be wasted by burning them as fuel second, biomass is low grade fuel. If burnt directly, only about 10% of its energy content is utilised, and the remaining gets waste. An appropriate technology for the rural community will be one which extract high grade fuel value from biomass and also ensure that it does not lose its fertiliser.

Concepts

Biomass is abundantly available in villages. If all kinds of cellulosic wastes material (or biomass) available in a village are collected together and treated in a common ferment or, the gas produced from such a plant may be sufficient to cater to the energy needs of the entire village. There is another reason in favour of community biogas plants. Lack of private toilets in rural areas, which forces people in the villages to develop the unhealthy habit of going to the field to relive themselves.

A suitably designed and conveniently located community biogas plant can solve the aforementioned problems and will have the following advantages.

1. Land economy: A community biogas plant occupies a much smaller area of land.
2. Toilet facility: Community toilets can be constructed and attached to biogas plant. This will improve the hygiene condition of the village on one hand and allow for the utilisation of the waste material for production of gas and fertiliser on the other hand.
3. Maintenance problem: The smooth operation of a gas plant depends on its proper maintenance. It will be less troublesome and more economical to maintain a single large unit than a large number of small units.

Various factors their need to be considered while deciding the size of a community biogas plant.

Size: Size of a biogas plant depends on various factors.

1. Nature and quantity of biomass available in a village, purpose of utilisation of biogas.
2. Necessity of single unit or more than one in village.

The number of biogas units may be selected after considering the problem related to the collection of biomass.

Retention time: Another important factor that influence the size of community gas plant is the retention time.

The destruction of the pathogenic bacteria present in the biomass fed into the digester should be one of the prime concerns in dividing the retention time.

Economic analysis of family size biogas plant

The economic analysis of any venture involve expenditure and statements. To evaluate the cost benefit viability of any viability of any project, the total investment incurred in the venture and the annual earnings therefore are to be necessarily considered.

Environmental laws and policies in India

Environmental legislation provides a legal tool for regulating the undesirable activities affecting the environment. Currently three approaches are being used.

1. The first method is limited in scope for example water pollution control, air pollution control, noise pollution control come under this category.
2. The law for prevention and control of water pollution and air pollution were enacted in 1974 and 1981.
3. The second approach for environmental pollution control is more comprehensive in nature. This policy covers will all type of pollution, namely water, air, land, noise, under a single legislated.
4. The third approach is the best. It envisages the integration of environmental protection with national development planning. In this approach environmental protection it integrated with the national plans for economic development.

Social aspect of waste treatment

Ethical issues involved in environmental biotechnology: Ethics is the science of morals as found in human conduct or behaviour and is related to the study of moral principles of human behaviour in a society.

Many individuals feels that nature and environment exist for the benefit of human being alone. Therefore they indiscriminately use plants, animals, and other environmental resources to meet their selfish purposes.

However there is also a parallel attitude which demands that nature be considered a sacred creation and that it must be respected and not tampered with mean that human beings should not manipulated nature.

Ethical issues

1. Impact of biotechnology on human health and safety and on the environment.
2. The extent of undesirable intrusion into the natural order.
3. Issues of right justice and the economics of biotechnology application.

The specific issues of concern about the development and application of biotechnology include damage to the environment, injury to human health, food safety and socio-economics. There is a growing concern about the destruction of the aesthetic value of nature and the survival of wild animals and plants being put at stake by destroying their natural habitat. It becomes our moral obligation to take care of and preserve nature. Intellectual Propriety Right (IPR) is an ethical issues that a society observes to insure that an inventor is protected from unfair use of his/her invention by any unauthorised person. This ethical principle is supported by law. Copy right trademarks, patents, etc. Come under IPR. Music paintings, software, literature work, customary protection of published data in the area of biotechnology, etc., are covered under copy right.

Biogas scheme – scope for rural employment

Biogas plant can be considered as the starting point of advancing rural development. Biogas plants can bring many positive changes both at the family and society levels.

A few considerations are:

1. Waste and dung pits, which are breeding grounds for flies and insect, can be eliminated.
2. Hygiene conditions can be improved by building toilets, which may be connected to the biogas plants.
3. Immediate ready-to-use hearth for cooking can be provided doing away with the troublesome smoky kitchens.
4. From the fermented decomposed sludge, organic manure of very high grade in obtained, which can be used for enhancing the fertility of the soil.

In villages most families do not have sufficient cattle heads to operate their our biogas plants. In this context community biogas plant will prove to be beneficial, especially to the weaker sections of the rural population.

Value Added Products from Organic Waste

12.1　Introduction

Agriculture is the principal economic activity on which about three-fourths of the population of the country depends. This is the only sector which is responsible for meeting the basic needs of the growing population. The adoption of the package approach in the late sixties has changed the scenario of Indian agriculture dramatically.

Considerable advances have been made in the modernisation of Indian agriculture during the last four decades. The use of chemical fertilisers, high-yielding varieties and mechanised agricultural practices have resulted in tremendous development in the agriculture sector. Although by use of chemical fertilisers, farmers have increased food grain production; but their excessive use is now decreasing not only crop yield but imbalance of nutrients in the soil occurs. Now-a-day's intensive crop cultivation requires the use of chemical fertilisers. Chemical fertilisers are costly industrial products, and limited supply is available. In this critical situation biofertilisers are an excellent alternative. They are low-cost inputs, renewable and pollution-free. Biofertilisers are useful as a supplement to chemical fertilisers.

The balanced use of chemical fertilisers along with the integrated use of all available sources of nutrients is the need of the present agriculture system. The controlled use of chemical, organic and biological sources of plant nutrients and their efficient management have shown promising results not only in sustaining productivity and soil health but also in meeting a part of the chemical fertiliser requirement of different crops. Hence, the adoption of the Integrated Plant Nutrient Supply (IPNS) System for the safe and sustainable use of key agricultural inputs for maximisation of crop yield, stabilisation of the agrosystem and minimisation of industrial input demand is the need of today.

12.2　Biofertilisers

Biofertilisers are low-cost, effective, and renewable sources of plant nutrients used to supplement chemical fertilisers. The role of biofertilisers in agriculture production assumes special significance, particularly in the present context of the escalating cost of agriculture inputs.

Biologically active products containing selective strains of micro-organisms which can contribute to plant nutrients through microbial activity are known as biofertilisers. Biofertilisers are mixture containing specific strains of micro-organisms like bacteria, fungi, algae or their combinations. When these preparations are incorporated with seeds, setts, seedlings or soil, they enhance crop productivity and soil health, by way of biological nitrogen fixation, solubilisation and uptake of other nutrients and synthesis of growth-promoting substances. Biofertilisers have a number of advantages over chemical fertilisers. Biofertilisers are very cheap. They supply other nutrients, may control plant pathogens, also supply vitamins and plant growth hormones and prevent soil erosion by producing capsular polysaccharides. They also convert immobilised chemical into soluble forms and make them available to the plants.

12.2.1 Advantages of biofertilisers

The biofertilisers are found to make their contribution as agriculture inputs due to the following advantages:

1. Biofertilisers are supplements to chemical fertilisers.
2. Biofertilisers are low cost and can help to reduce consumption of such fertilisers.
3. They contain micro-organisms which provide biological nitrogen directly to plants.
4. They help in solubilisation and mineralisation of other plant nutrients like phosphates.
5. They improve plant growth due to better sysnthesis and availability of hormones, vitamins, auxins and other growth-promoting substances.
6. On an average crop yield increases by 10–20 per cent with their use.
7. They control and suppress soil-borne diseases.
8. They help in the proliferation and survival of beneficial micro-organisms in the soil.
9. They improve soil texture by increasing amount of humans and maintain soil fertility.
10. They are eco-friendly and pollution free.

Broadly, biofertilisers are categorised into two main groups, viz., biological nitrogen fixing biofertilisers and phosphate solubilising or mobilising biofertilisers. Biological nitrogen fixing biofertilisers consist of micro-organisms which have the ability to fix biological molecular nitrogen (N_2) either symbiotically or asymbiotically in the plants; whereas, phosphate solubilising biofertilisers are capable of solubilising or mobilising the fixed insoluble phosphates of the soil.

12.3   Types of biofertilisers

Broadly biofertilisers are divided into five main categories. These five types are again divided in sub-types as follows:

12.3.1   Nitrogen fixers

1. Symbiotic: *Rhizobium, Frankia, Anabaena azollae.*
2. Free living: *Azotobacter, Clostridium, Blue green algae, Azolla, Acetobacter, Nostoc, Anabaena.*
3. Associative symbiotic: *Azospirillum.*

12.3.2   Phosphate supplier

1. Phosphate solubiliser:
   Bacteria: *Bacillus megaterium, Phosphaticum, Bacillus circulans, Pseudomonas striata, Pseudomonas* sp..
   Fungi: *Penicillium sp, Aspergillus awamori.*
2. Phosphate absorber biofertilisers:
   Arbuscular mycorrhiza: Glomus sp., Gigaspora sp., Acaulospora sp., Scutellospora sp. and *Sclerocystis* sp.
   Ectomycorrhiza: Laccaria sp., Pisolithus sp., Boletus sp., Amanita sp.
   Orchid mycorrhiza: Rhizoctonia solani.

12.3.3   Sulphur supplier

Thiobacillus novellus, Aspergillus.
   Micronutrients supplier: Silicate and Zinc solubilisers: *Bacillus* sp.
   Plant growth promoters: Pseudomonas: *Pseudomonas fluorescens.*

12.3.4   Organic matter decomposer and microbial cell mass

Cellulose decomposer, Lignin decomposer.

12.4   Production of biofertilisers

12.4.1   Nitrogen fixers

Rhizobium

Rhizobium is a gram negative rod shaped bacteria, it fixes atmospheric nitrogen symbiotically by forming the nodules on the roots of leguminous plants. The root nodule formation process is highly specific. *Rhizobium* isolated from root nodules of bean group plant, do not induce root nodule in the pea group plant. It is essential to use specific *Rhizobium* species as a fertiliser for specific plant.

Mass cultivation

Sterilise the growth medium and add the pure culture of *Rhizobium* to prepare inoculum. Incubate on a shaker at 30 to 32°C for 3–4 days. Transfer this inoculum under sterile precautions to a large fermenter; incubate under aeration for 4–9 days. Rhizobium biomass is cultivated and mixed with lignite, charcoal powder, peat or farmyard manure. These materials will act as carrier. Lignite is most commonly used. Lignite is obtained from mine. It is sieved through a sieve of 85 mesh sterilised and cooled.

The pH is adjusted to 6.5 to 7.5 by using sterile $CaCO_3$ or lime. Lignite has 30–40 per cent moisture which prevents death of bacteria during storage. *Rhizobium* mass is thoroughly mixed with carrier by using rotatory drum. This mixture is allowed to stabilise for 24 hours. Then it is packaged in polyethylene bags and properly sealed, otherwise, carrier get dried leading to the death of micro-organisms during storage.

Methods of application

On the seed surface: Mix the fertiliser in clean water to prepare a thick slurry. Use 250 grams of fertiliser for 10 kg seeds. It is recommended to mix 10 per cent sugar or jaggery or 4 per cent gum in the slurry. Spray uniformly this slurry on the surface of seeds. Intermittent mixing of seeds helps for uniform distribution. Dry seeds in the shade and sow immediately.

Frankia (Actinorrhiza)

Frankia belongs to actinomycetes. *Frankia* is also a symbiotic nitrogen fixer. It is a filamentous bacterium and bears spores in chain. It forms root nodules in the forest crops. 24 genera and 8 Angiosperm families of forest crops are known to possess actinorrhizal root nodules. *Casurina sitophilia* and *Alnus*, forest crops common in India bear actinorrhizal root nodule. Root nodule formed by *Frankia* are hard like wooden and large (5 to 6 cm in diameter) resembling a tennis ball.

Mass cultivation

Cultivation is done by using specific medium under microaerophilic condition incubating at 28–30°C at least for 4 weeks. *Frankia* is a slow grower. The medium used for cultivation of *Frankia* is shown is Table 12.1.

Table 12.1: Medium used for cultivation of *Frankia* (g/litre).

Component	Concentration
K_2HPO_4	0.591
NH_4Cl	0.267
KH_2PO_4	0.952
$MgSO_4. \ 7H_2O$	0.005
$CaCl_2. \ 2H_2O$	0.010
Trace elements	1 ml

Azotobacter

Azotobacter is non-symbiotic nitrogen fixing bacterium commonly present in soil. *Azotobacter* is gram negative, small rod and forms microcyst as a resistant structure in old culture. *Azotobacter species: A. chrococcum, A. vinelandi, A. beijerinckii, A. macrocytogenes. B. A nitrocaptans.*

Mass cultivation

Azotobacter is isolated from soil by using suitable nitrogen free medium. Procedure for mass cultivation and mixing is similar to that of *Rhizobium*.

Application

1. On the surface of roots: 250 grams *Azotobacter* is mixed in 10 litres of water. Roots of transplanting crops or potatoes or sugar cane pieces are dipped in this mixture for 2–3 minutes, just before the transplantation.
2. In the soil: This method is rarely used. Mixture of fertiliser in fine soil is sprayed on the soil having grown up crop. Then biofertiliser is mixed in the soil by using spade.

Azospirillum

It was found that some tropical forage crops like maize, wheat, sorghum and rye possess nitrogen fixing potential due to activity of Spirillum in their roots, Spirillum was then re-examined and named as *Azospirillum*. *Azospirillum* reside inside the roots and aerial parts of plants. They are absent in dicotyledons.

Azospirillum species: *A. brasilense, A. lipoferum, A. halopraeferans* and *A. amazonens. A. amazonense* are observed in acidic soil, *A. halopraeferans* are found in salaine soils.

Mass cultivation

It is similar to that of *Rhizobium* except the chemical composition of media for mass cultivation is different.

Application

Application of *Azospirillum* in the field is similar to *Azotobacter.*

Blue green algae (cyanobacteria)

Blue green algae like *Aulosira, Anabaena, Tolypothrix, Cylindrospermum, Nostoc, Plectonema* fix the atmospheric nitrogen. They usually represent 30 per cent of the total algae occurring in the soil.

Cyanobacteria population may be 70 per cent of total algae occurring in moist soil. Blue green algae, bear heterocyst, a site of nitrogen fixation. Cyanobacterial growth is favoured by excess of water which is a need of rice crop.

Mass cultivation

A small pit (m^2) is prepared in the soil and lined with polythene sheets, 10 kg of sieved soil, 250 grams super phosphate, 19 grams sodium molybdate are added in the pit. Water is added in the soil to maintain the level 7–10 cm depth. Furadon or carbifuron may be added as pest control. The pH is adjusted to 7.0 by lime. 0.15 gram inoculum containing mixture of different cyanobacterial genera is added in the pit. Incubated for one week. Cyanobacteria grow and form scum on water surface. When it dries out, scum is scrapped, dried, powdered and stored in bags.

Application

10–20 kg/ha dried algae is sprayed in rice field a week after transplantation of rice seeding.

Azolla

Azolla is an aquatic fern. It has mainly three parts, stem, small leaves and fine rootlets. Leaves contain an endophytic cyanobacterium. *Anabaena azollae* in its small leaf cavity on upper surface. *A. azollae* fixes the atmospheric nitrogen and supplies to the plant, whereas algae derives some nutrients from plant. *Azolla* have 94 per cent water, 5 per cent nitrogen and 1 per cent minerals. Being watery it decomposes rapidly in the soil.

Azolla species: *A. caroliniana, A. mexicana, A. microphylla, A. nilitica, A. pinnata* and *A. rubra. A. pinnata* is commonly found in India.

Mass cultivation

Prepare a microplot (20 m^2) with tin or cement. Add water 5–10 cm in depth. Add superphosphate 4–20 kg/ha, fresh *Azolla* 0.5 to 1.0 kg/m^2 to the water.

Adjust the pH of water 8.0, optimum temperature is 14–30°C. Furadon may be added as insecticide *Azolla* grows on the surface forming a mat. Harvest the *Azolla* after full growth usually after 20 days and dry.

Application

Cultivate the *Azolla* either before or after transplantation of rice in the field. Inoculate 0.5 kg/m^2 allow to grow and then water is drained to mix the *Azolla* in soil.

Limitations

In summer it is very difficult to maintain the level of water for growth of *Azolla*, growth stops as it touches to soil. *Azolla* may be washed out due to heavy rain. At temperature above 30°C, growth of *Azolla* is markedly reduced. *Azolla* mass is bulky and difficult to transport.

Advantages

Azolla shows tolerance against heavy metals, so it is the best fertiliser in the soils polluted due to metal wastes.

Acetobacter diazotrophicus: Micro-organism resides in the leaves, stem and roots of sugarcane plant, utilise sugar of the plant and fix atmospheric nitrogen. These have 20 times more efficiency to fix atmospheric nitrogen than *Azotobacter*.

12.4.2   Phosphate suppliers

The phosphorus is second important plant nutrient. There are two types of micro-organisms making available this plant nutrient.

Phosphate solubilisers

Soil contains large amount of insoluble inorganic phosphates and immobilised organic phosphorus also. Phosphate solubilising micro-organisms (bacteria, algae) solubilise tricalcium, aluminium, iron and rock phosphate and organic phosphorus. These micro-organisms easily convert these minerals in to easily available form to the crops in the soil.

PSM

Bacteria: Bacillus megaterium Var. *phosphaticum. Pseudomonas striata, P. fluorescens, Achromobacter*.

Fungi: Aspergillus, avamori, A. niger, A. flavus, Penicillium digitatum, cephalosporium.

Algae: Chlorella sp., *Anabaena, novecularis, Tolypotherix tennius.*
Actinomycetes: *Streptomyces* sp., *Actinomyces* sp.

Mass cultivation

B. megaterium var *phosphaticum and Pseudomonas striata* are generally
cultivated as fertilisers. Mass cultivation and mixing with carrier is similar to
that *Rhizobium* by using medium.

Application

Very similar to *Rhizobium* application on the seeds or transplantable crops
Vesicular arbuscular mycorrhiza (VAM). The symbiotic association between
fungus and root systems of higher plants is called mycorrhiza, which literally
means fungus roots. VAM fungi: *Glomus, Sclerocystis, Gigaspora, Endogone,
Acaulospora. VA. mycorrihizae* develop special characteristic structures called
arbuscles and vesicles. The finger like projections, arbuscles, help in the transfer
of nutrients (especially phosphates) from the soil into the root system. Absorbed
phosphate is stored in circular or ellipsoidal or rectangular vesicles. *VA.
mycorrhizae* are type of endomycorrhizae. In endomycorrhizae, the fungus
lives within the cells of the root and establishes direct connections between
the cells of the root and the surrounding soil. *VA. mycorrhizae* occur in roots
of most angiosperms, pteridophytes and bryophytes, which includes onion,
tomato, brinjal, jowar, bajra, sunflower and groundnut.

Mass cultivation

Mass cultivation of *VA mycorrhizae* is difficult. These fungi are obligate
symbionts and have not been cultivated in pure culture. The root biomass
heavily infected by a specific VAM fungus serves as the inoculum for mass
cultivation. Mass cultivation is carried out by cultivating plant roots, in sterilised
soil, in prior sterilised room. Temperature 25 to 28°C, relative humidity 70–
80 per cent and light intensity 10 to 15 kilo lux are maintained in the room.
Root pieces carrying mycorrhizae and soil around is used as inoculum and
mixed in the soil. Seeds are sown. After approximately 65 to 90 days
mycorrhizae grow luxuriantly in plant roots. During this period enough water
is supplied for plant growth. Then this soil along with root pieces are mixed
together and used as biofertiliser.

Advantages

VAM fungi also supply other nutrients like MO, Ca, Zn, Fe, Cu, Mg, to the plants.
VAM fungi absorb water from soil and supply to plant. VAM fungi also prevent
infection of plant pathogen. VAM fungi is the best fertiliser in acidic soil.

12.4.3   Sulphur supplier

Micro-organisms are known to increase the availability of sulphur in the soil for absorption by plants. Large amount of sulphur in the soil is insoluble in water and hence can not be absorbed by plant roots. Sulphur oxidising bacteria convert this insoluble sulphur to sulphate, which is absorbed by plant roots. Sulphur oxidiser: *Thiobacillus, Thiothrix, Thioploca, Aspergillus, Penicillium microsporeum. Thiobacillus thioxidans* and *T. novellus*, are commonly used as sulphur biofertilisers.

Advantages

If these are inoculated in alkaline soils, these produce H_2SO_4 and drop the pH of soil, making it fit for plant cultivation.

12.4.4   Organic matter decomposer

Large amount of complex organic matter is added in the soil in the form of plant leaves or bagasse. Micro-organisms having cellulolytic activity and lignolytic activity if added as a fertiliser, they decompose complex organic matter into simpler form and increase the fertility of soil. Cellulolytic micro-organisms like *Trichoderma, Cellulomonas* and lignolytic micro-organisms like *Arthrobacter* can be cultivated in the laboratory and added in the soil as a biofertiliser.

12.5   Microbial mass

Saprophytic microbial mass can be used as bio-organic fertiliser. Micro-organisms during growth produce different enzymes for conversion of complex substrates. Microbial mass is derived from the growth of *Penicillium* by using peanut meal, cotton seed meal, cornsteep liquors, ammonium sulphate, potassium phosphate, sulphate, phenyl, acetic acid as precursor; and zinc, iron, manganese etc., as trace element along with continuous supply of sugar solution. Microbial mass consists of protein, enzymes, vitamins, organic acids, plant growth hormones. Chitin present in it chelates the toxic metals present in soil. Micro-organisms in microbial mass also consume the waste products liberated by roots of the plants, and thus enhance the growth of plants.

12.6   Problems with biofertilisers

1. Microbial fertilisers are supplementary to chemical fertilisers but not substitute to it. Microbial fertilisers, usually cause 20 to 30 per cent

increase in crop production. They do not cause marked increase in productivity like chemical fertiliser.

2. Specific fertilisers are to be used for specific crops. This is more applicable to symbiotic micro-organisms. If non-specific *Rhizobium* is used as fertiliser, they do not cause root nodulation and increase in crop production.

3. Strict aseptic precaution is required during production of microbial fertiliser. Contamination is a common problem during microbial mass production.

4. Microbial fertilisers are sensitive to sunlight exposure. They get killed if exposed for long time in sunlight.

5. Microbial fertiliser must be used within six months after production when stored at room temperature. They can be used within two years if stored at chilling temperature.

6. Efficiency of microbial fertiliser is markedly dependent on soil character, e.g., moisture content, pH, temperature, organic matter and types of resident micro-organisms. When these factors are unfavourable microbial fertiliser may not be effective in increasing the soil fertility.

Composition of media of cultivation of bacteria (gm/l) are shown in Table 12.2.

Table 12.2: Composition of media of cultivation of bacteria (gm/l).

Component	Azotobacter	Azospirillum	Bacillus megaterium	Rhizobium
Yeast extract	–	–	0.5	1.0
Manitol	–	–	–	10
Malic acid	–	5.00	–	–
Glucose	–	–	10	–
Sucrose	20	–	–	–
$CaCl_2.2H_2O$	–	0.001	–	–
$FeSO_4.7H_2O$	–	0.05	5.00	–
K_2HPO_4	1.0	0.50	–	0.50
$MgSO_4.7H_2O$	0.50	0.10	0.10	0.20
NaCl	0.50	–	–	0.10
$FeSO_4$	0.10	–	0.0020	–
Na_2MoO_4	–	.0020	0.50	–
KOH	–	4.00	–	–
$CaCO_3$	2.00	–	–	–
$(NH_4)_2SO_4$	–	–	0.50	–

12.7   Single cell protein

12.7.1   Production of single cell protein (SCP)

In olden days people used filamentous blue green algae '*spirulina*' from lake, dried it in Sun light and used as food. First industrial production of single cell protein in 'World War I' Torula yeast (*Candida utilise*) was produced in Germany and used in soups and sausages.

SCP may be used directly as human food supplement. It may be used in animal food.

Micro-organisms used: Algae, filamentous fungi (yeast) and bacteria are used for SCP production.

Algae: (Used as feed) in Japan, Taiwan, and Maxico. *Chlorella, Scenedesmus, Spirulina.*

Yeast: Candida utilis (Torula yeast), *Saccharomyces cerevisia* (used as food) in UK, Russia, France.

Mold: Chaetomum cellulolyticum, Fusarium graminearuam.

Bacteria: Brevibacterium, Methylophillus methylotrophus (used as feed) in UK.

Substrace: Industrial effluents, confectionary effluents, whey, molasses, cellulosic wastes, sulphites liquor (wood pulpmills), distilleries, agrowastes, food wastes.

Production steps

1. Provision of carbon source, it may need physical/chemical pretreatment.
2. Addition to carbon source, nitrogen, phosphorus, other. Nutrients needed to support optimum growth of micro-organism.
3. Prevention of contamination.
4. The selected micro-organism is inoculated in a pure state.
5. Highly aerobic process (except algae) so aerate must be provided.
6. Microbial biomass is recovered from the medium (down stream processing).
7. Biomass production is carried out in the continuous mode to maximise yields and economics returns.

Recovery: Bacterial mass – flocculation, floatation with centrifugation.

Yeast: Centrifugation.

Filamentous fungi: Filtration.

Advantages of SCP

1. Rich in high quality protein, poor in fat, can be produced, good source of vitamins (B-group of vitamins), SCP can bridge the gap set requirement and supply of protein.
2. Basett Ltd. UK uses 'Candida utilise' to treat 140000 L confectionary effluent/day by continuous fermentation and produce 1.5 T of day yeast/day BOD of the effluent is reduced by 81%.
3. Sulphite liquor is widely used for SCP production in North America, Europe and Soviet Union.
4. Fungus *'Paecilomyces Varioti'* being used on an in industrial scale in Finland.
5. Cellulosic wastes fermented with fungus *Chaetomium.*

12.8   Mushroom

It is a food stock from agriculture and other highly organic waste material.

12.8.1   Micro-organism used in mushroom

Fungi

Agaricus bisporus for buttom mushroom *Pleurotus ostreatus* (India, China, East Asia) *Volvariella volvacea* (China, South Asia).

Substrate used

Cellulosic wastes, rice straw, sour dust, rice bran, straw paper, cotton, horse manure.

Production

These are following steps in production of mushroom:

1. Prepare straw compost (wheat straw 300 kg, wheat bran 25 kg, ammonium sulphate 9 kg, super phosphate 3 kg, urea 3 kg, gypsum 30 kg, V-BHC 1 kg, malatheon 200 ml.
2. Straw wetted for 45 hours, compost for 24 hour. Then mixed both, watering for 22.30 days, gypsum added and insecticides added in last.
3. Compost filled in 1×1/2×1/4 m wooden trays up to depth 16–18 cm, for temperature 60°C for 2 day for sterilisation.
4. Transfer to production room, at 24°C, inoculate and covered with news paper.

5. 10–15 days cottony mycelia growth occurs. Compost bed is covered with 1.5–2 cm thick layer of soil and sand (3:1) pH = 7 called 'casting'.

6. Watering regularly at 15°C, 70–80% humidity. Fruiting body appears other one month of casing. Harvested in 'button stage'.

Advantages

1. Protein rich (51% dry weight).
2. Rich in vitamin (Nicotinic acid, Riboflavin).
3. Lack of stack so good for diabetic patient.

12.9   Enzymes

The role of enzymes in many processes has been known for a long time. Their existence was associated with the history of ancient Greece where they were using enzymes from micro-organisms in baking, brewing, alcohol production, cheese making etc. With better knowledge and purification of enzymes the number of applications has increased manyfold, and with the availability of thermo stable enzymes a number of new possibilities for industrial processes have emerged.

12.9.1   Classification of enzymes

1. Oxidoreductases: All enzymes catalysing oxidation reduction reactions belong to this class. The substrate that is oxidised is regarded as hydrogen donor.

2. Transferases: Transferases are enzymes which transfer a group, e.g., a methyl group or a glycosyl group, from one compound (generally regarded as donor) to another compound (generally regarded as acceptor).

3. Hydrolases: These enzymes catalyse the hydrolytic cleavage of C–O, C–N, C–C and some other bonds, including phosphoric anhydride bonds.

4. Lyases: Lyases are enzymes cleaving C–C, C–O, C–N, and other bonds by elimination, leaving double bonds or rings, or conversely adding groups to double bonds.

5. Isomerases: These enzymes catalyse geometric or structural changes within one molecule.

6. Ligases: Enzymes that catalyse the joining together of two molecules coupled with the hydrolysis of a diphosphate bond in ATP or a similar triphosphate.

Different enzymes and their industrial applications are given in Table 12.3.

Table 12.3: Enzymes and their industrial applications.

Industry	Applications	Enzyme
Leather	Bating, unhairing,	Proteases, mucolytic proteases
Meat	Meat tenderising	Protease
Paper	Starch modification for paper coating	Amylase
Starch and syrup	Corn syrup, production of glucose	Amylase, dextrinase, Amyloglucosidase
Pharmaceutical	Digestive aids, cold swelling laundry starch	Amylase, protease, lipase, cellulase
Baking	Bread baking	Amylase, protease
Beer	Mashing	Amylase, protease
Carbonated beverages	Oxygen removal	Glucose oxidase
Chocolate, coffee	Syrup, coffee bean fermentation	Amylase, pectinase, hemicellulase
Dairy	Cheese production, evaporated milk, whole milk, ice cream, frozen desserts, whey concentrate	Lactase, protease, glucose oxidase renin, catalase
Distilled beverages	Mashing	Amylase
Textile	Desizing of fabrics	Amylase, protease
Vegetable	Liquefying purees and soups, dehydrated vegetables, restoring flavour	Amylase
Wine	Pressing, clarification, filtration, high test molasses	Pectinase, invertase, protease

Global Environmental Issues at National and International Level

13.1   Introduction

The global environment is affecting continuously day by day by changes in weather and land use which is creating direct impact on individuals and communities. If consider globe as whole, conflicts and interests in one area can provoke actions and reactions on the other side of the world.

The traditions in the industrialised world of consumption and economic growth have created many issues while following concept and idea of economic growth. Primarily economic focus limits the scope of sustainability and may obscure the important issues of equity within generations. There is the need of biological diversity and social equity to resist poverty in the developing and industrialised world.

People have common need of the Earth's resources, including a clean, safe and healthy environment. The quality and quantity of these basic requirements are under threat from climate change and environmental degradation. These challenges are considered as providing the greatest priority for global cooperation. As we are all aware that the world's resources are limited and are damaging by pollution and consumption patterns of these resources all over the world. Pollution is rapidly spreading its effects from one country to another country, we can not stop it by making boundary out side country. We should decrease the emission of pollutants to decrease its adverse effects. The critical condition of the physical environment requires a holistic approach. The rapidly changes in the environment significantly affects the planet as whole.

13.2   Climatic changes

Change in climate is also considered as global warming, rise in average surface temperatures on Earth. Climate change is due to the use of fossil fuels, which emits carbon dioxide and other greenhouse gases into the air. The gases trap heat within the atmosphere, which creates adverse effects on ecosystems, including rising sea levels, weather flactuations, and droughts. Climate change is caused by human activities. Human activity is affecting natural variations in Earth's climate and temperature. In any case, economists agree that acting to reduce fossil fuel emissions would be less expensive than dealing with the consequences climate change.

13.2.1 Causes of climatic change

Evidences from all around the world indicate that the planet is warming, and over the last half century, this warming is occurring due to human activity predominantly the burning of fossil fuels.

The major cause of climate change is the burning of fossil fuels, such as oil and coal, which emits greenhouse gases into the atmosphere particularly carbon dioxide. Other human activities, such as deforestation, also contribute to the multiplication of greenhouse gases that cause climate change.

Although some quantities of these gases are a naturally occurring, the atmospheric concentration of CO_2 did not rise above 300 ppm between the origin of human civilisation roughly 10,000 years ago and 1900. Today it is at about 400 ppm, which is problematic.

13.2.2 Effects of climate change

Climate change is affecting the people across regions and in many sectors important to society such as human health, agriculture and food security, water supply, transportation, energy, ecosystems, and others and are expected to become increasingly disruptive throughout this century and further.

Small change in Earth's temperature due to climate change can have severe effects. The earth's average temperature has gone up 1.4°F over the past century and is expected to rise as much as 11.5°F over the next. The average temperature during the last ice age was about 4°F lower than it is today.

Rising sea levels due to the melting of ice (again, caused by climate change) contribute to greater storm damage, warming ocean temperatures are associated with stronger and more frequent storms, additional rainfall, particularly during severe weather events, leads to flooding and other damage; an increase in the incidence and severity of wildfires threatens habitats, homes, and lives, and heat waves contribute to human deaths and other adverse effects.

Global warming

A number of gases present in the atmosphere are considered as greenhouse gases. These gases trap heat from the sun that is normally reflected back from the Earth surface. Due to this activity they act like the glass panels in a greenhouse. In the last 20 years, concern has grown that the increase of greenhouse gases and global climate change or global warming are associated with each other, which could have adverse effects such as rising sea levels and the extinction of plant and animal species that cannot adjust with the change. It has been discussed at different platforms that the Earth has warmed up by about 0.6°C in the last 100 years.

Ozone layer depletion

The ozone layer: The Earth's atmosphere is covered with several layers. The lowest layer, the troposphere, extends from the Earth's surface up to about 10 kilometers in altitude. All human activities occur in the troposphere. The next layer, the stratosphere. This is region of the atmosphere above the troposphere. The stratosphere ranges from about 10 km to about 50 km in altitude. Airlines fly in the lower stratosphere. The stratosphere temperature is rising from lower to higher altitudes. This warming is caused by ozone absorbing ultraviolet radiation. Warm air remains in the upper stratosphere, and cool air remains lower, so there is much less vertical mixing in this region than in the troposphere. Most commercial aeroplanes fly in the lower part of the stratosphere.

Atmospheric ozone is concentrated in a layer in the stratosphere, about 15 to 30 km above the Earth's surface. Ozone molecule contains three oxygen atoms. At any given time, ozone molecules are continuously generating and destroyed in the stratosphere. The total amount has remained relatively stable during the decades that it has been measured.

Due to presence of this ozone layer , stratosphere absorbs a portion of the radiation from the sun, preventing it from reaching the planet's surface. Most importantly, it absorbs the portion of UV light. UV band of ultraviolet radiation with wavelengths from 280–320 nanometers produced by the Sun. UV is a kind of ultraviolet light from the sun that has several harmful effects. UV is so effective to damage DNA. It is also responsible to cause melanoma and other types of skin cancer. It can also damage to some materials, crops, and marine organisms. The ozone layer protects the Earth against most UV light coming from the sun. It is always important to protect all of us against UV, even in the absence of ozone depletion. For this, we are wearing hats, sunglasses, and sunscreen to protect from UV light.

Ozone depletion: Ozone layer is depleting due to destruction of ozone molecules. When chlorine and bromine atoms come into contact with ozone in the stratosphere, they destroy ozone molecules. One chlorine atom can destroy over 100,000 ozone molecules before it is removed from the stratosphere. Ozone can be destroyed more quickly than it is naturally created, that's why ozone layer is depleting.

Several chemical compounds release chlorine or bromine when they are exposed to intense UV light in the stratosphere, known as ozone depleting substances. These compounds contribute to ozone depletion, that release chlorine include chlorofluorocarbons (CFCs), hydrochlorofluorocarbons (HCFCs), carbon tetrachloride, and methyl chloroform. Ozone depleting substances that release bromine include halons and methyl bromide. Although Ozone depleting substances are emitted at the Earth's surface, they are eventually carried into the stratosphere in a process that can take as long as two to five years.

In the 1970s, concerns about the effects of ozone-depleting substances (ODS) on the stratospheric ozone layer sensitise several countries, including the United States, to ban the use of chlorofluorocarbons (CFCs) as aerosol propellants. Production of CFCs and other ODS continued to grow rapidly as new uses were found for these chemicals in refrigeration, fire suppression, foam insulation, and other applications.

Effects on human health: Ozone layer depletion increases the amount of UV radiation that reaches the Earth's surface. Research studies demonstrate that UV radiation causes non-melanoma skin cancer and plays a major role in malignant melanoma development. Also, UV radiation has been linked to the development of cataracts, a clouding of the eye's lens. Because all sunlight contains some amount of UV radiation, even with normal stratospheric ozone levels, so it is important to protect our skin and eyes from the sun.

Effects on plants: UV radiation also affects the physiological and developmental processes of plants. Plant growth and development can be directly affected by UV radiation while repair these effects and an ability to adapt to increased levels of UV radiation. Indirect changes such as changes in plant form, distribution of nutrients within the plant, timing of developmental phases and secondary metabolism takes place due to UV radiation. These changes can have important implications for plant competitive balance, plant diseases, and metabolic pathways.

Effects on marine ecosystems: Aquatic plant are considered as Phyto-plankton. They form the foundation of aquatic food webs. Phytoplankton productivity is limited upto the euphotic zone. Euphotic zone is the upper layer of the water column in which there is sufficient sunlight to support net productivity. Exposure to solar UV radiation has been shown to adversely affect both orientation and motility in phytoplankton. This results as reduced survival rates for these organisms. Scientists have demonstrated a direct reduction in phytoplankton production due to ozone depletion related increases in UV radiation. It has been seen that UV radiation also affects aquatic creatures such as cause damage to early developmental stages of fish, shrimp, crab, amphibians, and other marine animals. The most severe effects are decreased reproductive capacity and slow larval growth. Small increases in UV exposure could result in population reductions for small marine organisms with implications for the whole marine food chain.

Effects on biogeochemical cycles: Increases in UV radiation could affect both terrestrial and aquatic biogeochemical cycles. Therefore altering both sources and sinks of greenhouse and chemically important gases such as carbon dioxide, carbon monoxide, carbonyl sulphide, ozone, and possibly other gases. These potential changes would contribute to biosphere-atmosphere feedbacks that enhance the atmospheric concentrations of these gases.

Effects on materials: Material such as synthetic polymers, naturally occurring biopolymers, as well as some other materials of commercial interest are adversely affected by UV radiation. Advanced materials are somewhat protected from UV radiation by special additives. Yet, increases in UV levels will accelerate their breakdown and thus reducing their life.

Acid rain

Acid rain, or acid deposition, includes any form of precipitation with acidic components, such as oxides of sulphur and oxide of nitrogen form sulphuric or nitric acid that fall to the ground from the atmosphere along with rain water or in dry forms. This can include snow, fog, hail or even dust that is acidic. Acid rain results when sulphur dioxide (SO_2) and nitrogen oxides (NO_x) are emitted into the atmosphere and transported by wind and air currents. The SO_2 and NO_x react with water, oxygen and other chemicals to form H_2SO_4 and HNO_3. These acids then mix with water and other materials before falling to the ground. Some part of the SO_2 and NO_x that cause acid rain is coming from natural sources such as volcanoes, most of it comes from the burning of fossil fuels. The major sources of SO_2 and NO_x in the atmosphere are burning of fossil fuels to generate electricity. Two thirds of SO_2 and one fourth of NO_x in the atmosphere come from electric power generators, vehicles and heavy equipment, manufacturing, oil refineries and other industries.

Winds can blow SO_2 and NO_x over long distances from source of origin, some time across the borders making acid rain a problem for everyone. Due to entry of acids in atmosphere, pH of atmosphere vary, that can be measured as acidity and alkalinity using a pH scale for which 7.0 is neutral. The lower a substance's pH than 7, more acidic it is and the higher a substance's pH greater than 7, the more alkaline it is. Normal rain has a pH of about 5.6; it is slightly acidic because carbon dioxide (CO_2) dissolves into it forming weak carbonic acid. Acid rain usually has a pH between 4.2 and 4.4.

Effects of acid rain on fish and wildlife: The effects of acid rain are most clearly seen in aquatic environments, where it can be harmful to fish and other wildlife. As it flows through the soil, acidic rain water can leach aluminium from soil clay particles and then flow into streams and lakes. If level of acid will rise that leads to increase the release of aluminium in to the ecosystem. In nature, some plants and animals are able to tolerate acidic waters and moderate amounts of aluminium. Those do not resist, called acid-sensitive and will be lost as the pH declines. Normally young members of plant and animals are more sensitive to environmental conditions than adults. For example, most fish eggs cannot hatch at pH 7. At lower pH levels, some adult fish die. Some acidic lakes have no fish.

Effects of acid rain on plants and trees: Acid rain leaches aluminium from the soil. That aluminium may create harmful effects to plants as well as animals. Acid rain also removes minerals and nutrients from the soil that trees need to grow. Acidic fog and clouds might strip nutrients from trees foliage, leaving them with brown or dead leaves and needles at high altitude. The trees are then less able to absorb sunlight, which reduce photosynthetic capability and makes them weak and less able to withstand freezing temperatures.

Effects of acid rain on materials: It is very interesting that all acidic deposition is not wet as name suggest acid rain. Dust particles can be acidic as well, and this is called dry deposition. This occurs when acid rain and dry acidic particles fall to earth, the nitric and sulphuric acid that make the particles acidic can land on statues, buildings, and other manmade structures, and damage their surfaces. The acidic particles corrode metal and cause paint and stone to deteriorate more quickly. They also dirty the surfaces of buildings and other structures such as monuments. For example, historic monument Taj Mahal is adversely affected by dry acidic particles released from Mathura refinery.

13.3   Sustainable development challenges

There are three dimensions of sustainable development such as economic, social and environmental. The world is facing challenges in all three dimensions of sustainable development. More than 1.5 billion people are still living in extreme poverty in many countries and it is rising. On the other hand, unsustainable consumption and production patterns have resulted in huge economic and social costs and may endanger life on the planet. Achieving sustainable development will require global actions for economic and social progress. It is required for growth and employment, and at the same time protecting environment.

Sustainable development requires care of the poorest person and most vulnerable natural resources. Developmental strategies should be action-oriented and collaborative, and to adapt to different levels of development. They must need to systemically change consumption and production patterns, encourage the preservation of natural endowments; reduce inequality; and strengthen economic governance.

Poverty, unemployment, climate change, conflict and humanitarian aid, building peaceful and inclusive societies, building strong institutions of governance, and supporting the rule of law are the main challenges to sustainable development. United Nations Framework Convention on Climate Change, has proposed the following aims for its Sustainable Development Goals (SDGs):

1. Ending of poverty in all its forms everywhere by year 2030.
2. Ending hunger, achieving food security and improved nutrition by year 2030.
3. Ensuring inclusive and equitable quality education and promoting life-long learning opportunities for all by year 2030.
4. Ensuring availability and sustainable management of water and sanitation for all by 2030.
5. Ensuring access to affordable, reliable, sustainable, and modern energy for all by 2030.
6. Promoting sustained, inclusive and economic growth, full and productive employment.
7. Sustaining per capita economic growth, at least 7 per cent per annum GDP growth in the least developed countries.
8. Resilient infrastructure and promoting inclusive and sustainable industrialisation.
9. Encouraging innovation by developing quality, reliable, sustainable and including regional and transborder infrastructure, to support economic development.
10. Reducing inequality within and among countries by 2030.
11. Making cities and human settlements inclusive, safe and sustainable by 2030.
12. Ensuring sustainable consumption and production patterns.

13.4   Environmental protection acts and legislation

To solve environmental problems those we are facing now a day become most callenging and important task for ragulator agency. Environmental problems are creating global impacts and these are complex and often interrelated with social and economical factors. These problems are, such as water and air pollution, generation of solid and hazardous waste, soil degradation, deforestation, climate change and loss of biodiversity. These are cause of major threats to human safety, health and productivity. Due to these threats to human future, it is essential to address these problems.

Most important effort for environmental protection is raising public awareness and participation. The problems can only be properly addressed through cooperation among public sector along with the private sector, non-governmental organisations and the civil society such as public–private partnership (PPP) model. This requires national efforts as well as international collaboration on both bilateral and multilateral level and the active participation of all members of the international community.

For this purpose, international organisations such as the UN, the OECD, OSCE and other international financial institutions, global and regional forum, have been promoting and coordinating the efforts for the joint confrontation of global environmental problems. The United Nations Environment Programme (UNEP) was established in 1972, as one of the productive consequences of Stockholm conference on the human environment. The UNEP provides a basis for comprehensive consideration and coordinated action within the UN system on the problems of environment.

Major international agreements and conventions covering a wide range of environmental issues such as climate change, biological diversity, combating decertification, control of movements of hazardous wastes, ozone layer, illegal trade in endangered species, have been elaborated under UNEP's auspices.

India has been actively involved in international cooperation efforts to address environmental problems that are complex and mostly related to socioeconomic issues. India, taking into account its national interests and socioeconomics conditions, have become party to a number of conventions both at the global and regional level, with a view to contributing to address environmental problems. Following are the most effective environmental legislation, i.e., clean air act, the endangered species act, the montreal protocol, the clean water act, and reformation plan of 1970.

13.4.1 Clean air act

The first clean air act was established by Americans in December 1963, it was later amended in 1966, 1970, 1977, and 1990 America's air had been under siege for decades.

13.4.2 Endangered species act

This act was established to increase population of species whose population was very poor and comes under endangered species category. The population of Peregrine falcon, Key deer, Grizzly bear, Red wolf, etc. have been increased because of the Endangered Species Act (ESA). Bald Eagle Protection Act of 1940 is an example to follow Endangered Species Act (ESA).

13.4.3 Montreal protocol

This protocol signed in year 1987 and further revised seven times, and followed by 196 nations. Montreal protocol is officially known as the Montreal protocol on substances that deplete the ozone layer. It is considered as the single most successful international agreement to date. Ozone depleting substances are namely chlorofluorocarbons (CFCs) and hydrochlorofluorocarbons (HCFCs). CFCs were found in air conditioning systems, fire control solvents and hair spray canisters.

13.4.4 Clean water act

Clean water act was signed in 1972, the primary federal law addressing water quality standards for the nation's waterways. The act has been amended many times, most significantly in 1987 to control toxic pollutants, and in 1990 to more adequately address oil spills.

13.5 International policies, summits and declarations to protect environment

13.5.1 Earth summit

This provide a potential vision for moving toward sustainable development that is, toward both greater environmental protection and greater economic justice. The earth summit yielded two legally binding treaties:

1. The framework convention on climate change.
2. The convention on biological diversity.

13.5.2 Rio declaration

This is also a product of the summit which was a set of nonbinding general principles known as the Rio seclaration, a set of nonbinding principles on forest management. The 1992 Rio declaration on environment and development defines the rights of the people to be involved in the development of their economies, and the responsibilities of human beings to safeguard the common environment. The declaration builds upon the basic ideas concerning the attitudes of individuals and nations towards the environment and development, first identified at the United Nations Conference on the Human Environment

(1972). According to the Rio Declaration, long term economic progress is only ensured if it is linked with the protection of the environment. If this goal is to be achieved, then all countries must establish a new global partnership involving governments, their people and the key sectors of society. Together human society must assemble international agreements that protect the global environment with responsible development.

Number of principles have been developed by the Rio declaration. These are as follows:

1. People are entitled to a healthy and productive life in harmony with nature.
2. Development today must not threaten the needs of present and future generations.
3. Nations have the right to exploit their own resources, but without causing environmental damage beyond their borders.
4. Environmental protection shall constitute an integral part of the development process.
5. Solving poverty problem and reducing disparities in living standards in different parts of the world are essential if we are to achieve sustainable development.
6. Environment related issues are best handled with the participation of all concerned citizens.
7. The countries those are polluting the world at large , should bear the cost of pollution.
8. Sustainable development requires better scientific understanding of the problems. Nations should share knowledge and technologies to achieve the goal of sustainability.

13.5.3 Agenda 21

This agenda provides blueprint for sustainable development. The assembled governments also established the Commission on Sustainable Development (CSD) to integrate environment and development into the UN system while providing a forum to monitor the implementation of summit commitments.

US attention and leadership for global challenges

More than any developed and developing country, the United States is responsible for the existing gap between Rio's rhetoric of international environmental consciousness and the post Rio environmental reality. This is because of, US the world's only remaining economic and political superpower, it is also the largest polluter and the largest user of most important resources. Although the United States is often in the vanguard in recognising global environmental threats and in calling for a multilateral response, it often lags in changing its own behaviour. Once considered the leader in environmental regulation, the United States now lags well behind Germany and other European countries in adopting new and innovative regulatory approaches such as ecological taxes, extended product responsibility, and the precautionary principle on avoiding probable environmental damage.

As a leader in previous environmental conferences and negotiations, the United States almost single handedly undermined the Earth summit. Just days before the Rio summit opened, for example, the United States announced that it would not sign the biodiversity convention, despite provisionally adopting the draft version at the end of the negotiation session two weeks before. Instead, the United States emphasised the need to conserve the world's forests and offered what was considered a small, $150 million aid package to protect forests in developing countries. They were trying to divert attention from their failing elsewhere. For example, in the watering down of the climate change convention and their refusal to sign the biodiversity treaty.'

Getting the rules right regarding the climate regime

Climate change is the single most important environmental issue of the next few decades. In the Kyoto protocol, industrialised countries committed to reduce their net greenhouse gas emissions an average of 5% from 1990 levels by 2012 and further by 2030. In addition, the parties also established an international trading system in carbon emissions. It has been decided that tons of carbon emissions will soon trade like other commodities throughout the world termed as 'carbon trading'. Kyoto protocol may play crucial role and to be associate as many countries as possible. It is very important for conference of the parties to the protocol must address such issues as how to count the carbon emission by forests, landfills, and agricultural practices in calculating a country's net greenhouse gas emissions. It is also a task to find out, how to facilitate the trading of carbon emission credits between countries; and how to monitor and enforce such a trading system.

America holds position as the world's supreme carbon emitter and energy user, US leadership in getting these rules right will be critical if the climate regime is to have any hope of responding effectively to the threat of climate change. But America is pulling back its feet to follow rules and regulation decided. America is not agreed to provide advantage to India and China in reducing carbon emission and carbon credit issue, that have been seen recently.

Imposing liability and providing compensation

Montreal protocol and some other international environmental regimes have addressed the question of liability and compensation for harm caused to the environment. The Montreal protocol, widely viewed as the model for all international environmental treaties, effectively banned the production and use of most ozone depleting substances. But it did not hold those responsible for ozone depletion legally accountable, nor did it provide for compensating persons or countries that have suffered from ozone depletion.

Convention on biological diversity

Biological diversity should be conserved if we are even thinking of sustainable development in different part of the globe. The convention on biological diversity was signed by over 150 countries at the Rio Earth summit in 1992 and entered into action in 1993. It has become the driving force of international efforts to conserve the planet's biological diversity, ensure the sustainable use of biological resources, protect ecosystems and natural habitats, and promote the fair and equal sharing of the benefits arising from the utilisation of genetic resources. The convention was signed on June 4, 1993, but the United States has failed to ratified it.

Convention on climate change

Over 150 Nations signed the United Nations Framework Convention on Climate Change in June 1992 at the Rio Earth summit, recognising climate change as 'a common concern of humankind.' The convention aimed to reduce emission levels of greenhouse gases to 1990 levels by the year 2000 but failed to set binding goals. The United States signed the treaty on June 12, 1992, ratified it on October 15, 1992, and entered it into force in the United States on March 21, 1994.

Kyoto protocol to the united nations convention on climate change

The agreement sets, for the first time, to limits the emission of greenhouse gases that cause global warming. Under the protocol, 38 industrialised countries agreed to reduce their overall emissions to about 5% below 1990 levels by 2012, and a range of specific reduction requirements was set for other countries. The US signed the protocol on November 12, 1998, but has not yet ratified it.

Convention on international trade in endangered species (CITES)

CITES establishes international controls on global trade of endangered or threatened species of animals and plants. It prohibits all commercial trade in wildlife species threatened with extinction. It was ratified by the United States on January 14, 1974, and implemented as the endangered species act. Currently more than 125 countries are members of CITES.

Montreal protocol on substances that deplete the ozone layer

The Montreal protocol is the primary international regime for controlling the production and consumption of ozone depleting substances such as CFCs, halons, and methyl bromide. As of June 1994, 136 nations, including most developing countries, had become parties to the protocol. The United States signed the protocol on September 16, 1987, and ratified it on April 21, 1988. The protocol and its subsequent revisions modified the original 1985 Vienna convention for the protection of the ozone layer.

Aerobes: Group of organisms that require air or oxygen for their survival, growth and development.

Aerobic respiration: Respiration that occures in an oxygen rich environment.

Anaerobes: Group of organisms that can not bear the presence of air or oxygen, or survive in the absence of oxygen.

Abiotic stress: Conditions or factors (non-livings) which can cause harmful effects to plants, such as soil conditions, drought and extreme temperatures.

Absorption: The process by which one substance is taken into the body of another substance.

Acid rain: The precipitation of dilute solutions of strong mineral acids, formed by the mixing in the atmosphere of various industrial pollutants primarily sulphur dioxide and nitrogen oxides with naturally occurring oxygen and water vapour.

Actinomycetes: Filamentous bacteria, many of which are valuable in the production of antibiotics.

Activated sludge method: A method of sewage treatment in which wastes are degraded by complex populations of aerobic micro-organisms.

Adsorption: It is the adhesion of atoms, ions, or molecules from a gas, liquid, or dissolved solid to a surface. This process creates a film of the adsorbate on the surface of the adsorbent.

Advanced waste treatment: The removal of non-carbonaceous materials such as excess phosphorus and nitrogen. The term implies treatment beyond secondary treatment, and advanced treatment is most effective after the organic matter has been removed.

Aerobic organisms: Organisms that can utilise oxygen as the final electron acceptor during metabolism.

Aerosol: A suspension of small liquid or solid particles in gas.

Agro ecosystem: A community of micro-organisms, plants and animals, together with their abiotic environment, that occurs on farmed land, and including the crop species.

Agrobacterium: A genus of bacteria that includes several plant pathogenic species, causing tumour like symptoms.

Air pollution: Air is made up of a number of gases, mostly nitrogen and oxygen and, in smaller amounts, water vapour, carbon dioxide and argon and other trace gases. Air pollution occurs when harmful chemicals and particles are emitted to the air due to human activity or natural forces at a concentration that interferes with human health or welfare or that harms the environment in other ways.

Air quality: A measure of the level of pollution in the air.

Algae: A group of simple aquatic plants capable of photosynthesis. Simple rootless plants that grow in sunlight waters in proportion to the amount of available nutrients. They can affect water quality adversely by lowering the dissolved oxygen in the water. They are food for fish and small aquatic animals.

Algal biomass: Single-celled plants (e.g. *Chlorella* spp. and *Spirulina* spp.) grown.

Algal blooms: Sudden spurts of algal growth, which can affect water quality adversely and indicate potentially hazardous changes in local water chemistry.

Allergen: A substance, usually a protein that can cause an allergy or allergic reaction in the body.

Allergy: A reaction by the body's immune system after exposure to a particular substance, often a protein.

Alternative energy: Energy that is not popularly used and is usually environmentally sound, such as solar or wind energy (as opposed to fossil fuels).

Alternative fibres: Fibres produced from non-wood sources for use in paper making.

Alternative fuels: Transportation fuels other than gasoline or diesel. Includes natural gas, methanol, and electricity.

Alternative transportation: Modes of travel other than private cars, such as walking, bicycling, roller blading, carpooling and transit.

Amendment: A change or addition to an existing law or rule.

Ammonia fertiliser: A material with a high concentration of nitrogen compounds put on soil to stimulate plant growth.

Anabolism: The synthesis of complex molecules from simpler ones. All biosynthetic reactions in a living organism.

Anaerobe: An organism that grows in the absence of oxygen.

Antimicrobial agent: Any chemical or biological agent that harms the growth of micro-organisms.

Anaerobic: In absence of air or oxygen.

Archaebacteria: Most primitive type of micro-organism among prokaryotes.

Biochemical pathway: Various steps involved in any bioconversion process.

Biofuel: Fuel produced from biological source or action of micro-organism, e.g., hydrogen, ethenol, methane, biodiesel, etc.

Biogas: Gas produced after microbial digestion of organic waste under anaerobic conditions (in absence of air or oxygen). The major compositions of biogas are CH_4 and CO_2.

Bioleaching: Process of using micro-organisms to recover metals from their ores.

BOD: Biological oxygen demand. BOD quantifies the amount of oxygen required by micro-organisms to oxidise organic waste to CO_2 and H_2O.

Biomass: Total dry matter of all organisms in a particular sample, population or area.

Biological oxidation: The way bacteria and micro-organisms feed on and decompose complex organic materials; used in self-purification of water bodies and in activated sludge wastewater treatment.

Biomining: Process of recovering metals from ores using micro-organisms. It is also used for extraction of metallic pollutants from solid or liquid wastes.

Bioreactor: Apparatus used to carry out biological reactions or processes, especially on an industrial scale.

Bioremediation: Process of using organisms to degrade or consume to remove pollutants from environment.

Biocontrol: Pest control by biological means. Any process using deliberately introduced living organisms to restrain the growth and development of other organisms, such as the introduction of predatory insects to control an insect pest.

Bioconversion: Conversion of one chemical into another by living organisms, as opposed to their conversion by isolated enzymes or fixed cells, or by chemical processes. Particularly useful for introducing chemical changes at specific points in large and complex molecules.

Biodegradable: Capable of being biodegraded.

Biodegradation: The breakdown of substances by micro-organisms. Mainly aerobic bacteria.

Biodegrade: The breakdown by micro-organisms of a compound to simpler chemicals. Materials that are easily biodegraded are colloquially termed biodegradable.

Biodiesel: An alternative fuel for use in diesel engines that is made from natural renewable sources such animal fats or vegetable oils, and does not contain petroleum. It has similar properties to petroleum but releases fewer environmental pollutants in its emissions. Biodiesel can be used in diesel engines with little or no modifications, either as a diesel fuel substitute, or added to petroleum-based fuels to reduce their polluting effect. Examples include oils from soyabeans, rapeseed, sunflowers or animal tallow.

Biodiversity: The wide diversity and interrelatedness of earth organisms based on genetic and environmental factors.

Bio-energetics: The study of the flow and the transformation of energy that occur in living organisms.

Bioenergy: Energy choices using a wide range of biomass sources (for example, agriculture, forestry, industry and municipal waste) and conversion technologies such as fermentation (alcohol production) and co-firing (co-combustion of biomass and coal). Also identifies linkages to wider sustainable development outcomes, critical economic, environmental and security benefits (such as adding value to farm, forestry and other industries) and reducing fossil fuel use (product displacement), waste streams, emission of greenhouse gases and other pollutants.

Bioengineering: Engineering applied to biological and medical systems, such as biomechanics, biomaterials and biosensors. Bioengineering also includes biomedical engineering, as in the development of aids or replacements for defective or missing body organs.

Bio-enrichment: Adding nutrients or oxygen to increase microbial breakdown of pollutants.

Bioethics (and biomedical ethics): A discipline that studies the ethical implications of biological applications.

Biofilms: A layer of micro-organisms growing on a surface, in a bed of polymeric material which they themselves have made. Biofilms tend to form wherever a surface on which bacteria can grow is exposed to some suitable medium and a supply of bacteria.

Biofuel: A gaseous, liquid or solid fuel derived from a biological source, e.g. ethanol, rapeseed oil or fish liver oil.

Biogas: A mixture of methane and carbon dioxide resulting from the anaerobic decomposition of waste such as domestic, industrial and agricultural sewage.

Biohazard: A biological agent, such as an infectious micro-organism, or a condition that constitutes a threat to humans, especially in biological research or experimentation. The potential danger, risk, or harm from exposure to such an agent or condition.

Bioinformatics: The generation/creation, collection, storage (in databases), and efficient use of data/information from genomics from biological research to accomplish an objective (for example, to discover a new pharmaceutical or a new herbicide).

Bioleaching: The recovery of metals from their ores, using the action of micro-organisms, rather than chemical or physical treatment. For example, *Thiobacillus ferroxidans* has been used to extract gold from refractory ores.

Biological control: The control of a population of one organism by another organism. Generally the controlling organism is a predator or disease-causing organism of the species being controlled.

Biological products: Any virus, therapeutic serum, toxin, antitoxin, or analogous product used in the prevention, treatment or cure of diseases or injuries in humans.

Biomass concentration: The amount of biological material in a specific volume.

Biomass: Any organic matter, particularly available on a renewable or recurring basis such as trees and plants (residues and fibres containing cellulose or lingo-cellulose), but also poultry litter and animal residues and waste, and industrial and municipal solid waste (for example, sawdust, wood chips, paper, grass and leaf compost).

Biomimetic materials: Employed to describe synthetic analogues of natural materials with advantageous properties. For instance, some synthetic molecules act chemically like natural proteins, but are not as easily degraded by the digestive system. Other systems such as reverse micelles and/or liposome exhibit certain properties that mimic certain aspects of living systems.

Biopesticides: A product made from natural sources such as bacteria, animals or plants that is used for pest control. They tend to have less of an impact on the environment and human health because they are less toxic than conventional pesticides and usually affect only one specific pest instead of being broad-range. They can also work in low amounts, they break down quickly and when used properly, they can reduce the use of conventional pesticides while maintaining crop yields.

Biopharmaceuticals: This term is sometimes used for biologic drugs produced through rDNA technology, but essentially they also fall under the regulatory definition of a biologic.

Biopiracy: The patenting of genetic stocks, and the subsequent privatisation of genetic resources collections. The term implies a lack of consent on the part of the originator.

Bioprocess: Any process that uses complete living cells or their components (e.g., enzymes, chloroplasts) to effect desired physical or chemical changes.

Bioreactor: A tank in which cells, cell extracts or enzymes carry out a biological reaction. Often refers to a fermentation vessel for cells or micro-organisms.

Biorecovery: The use of micro-organisms for the recovery of valuable materials (metals or particular organic compounds) from complex mixtures. See: biodesulphurisation, bioleaching.

Bioremediation: The use of plants and micro-organisms to consume or otherwise help remove materials (such as toxic chemical wastes and metals) from contaminated sites (especially from soil and water). A natural process in which environmental problems are treated by the use of bacteria or other micro-organisms that break down a problem substance, such as oil, into less harmful molecules.

Biosafety protocol: An internationally agreed protocol set up to protect biological diversity from the potential risks posed by the release of genetically modified organisms. It establishes a procedure for ensuring that countries are provided with the information necessary to make informed decisions before agreeing to the import of such organisms into their territory.

Biosafety: Referring to the avoidance of risk to human health and safety, and to the conservation of the environment, as a result of the use for research and commerce of infectious or genetically modified micro-organisms.

Biosensing: Technology for the detection of a wide range of chemical and biological agents, including bacteria, viruses and toxins, in the environment and humans.

Biosensor: A device that uses an immobilised biologically-related agent (such as an enzyme, antibiotic, organelle or whole cell) to detect or measure a chemical compound. Reactions between the immobilised agent and the molecule being analysed are converted into an electric signal.

Biosilk: A biomimetic fibre produced by the expression of the relevant orb-weaving spider genes in yeast or bacteria, followed by the spinning of the expressed protein into a fibre.

Biosorbents: Micro-organisms which, either by themselves or in conjunction with a substrate are able to extract and/or concentrate a desired molecule by means of its selective retention.

Biosphere: The part of the earth and its atmosphere that is inhabited by living organisms.

Biosynthesis: Synthesis of compounds by living cells, which is the essential feature of anabolism.

Biotechnologists: Scientists who use biological processes to develop novel products.

Biotechnology: The scientific manipulation of living organisms, especially at the molecular genetic level, to produce useful products. Gene splicing and use of recombinant DNA (rDNA) are major techniques used.

Bioterrorism: The use of bacteria, viruses or toxins with the intent of causing harm to people, animals or food to achieve certain political, religious or ideological goals through intimidation.

Biotic stress: Living organisms which can harm plants , such as viruses, fungi, and bacteria, and harmful insects. See Abiotic stress.

Biotransformation: The conversion of one chemical or material into another using a biological catalyst: a near synonym is biocatalysis, and hence the catalyst used is called a biocatalyst. Usually the catalyst is an enzyme, or a fixed whole, dead micro-organism

Biotreatment: The treatment of a waste or hazardous substance using organisms such as bacteria, fungi and protozoa.

Biosensor: Analytical device used to determine the concentration of substances by converting a biological response in to an electrical signal.

Catabolism: Breakdown of complex biological molecules in to simpler ones, usually accompanied with the release of energy in the form of ATP.

COD: Chemical oxygen demand. COD quantifies the amount of oxygen required to convert all the oxidisable chemicals in wastes to stable end products such as CO_2, H_2O and NO_3.

Co-enzyme: Organic molecule that bineds to an enzyme and is required for its catalytic activity.

Corrosion: Destruction of metal by chemical, electrochemical or biological action.

Compost: A rich soil-like material produced from decayed plants and other organic matter, such as food and animal waste, that decomposes (breaks down) naturally. Most food waste can be put into compost, but you should not include meat, bones, cheese, cooking oils and fish. These may take a long time to break down and attract unwanted pests.

Coliform: Gram negative rods resembling *E. Coli* and similar species that normally in habit the colon.

Coliform bacteria: A group of bacteria that are normally abundant in the intestinal tracts of humans and other warm-blooded animals and are used as indicators when testing the sanitary quality of water.

Colonisation: Establishment of a site of reproduction of microbes on a material, animal, or person without necessarily resulting in tissue invasion or damage.

Colony: A group of bacteria in a culture derived from the multiplication of single cell ; usually visible to the unaided eye.

Contaminant: Any physical, chemical, biological, or radiological substance or matter that has

an adverse affect on air, water, or soil.

Conservation: The preservation or protection from decay or destruction of anything whose loss it is desirable to prevent.

Community: Any naturally occurring group of organisms that occupy a common environment. The term is a general one, covering groups of various sizes. A grouping of interacting populations in a particular habitat.

Cross: The mating of two individuals or populations.

Cross hybridisation: The annealing of a single-stranded DNA sequence to a single-stranded target DNA to which it is only partially complementary. Often, this refers to the use of a DNA probe to detect homologous sequences in species other than the origin of the probe.

Cross pollination: Application of pollen from one plant to another to effect the latter's fertilisation.

Cross pollination efficiency: The ease with which cross pollination can be achieved. Generally measured by the number of hybrid progeny generated per flower pollinated.

Cross-breeding: Mating between members of different populations (lines, breeds, races or species).

Crossing over: The process by which homologous chromosomes exchange material at meiosis through the breakage and reunion of non-sister chromatids.

Cryobiological preservation: The preservation of germplasm resources in a dormant state by storage at ultra-low temperatures, often in liquid nitrogen. Currently applied to storage of plant seeds and pollen, micro-organisms, animal sperm, and tissue culture cell lines.

Culture: A growth of micro-organisms.

Culture medium: A preparation containing nutrients and growth factors suitable for the cultivation of micro-organisms.

Cyanobacteria: Blue-green algae.

Cyclone collector: A device that uses centrifugal force to pull large particles from polluted air.

CRT: Cell retention time. It indicates the duration for which active cell mass remains inside a bioreactor before it is decomposed.

Digester: In wastewater treatment, a closed tank; in solid waste conversion, a unit in which bacterial action is induced and accelerated to break down organic matter and establish the proper carbon-to-nitrogen ratio.

Disposal: In this guide, getting rid of waste by discarding it into a bin and, when it is collected, by incinerating it or sending it to landfill.

Denitrification: The anaerobic biological reduction of nitrate nitrogen to nitrogen gas.

Domestic charges: Fees paid to local authorities for providing services such as collecting domestic waste.

Decomposition: The breakdown of matter by bacteria and fungi; changes the chemical makeup and physical appearance of materials.

Domestic waste: Waste produced within the home, including garden waste.

Dissolved solids: Disintegrated organic and inorganic material contained in water. Excessive amounts make water unfit for drinking or for use in industrial processes.

Dry wastes: Which can be collected by the containers for valuable materials such as glass, paper, cardboard, plastics, metals and similar recyclable wastes.

Dumping: Disposing of waste illegally by not using bins or official recycling centres, civic amenity sites or landfills.

Enzyme: Protein based substance produced by living cells to catalyse biochemical reactions.

Environment: It is an outer media in which human or another living being sustain own interactions during their life. The physical elements of this media are air, water and soil; the biological elements are producers (plants), utilisers (animals) and decomposers (bacteria and fungus); the economical environmental elements are the activities of human, which are related with utilisation and operation of natural, human, economical and materialistic sources; the social elements are demographic structure, and historical and cultural infrastructure of human, and the type of life with respect to accommodation, health, education and culture demands. The physical, chemical and biotic conditions surrounding a living organism.

Environmental Protection Agency (EPA): The federal agency of the US government, established in 1970, that is responsible for dealing with the pollution of air and water by solid waste, pesticides and radiation and with nuisances caused by noise.

Effluent: Wastewater treated or untreated that flows out of a treatment plant, sewer, or industrial outfall; generally refers to wastes discharged into surface waters.

Ecosystem: The interacting system of a biological community and its non-living environmental surroundings.

Environmental quality standards: The maximum limits or concentrations of pollutants that are permitted in specific media.

Ecology: The relationship of living things to one another and their environment, or the study of such relationships.

Environmental protection: That part of resource management which is concerned with the discharge into the environment of substances that might be harmful, or that might have harmful physical effects and with safeguarding beneficial uses.

Escherichia coli: A commensal bacterium inhabiting the human colon that is widely used in biology, both as a simple model of cell biochemical function and as a host for molecular cloning experiments.

Flocculation: The process by which clumps of solids in water or sewage are made to increase in size by biological or chemical action so that they can be separated from the water.

Filtration: A treatment process, under the control of qualified operators, for removing solid (particulate) matter from water by passing the water through porous media such as sand or a manmade filter. The process is often used to remove particles that contain pathogenic organisms.

Fermentation: Enzyme catalysed reaction in which molecules are broken down under anaerobic or aerobic condition.

Fertiliser: Any substance that is applied to land as a source of nutrients for plant growth. It may be a waste that is being recycled (e.g., farmyard manure, crop residues or compost) or produced industrially.

Fly ash: Noncombustible residual particles from the combustion process carried by flue gas.

Field trial: A test of a new technique or variety, including biotech-derived varieties, done outside the laboratory but with specific requirements on location, plot size, methodology, etc.

Fossil fuel: A fuel, such as coal, oil, and natural gas, produced by the decomposition of ancient (fossilised) plants and animals; compare to alternative energy.

Fungicide: An agent, such as a chemical, that kills fungi.

FOTE: Field oxygen transfer efficiency. It is the practical value of the amount of oxygen transferred to wastewater per unit power consumption.

Gas chromatography: Analytical technique used to separate compounds from a mixture, based primarily on their volatilities. It can also used to analyse gaseous mixture.

Glycolysis: Metabolic process in which sugars are broken down in to smaller compounds along with the release of energy.

General waste: No special treatment is necessary for this waste which can be disposed of with municipal waste. Food waste from tuberculosis or similar category treatment areas should be autoclaved before disposal.

Genetic modification (GM): Any process that alters the genetic material of living organism. This includes duplicating, deleting or inserting one or more new genes or altering the activities of an existing gene. It can be performed on microbes, plants or animals (humans included). Where this is done in humans, it is gene therapy, and only human genes are used.

Genetically modified organism (GMO): An organism (plant, animal, bacteria, or virus) that has had its genetic material altered, either by the duplication, insertion or deletion of one or more new genes, or by changing the activities of an existing gene.

Genetic engineering: The technique of removing, modifying or adding genes to a DNA molecule to change the information it contains. By changing this information, genetic engineering changes the type or amount of proteins an organism is capable of producing. Genetic engineering allows scientists to isolate a specific gene for a particular trait - such as resistance to insect attack in a plant or animal, and transfer it into another plant.

Gene therapy: An evolving technique used to treat genetic diseases. The medical procedure involves replacing, manipulating or supplementing non-functional genes with healthy genes so that they can function normally.

Geiger counter: An electrical device that detects the presence of certain types of radioactivity.

Greenhouse effect: The warming of the Earth's atmosphere caused by a buildup of carbon dioxide or other trace gases; many scientists believe that this buildup allows light from the sun's rays to heat the Earth but prevents a counterbalancing loss of heat.

HPLC: High-pressure liquid chromatography. It is based on their chemical or molecular properties, chemical compounds can be separated through specific stationary and mobile phases of HPLC. HPLC is mainly used as an analytical technique in biotechnological, biomedical and biochemical research and in pharmaceutical industries.

HRT: Hydraulic retention time. It is the ratio of the effective volume of a reactor to the volumetric flow rate of feed in to the reactor under steady state conditions.

Hazardous waste: Waste that poses a risk to human health or the environment and needs to be handled and disposed of carefully. Examples include oil-based paints, car batteries, weed killers, bleach and waste electrical and electronic devices.

Habitat: The place where a population (e.g., human, animal, plant, or micro-organism) lives, and its surroundings, both living and non-living.

Herbicide: A substance that kills plants. Used in agriculture, horticulture and gardening. Can be selective (kill selected species) or non-selective (broad spectrum - kill all plants).

Household waste: Waste that contains paper, cardboard, textiles (for example fabric or carpet), timber, food, garden clippings, glass, plastic and other manufactured materials.

In situ: In the natural or original position.

In vitro: In an artificial environment.

Inversion: An atmospheric condition that occurs when a layer of warm air prevents the rise of cooling air trapped beneath it. This in turn prevents the rise of pollutants that might otherwise be dispersed and can cause an air pollution episode.

In vivo: In a living organism.

Incineration: Burning of garbage in special facilities utilising inherent thermal values of solid wastes.

Incinerator: A device in which solid, semi-solid, liquid or gaseous combustible material is burnt as a means of disposal. If the material does not support combustion auxiliary fuel is added. Many types of industrial and domestic wastes are incinerated and there are many types of incinerator to deal with different wastes.

Lysis: Process of cell disintegration or membrane rupturing.

Landfill: The disposal of refuse by tipping it on land. Often the refuse is used to fill in old mine workings or low-lying land, to reclaim land from water or to create a feature on flat land. If the refuse is deposited in prepared trenches or holes, over which earth can be heaped at the and of each day, this is called controlled tipping in the UK and Sanitary Land-Fill in the USA.

Land use: The deployment of land for any use. Competition for limited areas of land requires the establishment of priorities among claims, which is the object of land use planning.

Latent: Currently inactive but capable of becoming active.

Leachate: Water that has percolated through soil, or a filter material, containing soluble substance and that, therefore, contain amounts of these substances in solution.

Leaching: The removal of the soluble constituents of a rock, soil or ore (that which is leached being known as the leachate) by the action of percolating waters. Leaching is a major process in the development of porosity in limestones in the secondary enrichment of ores and in the formation of soils.

Litter: Waste that is thrown away carelessly, mainly made up of plastic, metal, glass, paper or food. Common examples are chewing gum and cigarette butts.

Monosaccharides: Chemical building blocks of carbohydrates with the empirical formula $(CH_2O)n$.

Mutagen: Chemical or physical agent capable of producing a genetic mutation in a living organism.

Mutant: Product of a mutation or heritable genetic change.

MBT: Short for 'mechanical biological treatment', which is a way of sorting and treating waste. The waste is first sorted mechanically into materials that can and cannot be recycled. Any waste that can be recycled is then broken down biologically, often through composting, while the rest is usually sent to landfill.

Micronutrient: For growth media: An essential element normally required in concentrations < 0.5 millimole/litre.

Micro-organism: Organism visible only under magnification.

Mixed liquor: A mixture of activated sludge and water containing organic matter undergoing activated sludge treatment in an aeration tank.

Municipal waste: Substances discarded as unusable by private households, offices, shops, etc., but not the waste products of industrial processing or manufacturing. Municipal waste is composed typically of paper, organic matter, plastics, metals and non-metallic minerals (e.g., ash).

Mycorrhizae: Fungi that form symbiotic relationships with roots of more developed plants.

Nitrification: The process whereby ammonia in wastewater is oxidised to nitrite and then to nitrate by bacterial or chemical reactions.

Nitrogenous wastes: Animal or vegetable residues that contain significant amounts of nitrogen.

Nonpoint sources: Pollution sources that are diffuse and do not have a single point of origin or are not introduced into a receiving stream from a specific outlet. The pollutants are generally carried off the land by storm-water runoff. The commonly used categories for nonpoint sources are agriculture, forestry, urban, mining, construction, dams and channels, land disposal, and saltwater intrusion.

Neutralisation: Decreasing the acidity or alkalinity of a substance by adding to it alkaline or acidic materials, respectively.

Ologosaccharide: Relatively short molecular chain consisting of 10 to 100 simple sugar units.

Organelles: Membrane bound structures with distinct functions contained in eukaryotic cells.

OUR: Oxygen uptake rate. It is the amount of oxygen consumed per unit time to stabilise waste.

Photosynthesis: It is the process in green plants of converting carbon dioxide and water into sugar using light as the source of energy.

Oil spill: The harmful release of oil into the environment, usually through water, which is very difficult to clean up and often kills birds, fish and other wildlife.

Organic: In this guide, matter from living, or once-living, things.

Organic farming: Farming without the use of industrially made fertilisers and pesticides.

Organic matter: Amount of remainder after drying and incinerating of a sample into an oven at 625°C for 3 hours, which is taken from solid wastes or composts.

Organophosphates: Pesticide chemicals that contain phosphorus; used to control insects. They are short-lived, but some can be toxic when first applied.

Oxidation pond: A man-made lake or body of water in which liquid waste is consumed by bacteria. It is used most frequently with other water-treatment processes. An oxidation pond is basically the same as a sewage lagoon.

Organism: Any living thing, from bacteria and fungi through to insects, plants, animals and humans.

PCR: Polymerase chain reaction. Reaction that uses DNA polymerase to catalyse the amplification of a DNA strand through repeated cycles of DNA synthesis.

Polysaccharides: Long chain molecule composed of multiple units of monosaccharides.

Prokaryotes: Primitive type of micro-organism.

Particulates: Fine liquid or solid particles, such as dust, smoke, mist, fumes, or smog, found in air or emissions.

Particulate matter: Fine solid or liquid particles that pollute the air and are added to the atmosphere by natural and man-made processes at the Earth's surface. Examples of particulate matter include dust, smoke, soot, pollen and soil particles.

Pesticides: A general term for any chemicals that are used to kill weeds, fungi, insects or other pests.

Post-consumer waste: Waste collected after a consumer has disposed of it, for example sweet wrappers or packaging from small electronic goods such as mobile phones or MP3 players.

Pathogen: An agent that causes disease, especially a living micro-organism such as a bacterium or fungus.

Pesticide: A broad term that defines all chemical substances used to control insects, diseases, weeds, fungi and other 'pests' on plants, fruits, vegetables and animals, and in buildings. Fungicides, herbicides, sanitisers, growth regulators, rodenticides, soil fumigants and insecticides are all pesticides.

Primary wastewater treatment: First steps in wastewater treatment; screens and sedimentation tanks are used to remove most materials that float or will settle. Primary treatment results in the removal of about 30% of carbonaceous biochemical oxygen demand (BOD) from domestic sewage.

Precipitators: Air pollution control devices that collect particles from an emission.

Phytoplankton: That portion of the plankton community comprised of tiny plants, e.g., algae, diatoms.

Plume: (i) Visible or measurable discharge of a contaminant from a given point of origin; can be visible or thermal in water or visible in the air as, for example, a plume of smoke, (ii) the area of measurable and potentially harmful radiation leaking from a damaged reactor, (iii) the distance from a toxic release considered dangerous for those exposed to the leaking fumes.

Pollutant: Generally, the presence of matter or energy whose nature, location, or quantity produces undesired environmental effects. Under the US. Clean Water Act, for example, the term is defined as the man-made or man-induced alteration of the physical, biological, and radiological integrity of water.

Putrescible: Able to rot quickly enough to cause odours and attract flies.

Photosynthesis: The manufacture of carbohydrates and oxygen by plants from carbon dioxide and water in the presence of chlorophyll, using sunlight as an energy source.

Pyrolysis: Decomposition of a chemical by extreme heat.

RDT: Recombinant DNA Technology. Technology of cutting and recombining DNA fragments from different sources.

Recycling: Procedure which is carried out without any chemical and biological treatment for some reusable materials such as paper, plastic, glass and can. These materials can be returned into economical processes.

Renewable resource: A resource that can be exploited without depletion because it is constantly replenished. The includes agricultural crops and fish, provided stocks are not over fished, and is extended to cover the energy of solar radiation, wind, waves and tides.

Renewable energy: Energy from renewable resources such as wind power, solar energy or biomass.

Reuse: To use an item more than once for the same purpose, which helps save money, time, energy and resources.

Risk assessment: The qualitative and quantitative evaluation performed in an effort to define the risk posed to human health or the environment by the presence or potential presence and use of specific pollutants.

Recycle/reuse: The process of minimising the generation of waste by recovering usable products that might otherwise become wastes. Examples are the recycling of aluminium cans, waste paper, and bottles.

Rhizophere: The part of the soil immediately surrounding roots. Roots alter the nutrient status of the soil close to them by absorbing minerals and releasing other substances. This leads to an increase in the numbers of micro-organisms and often alters the relative proportions of the different kinds of micro-organisms present.

Run-off: Water from rain or snow that runs off the surface of the land and into streams and rivers.

Rubbish: Solid waste, excluding wood waste and ashes, from homes, institutions, and workplaces.

SOTE: Standard oxygen transfer efficiency. It is the theoretical value of the amount of oxygen transferred to wastewater per unit power consumption.

Stoichiometry: Science of balancing the material and energy involved in a chemical or biological conversion process.

Sewage: Liquid wastes from communities, which may be a mixture of domestic effluent from homes and liquid waste from industry.

Smog: Air pollution consisting of smoke and fog, which occurs in large urban and industrial areas and is mainly caused by the action of sunlight on burned fuels, mostly from car exhausts. Smog can cause eye irritations and breathing problems and damage plant life.

Suspended solids: Small particles of solid pollutants that float on the surface of or are suspended in sewage or other liquids. They resist removal by conventional means.

Solid waste management: Supervised handling of waste materials from their source through recovery processes to disposal.

Solid wastes: Non-liquid, non-soluble materials, ranging from municipal garbage to industrial Wastes that contain complex, and sometimes hazardous, substances. Solid wastes include sewage sludge, agricultural refuse, demolition wastes, and mining residues. Technically, solid wastes also refer to liquids and gases in containers.

Sterilisation: (i) In pest control, the use of radiation and chemicals to damage body cells needed for reproduction and (ii) the destruction of all living organisms in water or on the surface of various materials. In contrast, disinfection is the destruction of most living organisms in water or on surfaces.

Smoke: Particles suspended in air after incomplete combustion of materials.

Slurry: A watery mixture of insoluble matter that results from some pollution control techniques.

Sludge: A semisolid residue from any of a number of air or water treatment processes. Sludge can be a hazardous waste.

Stabilisation: Conversion of the active organic matter in sludge into inert, harmless material.

Sedimentation: Letting solids settle out of wastewater by gravity during wastewater treatment.

Secondary wastewater treatment: The second step in most publicly owned water treatment systems, in which bacteria consume the organic parts of the waste. It is accomplished by bringing together waste, bacteria, and oxygen in trickling filters or in the activated sludge process. This treatment removes floating and settleable solids and about 90% of the oxygen-demanding substances and suspended solids. Disinfection is the final stage of secondary treatment.

Scrubber: An air pollution device that uses a spray of water or reactant or a dry process to trap pollutants in emissions.

Screening: Use of screens to remove coarse floating and suspended solids from sewage.

Sand filters: Devices that remove some suspended solids from sewage. Air and bacteria decompose additional wastes filtering through the sand so that cleaner water drains from the bed.

Sewage: The waste and wastewater produced by residential and commercial establishments and discharged into sewers.

Settling tank: A holding area for wastewater in which heavier particles sink to the bottom for removal and disposal.

Toxic: Poisonous or harmful to the body (exotoxic relates to damage to the environment).

Toxin: A poisonous substance that can either be natural (produced by plants, animals or bacteria) or manufactured.

Trickling filter: A coarse biological treatment system in which wastewater trickles over a bed of stones or other material covered with bacterial growth. The bacteria break down the organic waste in the sewage and produce clean water.

Total suspended solids (TSS): A measure of the suspended solids in wastewater, effluent, or water bodies.

Toxicity: The degree of danger posed by a substance to animal or plant life.

Tertiary wastewater treatment: Advanced cleaning of wastewater that goes beyond the secondary or biological stage to remove nutrients such as phosphorus and nitrogen and most biochemical oxygen demand (BOD) and suspended solids.

USW: Unprocessed solid waste. It is solid waste that has not been processes to isolate organic constituents from inorganic constituents or subjected to any size reduction before being dumped in to an incinerator or any other treatment system.

Urban area: An urban area is characterised by higher population density and vast human features in comparison to the areas surrounding it. Urban areas may be cities, towns or conurbations, but the term is not commonly extended to rural settlements such as villages and hamlets.

Urbanisation: Urbanisation (or urbanisation) is the increasing number of people that live in urban areas.

Ultraviolet light; ultraviolet radiation (UV): The portion of the electromagnetic spectrum with wavelengths from about 100 to 400 nm; between ionising radiation (X-rays) and visible light. UV is absorbed by DNA and is highly mutagenic to unicellular organisms and to the epidermal cells of multicellular organisms. UV light is used in tissue culture for its mutagenic and bactericidal properties.

Volatile organic compound (VOC): Any organic compound that participates in atmospheric photochemical reactions; generally have a boiling point of less than 145°C.

Volatile: Description of any substance that evaporates readily.

Waste stabilisation: Process of reducing the BOD or COD of organic wastes to render them harmless.

Wash-out: The loss of the slower growing micro-organism when two organisms are being grown together.

Water pollution: The presence in water of enough harmful or objectionable material to damage water quality.

Wastewater: Spent or used water from individual homes, communities, farms, or industries that contains dissolved or suspended matter.

Waste management: The management of waste collection, handling, processing, storage and transport from where it is produced to where it is finally disposed.

Wastewater treatment plant: A facility containing a series of tanks, screens, filters, and other processes by which pollutants are removed from water.

Waste prevention: An aspect of waste management that involves reducing the amount of waste we produce and minimising the potential harm to human health or the environment from packaging or ingredients in products.

Wetlands: An area that is regularly saturated by surface water or groundwater and is subsequently characterised by a prevalence of vegetation adapted for life in saturated soil conditions. Examples include swamps, bogs, fens, marshes, and estuaries.

Xenobiotic: Group of chemicals unfamiliar or foreign to micro-organisms and thus not easily degradable by them.

References

A.K. Chatterji, *Introduction to Environmental Biotechnology*, PHI Learning Pvt. Ltd., New Delhi.

Alan H. Scragg, *Environmental Biotechnology*, Oxford University Press.

Bruce Rittmann, Perry L. McCarty, *Environmental Biotechnology: Principles and Applications*, Tata McGraw-Hill Education.

Daniel A., Vallero, *Environmental Biotechnology: A Biosystems Approach*, Academic Press.

Fulekar, M.H., *Environmental Biotechnology*, CRC Press.

Gareth Evans, Judy Furlong, *Environmental Biotechnology: Theory and Application*, John Wiley & Sons.

Garima Kaushik, *Applied Environmental Biotechnology: Present Scenario and Future Trends*, Springer.

Hans-Joachim Jördening, Josef Winter, *Environmental Biotechnology: Concepts and Applications*, John Wiley & Sons,

Indu Shekhar Thakur, *Environmental Biotechnology: Basic Concepts and Applications*, I.K. International Publishing House Pvt., New Delhi.

Milton Wainwright, *An Introduction to Environmental Biotechnology*, Springer.

P. K. Mohapatra, *Textbook of Environmental Biotechnology*, I. K. International Pvt Ltd., New Delhi.

Ram Lakhan Singh, *Principles and Applications of Environmental Biotechnology for a Sustainable Future*, Springer.

Raman Kumar, Anil Kumar Sharma, Sarabjeet Singh Ahluwalia, *Advances in Environmental Biotechnology*, Springer.

Rintu Banerjee, *Environmental Biotechnology*, Oxford University Press, New Delhi.

Sangeetha, Devarajan Thangadurai, Muniswamy David, Mohd Azmuddin Abdullah, *Environmental Biotechnology*, Apple Academic Press,

Sayler, Gary S., Fox, Robert, Blackburn, *Environmental Biotechnology for Waste Treatment*, Springer.

Winter, J., *Environmental Processes*, Wiley Publications.

Index